T0365676

MESSAGES OF IMPACT

Robert James Thomas Sr.

WESTBOW
PRESS®
A DIVISION OF THOMAS NELSON
& ZONDERVAN

This book is a work of non-fiction. Unless otherwise noted, the author
and the publisher make no explicit guarantees as to the accuracy of
the information contained in this book and in some cases, names
of people and places have been altered to protect their privacy.

WestBow Press books may be ordered through booksellers or by contacting:

WestBow Press
A Division of Thomas Nelson & Zondervan
1663 Liberty Drive
Bloomington, IN 47403
www.westbowpress.com
844-714-3454

Because of the dynamic nature of the Internet, any web addresses or
links contained in this book may have changed since publication and
may no longer be valid. The views expressed in this work are solely those
of the author and do not necessarily reflect the views of the publisher,
and the publisher hereby disclaims any responsibility for them.

Any people depicted in stock imagery provided by Getty Images are
models, and such images are being used for illustrative purposes only.
Certain stock imagery © Getty Images.

Scripture taken from the King James Version of the Bible.

ISBN: 978-1-6642-7910-0 (sc)
ISBN: 978-1-6642-7912-4 (hc)
ISBN: 978-1-6642-7911-7 (e)

Library of Congress Control Number: 2022917816

Print information available on the last page.

WestBow Press rev. date: 02/06/2024

CONTENTS

AUTHOR'S LETTER

Dear Enthusiastic Reader,

Many people have said Sunday-morning sermons are ineffective, irrelevant, archaic, boring, redundant, and just for show. Others have said Sunday sermons are just some charismatic preachers trying to attract members into their church but never really living what they preach. However, in my fifty-four years of living in this world, my experience with many of those Sunday sermons has been none of the above. Sunday sermons have been rewarding for me. I was raised in a home as the youngest of six children, and my family was faced with hard times; but with the love we shared for one another, we were able to push through tough times with our gifted entrepreneurial skills and with God on our side.

Eventually, my mom and dad separated because their loving relationship had turned into a violent and abusive marriage. This was due to some things done within the constraints of their holy matrimony, and those divided them for many reasons. Whatever the problem was, it wasn't really explained to me because I was the aftermath baby. Born in 1962, I finally brought some sunshine into the home during some of the upheaval before Mom and Dad had to separate.

So I lived through some of the pains associated with broken families and vowed to myself as a little child to aspire for something better. My mother kept me in church every Sunday, making me attend Sunday school, Sunday morning service, Sunday afternoon services, Sunday evening services, weekday prayer service, weekday Bible studies, revivals during the summers and winters, anniversary services, and youth services.

Church was my second home, since I was in church five days out of a seven-day week. It seemed overbearing and tedious, but the good news was that I had the pleasure of hearing thousands of good sermons and Bible studies over the years. Many of those sermons impacted my life in such a positive way; they helped me first to develop a personal relationship with our Lord Jesus Christ, and much later they gave me the ammunition to begin writing my own messages, which later led to this book, *Messages of Impact*, which will be presented as a trilogy.

God gave me several messages over the years, which were influenced and inspired by many of those old sermons I listen to all those years. My church experience brought forth many good things in my life. I found salvation. I was baptized and filled with the Holy Spirit. I found my first and only love in church, my wife, Marie Della Thomas. We have been married for thirty-five years and have four children, who love to worship in the house of the Lord.

God has been so good to me and my family. I'm utterly grateful to be able to tell this story. Today I can see the rewards of planting my feet in the house of the Lord during my youth years. Now my children attend church regularly as I did, and they are all musicians, preachers, and worship and praise leaders; and they all have their personal relationships with Christ, our Savior. Thank you, Jesus! It just didn't have to be. I, for one, don't deserve God's goodness and mercies. Trust me, all this didn't come easily; it came with a fight to do the right thing. There were some dreary and darkened days, which seemed like life had given me a distasteful plate to eat due to the bad decisions I had made in the past; but thank God, the good outweighed the bad, and this is why I write this book today—to share messages that will hopefully impact people's lives in a positive way.

Sunday sermons and Bible studies lifted my spirit and

motivated me to do better, work harder, pray often, and be thankful and content with all the things God has bestowed on me. Hearing those powerful words from the scriptures in the Holy Bible gave me hope; it promoted love, honesty, peace, righteousness, and faith. Finally, God's word spoken through those sermons made me the man I am today; it convinced me to be thankful for all God's goodness and kindness. Now I stand with praise on my lips and thanksgiving in my heart to God for all he has done for me and my family. Although my life hasn't been all peaches and cream, nor have I reached perfection, God's words impacted my life so much that I learned to be content in whatever state I'm in. I have witnessed and experienced some dark days due to my disobedience to God's word, but the good days have outnumbered the bad, and I am grateful to God for sparing my life to write this book and hopefully impact readers from all over the world.

Many people have demonized churches and their pastors, spreading untrue rumors about men and women of God. However, they are simply vessels God is using. But even if some of those rumors are true, they still don't negate the fact that much good has come from God's house of worship abroad, and the good outweighs the bad. Jesus started the Christian church and called it "his bride"; therefore, Jesus takes pride in his place of worship, and he will correct the things that need to be corrected.

God's church and our salvation have been established on a rock and a true foundation. Who is that rock? Jesus is the rock of our salvation. Yet during Bible days, religious leaders like the Pharisees and Sadducees sought to crucify Jesus for no apparent reason. These religious leaders concocted a theory that Jesus was committing treason, calling him an impostor because he claimed to be the Son of God and King of kings. The Roman Empire felt threatened by the many rumors of another king rising up while king Herod yet stood on the throne. These accusations created turbulence and caused the king to order that thousands of babies be killed so the rumor of a new king rising up would be obliterated. As far as the Jews were concerned, they were under the notion and frame of mind that if Jesus was the Son of God coming from heaven as the scriptures foretold, he would have brought forth warfare and destruction to the Roman Empire; instead, Jesus brought forth the gospel (good news) salvation and miracles to the world and all who would listen. The Jews wanted no part with the Son of God in this capacity. What the Jews didn't know was that Jesus did conduct warfare, but it was spiritual warfare; he used his word as a sword and shield to defeat more than just the Roman Empire. He destroyed the powers of sin, darkness, sickness and disease, evil, and finally death so all mankind could have the opportunity to be redeemed from their sins and live forever in heaven after death. The warfare Jesus brought on the earth wasn't visible to the Romans or the Jews.

Finally, after much determination and many allegations, the Jews and Romans concluded that crucifying Jesus was destined. Nevertheless, Jesus still remains the King of kings. He is the King above all kings; he is a Ruler above all those in power. He rose from the dead, and all power is in his hand. What prophet or religious leader do you know who could resurrect himself from death and hell? Jesus rose from the dead with all power in his hand, and because of Jesus's resurrection, everything dead should be resurrected in the name of Jesus Christ, the Son of the living God. So whatever is dead in your life can be resurrected. I pray that righteousness will be resurrected in your life in the name of Jesus Christ.

These Sunday sermons came from ordained ministers, who used the Holy Bible, King James Version, and life experiences along with much prayer. Most of all, their messages were inspired by God's Holy Spirit. Who else could know the topics that would pierce the hearts of men and women? Often some of these messages could have won a Dove Award for such a great presentation and research. More importantly, these messages inspired by God had such an impact on all who listened; they changed lives. They turned criminals into law-abiding citizens, haters into lovers, adulterers into faithful husbands and wives, liars into honest people, thieves into givers, and drunkards into sober people. They healed our sickness and diseases, delivered us out of bondage, and gave us the courage to face life circumstances with confidence and assurance that things would get better.

I'm a witness that these things are true; I was there. I literally witnessed some of these events, both in my life and in other people's lives too. God's word begins construction work on the bad behavior and dark deeds done in our lives. Those words from the Holy Scriptures literally perform an invisible operation on our hearts and minds so we can love others and forgive our brothers, sisters, and neighbors. God's word infuses power and courage within us to move forward into our destiny.

There is no book existing in the history of mankind or in any library of the world that could ever come close to the ultimate power, life-changing power, earth-shattering power, and supernatural power the Holy Bible gives to mankind. If there was such a book that could match the power of the Holy Bible, it would be the world's most sold book in history. Fortunately, the Holy Bible consistently remains the world's most sold book in the world. Hallelujah! You can't beat God. Who dares to compete with God Almighty? His words heal and cure more people than hospitals do. God's words from the Holy Bible rehabilitate more people than prisons and psychologists. The Holy Scriptures will lift those hung-down heads and give you hope and a reason for living.

There is no racism in God's word. There's no prejudice in God's word. There's no supreme nationality God loves more, "for God so loved the world he gave his only begotten son" (John 3:16). No dollar amount can buy God's love; it's free just like oxygen, which God gives to all mankind. Even criminals enjoy God's goodness. The Bible still contains the same power it had centuries ago; if anything, its power has intensified and become more potent. Its prophecies are awesomely accurate, and many of its prophecies have been revealed in the twenty-first century. Its stories are real and true (nothing but the truth) and impactful. Its laws and instructions apply to modern-day society. The Holy Bible influenced the Constitution of the United States of America. That's how impactful God's words from the scriptures are.

The Bible is full of truth, power, healings, love, miracles, and God's greatness, salvation, holiness, righteousness, instructions, wrath, mercy, and promises.

The Holy Bible, which represents words from God's mouth translated in all languages and written on paper with black ink by holy men, continues to change people's lives the more they read it's words will eventually and literally engraved its message of hope and salvation deeply in your heart and mind, submerging their lives in God's righteousness. This is truly the only book I know that can still impact people's lives positively today. It is written in the scriptures that "God's word will never return void(Isaiah 55:11)," meaning that whenever God's word is spoken, it will complete its task. When people hear the word of God often enough, eventually they will be affected by the power it carries and the impact it leaves, all of which will ultimately change their lives for good over time. This is similar to the rain that falls from the cloudy skies to the earth; we don't see all the good it brings to the earth, but after some time, beautiful flowers begin to blossom, and small plants grow into trees; so it is with the word of God. God attaches his words to our hearts, and over time they begin to rebuild our lives, attitudes, facial expressions, and behavior for the better.

During my fifty-four years on this earth, God has been speaking to me and giving me messages to share with the body of Christ and the world, messages that will impact people's lives in a positive way toward God. God inspired me many years ago to write down and publish these messages, which he would engrave on my heart. He has prompted me to publish *Messages of Impact* (1, 2, and 3) to bring glory to the kingdom of God and to uplift people from all walks of life. This is the reason I write simply to bring glory to God's kingdom, for the Spirit of God has inspired, stimulated, and motivated me to write and publish *Messages of Impact.* I have ministered to my immediate family, my church congregation, other congregations, and different groups throughout New York City and beyond for many years. I cannot hold back anymore because it's just like sitting on fire. I must spread the gospel through my writings. God's words planted in my spirit are that fire shut up in my bones to do the will of my father; I strongly believe and stand totally convinced that God has endorsed *Messages of Impact* to spread his words from the Holy Bible to the world. Thank you for choosing to read *Messages of Impact.*

ACKNOWLEDGMENTS

This book wouldn't have materialized if not for God the Father; his Son, Jesus Christ; and the Holy Ghost. First, I would like to thank my wife of thirty-two years, Marie Della Thomas, for her encouragement and support in all my business endeavors; without her, this project wouldn't have been possible. Thanks to my darling, Marie Della Thomas, whom I love very much. Thanks to my four children, whom I love very much.

- Bobby Jr., my eldest son (man of God, preacher, drummer, pianist, college grad, businessman)
- Latasha, my only daughter and princess (woman of God, college grad, soon-to-be lawyer, fashion designer, musician, and soloist)
- Daniel, my artist, musician, college grad, and preacher
- Last but not least, Mr. Joshua Thomas, a baby genius (wise as Solomon, the great king), a man of God, and soon to be a doctor

Thanks to all the Thomas family for your patience, prayers, and support. To the late Mrs. Katherine Thomas, my mom and the woman of God who kept me in church, the woman who stayed up late at night, praying for me when I was roaming the street with my crew—this book is for you, Mom, and I will always love you dearly. Thanks also to my siblings, the late Jeffrey Thomas and Ron Thomas, the business doctor and my mentor; to my late sister-in-law, the late Emily Thomas, and her surviving children (Melissa Thomas and Karen Thomas); to my big sister, Sandy Simone Pascal and the Pascal family, the pastor for today; to her children (Greg jr., Donna, and Jay); and to my sister, the late Kathleen Thomas. I will always love you.

This book is for my eldest sister, the late Ruby Melton, my poet. Before Ruby passed, she inspired me to write a book. This book is also for her late husband, Hubert Melton; may God keep you in his arms. I love you all, family.

Thanks also to the entire Stowers family, Lydia and Odell Stowers; to my church, Mission of Hope, with senior pastor Odis and pastor Sam Stowers; to my late Uncle Fred Ingram, who taught me how to play gospel music on the piano and his wife; to the late Martha Ingram, my darling auntie to the late Charles Crawford and surviving wife Gertrude Crawford and family; and to Pastor Thomas McCamery and his wife Betty Mc Camery and family.

A special thanks to all the family of God. l love you all, and when this book is a success, I want all of you to know I appreciate the contribution and impact you had on my life. May God bless you and your families. Please spread the word about this book and read it, absorb it, preach it, teach it, and use it as a sermon selector for your church. I pray that something said in my book will impact your life positively, just like you all have impacted my life. God bless you all, and may heaven smile upon you.

INTRODUCTION

In 1979, when I was seventeen years old, my pastor asked me to give a word or message to the congregation. He felt that since I'd been faithful to Bible study and prayer service, certainly God was speaking to me. I was a little surprised that he would ask me, a teenager, to speak in front of his congregation. He continued to ask me whether I had a word to share with the congregation. I finally answered him after much of his inquiring. My answer was, "There is something God has laid on my heart to share with the body of Christ." His face was filled with relief.

After much preparation, prayer, and Bible study, I heard the Lord speak to my heart, and he gave me a message, "The Dead Cannot Praise the Lord." Little did I know this message would transcend into the future through this book. As the words came out of my mouth, this audience hung on each word. Some people stood to their feet; others raised their hands in agreement with this message. The anointing of God was on every word and phrase I spoke.

It was a powerful moment in history. The audience wanted more of God's word. God was using me as a vessel; what a rewarding experience it was! This occurrence was like feeding a hungry multitude. Have you ever been so hungry to hear something that it would motivate you to do better? Thank God that in America there isn't a famine of God's word being dispensed; in fact, we can hear the gospel of our Lord Jesus Christ twenty-four hours a day. I wouldn't want to experience or witness a famine of God's word in America, but a famine of God's word could never happen as long as his word is hidden in our hearts. That's why God's word must be glued to our hearts and minds. As I stood preaching that day, you would have thought this audience had never heard this topic before. The congregation leaned forward to catch every word that came out of my mouth. They were hungry for the word of God. I could tell this congregation was hungry based on their facial expressions and body language. This congregation desperately wanted to hear an encouraging message that would enlighten their lives, a message they could live by and take home to share with others. They wanted to hear an impactful message they could apply to their daily life routines. The message began this way:

Praises are important to God, and they should be important to Christians. As a matter of fact, praise should be a common exercise for Christians—better yet, a way of life. Why? If you are a Christian, wouldn't you want to do the things God himself dwells in, because God inhabits the praises of his people? Praises are the ABCs of what Christians do when they enter the house of God—not only in the physical sanctuary but in our homes and wherever the body of Christ meets.

Jesus and the ark of God, which represents God's presence, aren't in a box anymore. In BC times, the ark of God represented the presence of God wherever it was carried. In ancient times the Israelites physically carried the ark of God wherever they dwelled, and only the holy priests were able to enter the ark to commune with God, but after the death and the resurrection of Jesus Christ, Christians are able to carry the presence of God within their hearts. God's presence is no longer in a box; the presence of God is in the hearts of his people. So with this in mind, we should be excited, cheerful, and full of praise, especially when entering his house of worship. Praise him, all ye people. Praise God, from whom all blessings flow. Let everything that has breath praise the Lord.

Sincere praises brings God to action and drives God to work swiftly in our favor. God's angels praise and worship him around the clock (24-7). The Bible teaches us that God inhabits the praises of his people (Psalm 22:3), which means where there's sincere praise being offered up to God, God will live there. Wherever God lives, miracles happen, prayers are answered, mountains are moved, sickness and disease are dissolved, and your enemies are destroyed. That's why our flesh and the forces of darkness try to hinder us from praising the God of the universe—because if we were ever to master or make praising the King of kings a part of our daily routine, our stress levels would be diminished. This world tries to weigh us down with heavy anxiety, societal pressures, and peer pressure, along with different circumstances and situations that smack us in our faces. These burdens can sometimes become too much to bear, and our financial failures lurk over our heads to choke and strangle the praises out of our systems and out of our churches. Just as God lives in the atmosphere of our praise, the enemy of our soul inhabits depression, frowns, pity parties, gloominess, hopelessness, doubt, and fear, which bring him glory and honor. Are you and I guilty of giving more honor and glory to the enemy of our souls than to God? In praise, there's rejoicing, freedom, and liberty, but in doom, gloom, doubt, stress, and fear there's torment. The only people legitimately exempt from praising God are dead people. So the message today is, "The dead cannot praise God!"

There's no glory in death. Death strips you of everything: mobility, human faculties, thoughts, memories, ideas, creativity, dreams, happiness, praises, imagination, strength, emotions, and all bodily activity. I repeat, there is absolutely no praise going on among the dead. Praises are for living beings, not for dead people. Are you alive today? Then you qualify to praise God (Psalm 150:1) Let everything that breathes praise the Lord. This scripture doesn't say only church people should praise God—it says everything that has breath should praise God. If you are breathing, you owe God some praise. Praising God is a choice you must make, and when you participate in praise, it brings about a connection with God. While you remain alive, choose whom you will serve, because in death there are no decisions being made, only destinations being set in place. Praising God empowers you; it releases stress, pain, and worry. It calms your fears and heals your spirit, and it expedites answers to your prayers. Don't you want your prayers answered? Lift your hands and elevate your voice and ring out, "Hallelujah! Thank you, Jesus! Glory to the King of kings." Sing unto the Lord God of your salvation. Clap your hands and cheer his name, which is the highest name ever to be called. Dance with happy feet, because being alive is a gift from heaven.

What could you or I do without this gift of life God has given us? Nothing! And nothing times itself equals nothingness. And procrastinating equals a big, fat zero too. Start praising God wherever you are, and be grateful for the small things in life—and the big things too. Sing praises to his name. Express your gratitude to God every day. Lift up your voice in your home; lift up your voice in the sanctuary. Jesus is worthy of praise. Praises will make you wear a smile. Learn to be happy within your heart, because that's where praises really come from. Don't allow yourself to enter the land of, and ministry of, whispering praises instead of lifting your voice like a trumpet and letting the world know whom you are praising. Hallelujah! Thank you, Jesus! For the Lord God is worthy of all the praises we can offer and then some. If the heavenly angels in heaven praise God around the clock, why would we, who are made lower than they, think that it's okay not to praise God at any time? Get over yourself, because even the animals and elements of the earth praise God every day. God is truly worthy of all accolades. Glory to his name.

Human resource departments all over the country can vouch for me when I say the most important thing that motivates employees is appreciation and praise for a job well done every now and then. So it is with God Almighty; he loves when his creation praises his name. Our praises unto God are like a rich and magnificent fragrance that fills the atmosphere, leaving an aroma for God to inhale. And when God smells this perfume, it pleases him so much that he inhabits the area where true praises are being conducted. In other words, God lives in the midst of the fumes of praises, and while he's there, he wants to answer our unanswered prayers, meet our needs, and heal our sickness and disease. Hallelujah! That is why we are to praise God more than being spectators and complainers. Praises aren't something done secretly; on the contrary, praise is boisterous, energetic, lively, and animated. What is this I hear about people called Christians becoming comatose, motionless, lifeless when it comes to praise and worship services? No! No! You should become alive! Be grateful for the very obvious: life, health, and a sound mind. These are things you cannot pay for because they all are gifts from God, and they represent the most valuable things in life. So with God's gift of life, we should choose to praise God every day he allows us to live above ground. Only the dead can't praise God. Are you dead? And what could you do without God's precious gift to humanity called "life"? If you are reading this book, that's proof you are alive, and you should praise your Creator. Give him some glory and praise; open your mouth and thank God.

From the beginning, we weren't created to die. When sin entered the world through Adam and Eve, God promised death to us. So every man and woman born into this world at an appointed time must die, according to the scriptures. King David said it best: "As I live and have my being I will sing praises to the Lord. While blood is running warm in my veins I will praise God." (Psalm 104:33) Praise him on the instruments, praise him with a timbre and dance. Let everything that has breath, praise God (Psalm 150:6). Praises aren't exclusively for Christians as some may believe but for anyone or thing that has breath! Let me add that praises are done openly and publicly; Jesus said, "But when you pray, pray in secret, pray in your closet and God will reward you openly (St. Matthew 6:6)"; therefore, praising and rejoicing are unrestricted to a place, event, or area; they are performed openly, the same way you cheer for the New York Yankees, New York Knicks, New York Rangers and the New York Islanders or your favorite team; so it is when you praise the almighty God.

I am tired of seeing church folks sitting quietly, waiting for the show to begin, trying to convince others that you can really praise God quietly, when in fact prayer is a quiet, sacred action between you and God. Making a joyful noise isn't self-contained; rather it is pumped up and lively, which is the opposite of deadness. Can the church say, "Amen"? Sunday service shouldn't be dead because we serve a living God. We don't serve a dead God or a statue. Meanwhile, many who do serve dead gods and statues make more noise than we who say we serve a living God. What's wrong with that picture? God's breath of life is actually in your mortal body, and that, my dear reader, is why you exist and are able to climb, dance, feel, hear, learn, move, jog, jump, move, run, see, talk, think, walk, and work; so lift your vocal cords loudly and give him cheer and ovation. God is truly worthy of all the praises! If we would only praise God with our vocal cords and limbs more than never, sugar diabetes, heart disease, arthritis, high blood pressure, and many other ailments would probably be foreign to us and be of no consequence. Yet praising God still remains a struggle for many Christians, so therefore we suffer and endure hardship. Jesus didn't die for us to be miserable Christians or a wretched people. Jesus puts smiles on people's faces, he puts running in people's feet, and he puts dancing in our feet; and we are to use the microphone of our vocal cords to dispense and elevate our praise and worship from the speakers of our mouths. Hallelujah! Wipe those forever frowns off your face and lift your voice and praise the Lord God Almighty.

Many of us continue to take the same posture we have at home and bring it to the house of God; sitting in our comfortable chairs as though we were watching television, sitting down as though we are at a Broadway show, or viewing a movie or sitting in a stadium, watching a boring game, and having very little or no emotion and energy. I have news for you: this posture you display in your home, do that in your home; but when you enter God's house, you are to get up out of your chairs and praise God. Elevate your voice, dance before the Lord God, sing songs to the Lord God, clap your hands in his presence, smile, and be joyful, for it is he who has made us and not we ourselves (Psalm 100:3). Always remember when you enter God's house that he said, "Let everything that have breath praise God." Get up out of your chair and praise God. Your feet should be dancing like happy feet. Clap your hands, all ye people (Psalm 47:1). The king of glory is here in this place. Stand to your feet and give God glory. Praise him! You and I don't deserve God's goodness anyway. Stand up for Jesus! You were created to praise God. Open your mouth and praise the King of kings. Who do you think you are coming in God's house with no praise or accolades toward your creator, who happens to be the only reason why you are alive today? God deserves all the praise, glory, and honor, for it is he who has made us and not we ourselves(Psalm 100:3). Get up and praise the King of kings and Lord of lords. The purpose of worship and praise service in church was never meant to be a funeral service but a type of invitation for God's Holy Spirit to come in our midst because God inhabits our praises; it should be a common thing that we pump up sincere but loud and powerful sounds of praises, which invites the presence of God in our midst. God's house is too quiet these days. *Our praises should be louder than all of our troubles.* Our praises should be louder than everything that comes against us. Our praises should be louder than everything we have been through and are going through. Our praises should be louder than everything we want to achieve. Our praises should be louder than all the gossip in our communities and churches. Our praises should be louder than our past sins and evil deeds we committed. And if it's not louder than what God brought us out of, maybe we really missed Egypt tremendously, which represents our past lifestyle. What and who in your past do you want more than God's presence in your life? Because whatever it is and whoever it is, it or he or she isn't worth your soul.

Some churches are heavily concerned with their church programs, offerings, attendance, guest speakers, and dress codes more than having God's presence in their midst, and that's why people leave services not healed, not delivered, depressed, full of jealousy and strife with one another, making themselves so easily acceptable to go astray from the faith, because it's not enough substance for them to hold on to. The world needs to see the Spirit of God in operation and needs to be filled with God's Spirit within them so they can be conquerors in life. Why? Because many churches have experienced too many Sunday services without the presence of God in their midst; therefore, they endure boredom, daydreaming, no spirit, no miracles, no healing, no uplifting, and no joy or peace; and many aren't coming to the knowledge of the truth. Coming out to Sunday services shouldn't be as painful and motionless as displayed in some churches. It almost seems that the many who have confessed coming out of darkness into the marvelous light of Jesus Christ salvation were happier and more vivacious in their previous lifestyle than in their current lifestyle. Is this true? Well, actions sometimes speak louder than words. Let's make the enemy of our souls a liar and give God some sincere and boisterous praise right now! Hallelujah!

Sin is like quicksand; it continues to pull you down every time you make strides to lift yourself up. This quicksand I speak of is the aftermath of indulging in sinful activities, which engulfs us into its influences and attractions, giving us the falsehood that it's a good thing to participate therein, only to face ramifications of our past, which destroys our lives and leave us with the memory of it all. This in itself is tormenting and continues to drown us in its bottomless pit of sinful distastefulness until we die. So the enemy of our souls' only purpose of doing such things to us is to continuously pull you and me downward into a pit of hellishness and a gutter lifestyle. Here's the good news. Jesus said that if you will begin to look up from where your help comes from and praise your God, he will lift you out of life's quicksand and plant your feet on a rock to stay.

Hallelujah, church of the highest God! We've been down too long; it's time to get up and praise the Lord. Lift the Savior up! Praise God from whom all blessings flow. Praise God! God's house isn't a movie theater, Broadway show, den of thieves, or the house of prejudice and hatred; nor is it a house of one race, a concert hall, or a house of political influence; neither is it a fashion show, but many people have made God's house these things. God's house isn't a playhouse, social club, nightclub, or dating club; and neither is it a Hollywood Academy Award show with a bunch of actors, directors, and cameras. Jesus said, "My house shall be called the house of prayer." Therefore, we should be praying, praising God, and hearing his word more than anything else. Let's stop making God's house everything we think it should be and nothing God said it ought to be. Lift your voice and praise your creator. Praises should be a natural thing for the righteous. Stand to your feet and praise God with everything you've got. I can't hear you? Let the praise flow from your lips.

During all the years I spent in church services, no matter how good the worship and praise singers sang and no matter how powerful and charismatic the preacher preached, there were always those who refused to praise God joyfully along with the congregation. If the angels in heaven created by God rejoice and praise God exceedingly (Psalm 68:3), how do you think God feels when he created all of us in his image but we refuse to rejoice and praise our creator? How do you feel when no one thanks you for all your hard work? Maybe now you can understand how God feels. Praising God has nothing to do with your religion, color or race, doctrine, church, financial status, or position in church or life; what it has everything to do with is your gratefulness to God personally for all he has done for you and all he has given you. You may ask, "What has God done for me lately?" The answer is, "He gave you life." Now tell me, what can you do or accomplish without it? I thought so!

To be grateful and full of praise is to be stress free. Stress is the number one element that destroys businesses, homes, families, churches, good ideas, marriages, companies, and our personal lives all over the world, namely in America. Most sicknesses are created from excessive stress over time. Let it go, people, and release your praises to God. Praise God when you wake in the morning. Praise God before you lie down to sleep. Praise God when things are going wrong. Praise God whenever things are just fine. Praise God for what you currently have. Praise God for food and shelter. Praise God for keeping you alive during COVID 19, one of the worst pandemics. Praise God when bills seem to have gotten out of control. Praise God while you walk the streets, shopping. Men ought to always praise and worship God(St. John 4:11). No matter what state you are in today, God deserves all the praise.

During my fifty-four years of being in church services, I observed several common reasons why people in my view refuse to praise God openly.

1. Some people are unfamiliar with praises in the house of God, probably because it was never performed or practiced in their homes; nor was it rehearsed by their parents, maybe because their parents never attended church or were part of any religion that praised God boisterously. As they witness others praise God openly and loudly, they feel no conviction or sense of urgency to praise God publicly because it's <u>unknown to them</u>. So their willingness to participate in praise and worship turns into a state of tranquility and silence and motionlessness because it is unknown to them. People sometimes become hushed

when they're unfamiliar with things. So, they sit frozen because it's something that's not practiced or conducted in their circle of life. They are unknown to praising God, and the only way they will participate in a praise and worship service is to observe fellow Christians as they praise and worship God amid the congregation. Lift your voice and shout, "Hallelujah." Say, "Thank you, Jesus." Thank God for the obvious: "health, strength, life, shelter, food, children, and your job." If you practice praising God at home, praising God sincerely in the church will become your edict. There is a real God in this world, and his name is Jehovah God. He deserves all the praise from your lips. Although God deserves all the praise from our lips, he won't force you to praise his name; he would much rather have rocks cry out, "Hallelujah" than to compel you to praise him with a loud voice. If praising God is still unknown and mysterious to you, fear not, brothers and sisters. You will still enjoy life's amenities. God isn't a dictator. God loves the praises from his people so much that he draws closer to you when you praise his name sincerely; maybe that's why people are very cautious about praising God aloud. It should always be a common response to give gratitude and accolades to someone who does kind things for you; with this in mind, give your creator some praise. The mere fact that God created you and me in his own image and likeness is enough to shout, "Hallelujah" to our awesome God.

2. Embarrassed are those who refuse to praise God openly because they become humiliated and even mortified. It makes them feel uncomfortable to shout out loudly in front of other people in their midst; even when there's no one around, it's difficult for them to raise their voices. They don't want attention drawn to themselves, so they choose to be a spectator, never disturbing other people's peace. So,

they feel no conviction or sense of urgency to praise God loudly, because they are worried about what others may say. They are scared to give loud cheers and accolades to the Lord Jesus Christ because doing so embarrasses them. Are you embarrassed to give your creator praise? If you are ashamed of the Lord Jesus Christ, he will be ashamed of you (St. Marks 8:38). There's another thing about these people who make you feel embarrassed to praise God vociferously in public; what have they done for you lately? Do they even know your name? Are they currently helping you to accomplish anything in life? Did they wake you up this morning? Did they allow your blood to run warm in your veins? Can any of these bystanders help you with your immediate needs and issues? I thought so. Cry aloud unto the Lord God. He is your helper; he is your strength. The very air you breathe comes from him. Lift your voice, get over yourself and the people you are surrounded by, and praise the Lord Jesus Christ. We freely give praises and great accolades to movie stars, our favorite teams in sports, and public figures and people in high authority, none of whom know our names or really care whether we live or die; but there's one who is greater than them all, and he loves us unconditionally with all our bad baggage, and he still allows us to breathe each morning and gives us strength to work and play. And he gives us the privilege to enjoy all life's ambiance while having our own free will to do as we please, and still that seems like not enough for us to give praises to his name aloudly. Why do we give our allegiance, praise, and boisterous accolades to people who don't have our best interest at heart? Oh, I know why—because we can't see Jehovah God with our naked eyes; therefore, it gives us the excuse to hush our vocal cords, but on occasion, we so willingly give great praise, ovation, and honor to people who don't even know our names; and if they did know our names, they wouldn't care anyway. Praises may have been unknown to you in the past, but now that you have been enlightened, what will you do now?

3. Whisperers are those who believe and stand firm on the fact that praises are supposed to be performed quietly or inwardly, never to interrupt other people's peace. But let us read Matthew 6:6. "But thou, when thou pray, enter into thy closet, and when thou hast shut the door, pray to the father which is in secret; and thy father which sees in secret shall reward thee openly." Prayer is supposed to be done in secret but not praise. Praises are to be open, loud, boisterous, and energetic. Praise is our way of giving God a sincere and thunderous sound of accolade and thankfulness for his goodness. There is no whispering in heaven; the angels rejoice and dance before the King of kings and Lord of lords. Usually, when whispering is conducted, it's because you don't want others to know what you're saying. But with praise we want others to know who we serve, adore, honor, and give great and loud accolades to. We want others to know how great God is. We want the world to know how good God is. Hallelujah! Glory to the Kings of kings! Shout praises to your God, all ye people, and for those who are in the whispering praise ministries, evidently you praise a small god and you don't want anyone to know who he is, because you are ashamed of him. He is evidently deaf and dumb and doesn't hear or answer your cry anyway. But if you serve the God of the universe, lift your voice unto the Lord God Jehovah. Just like you and I have pet peeves, so does God; when God hears sincere praises being lifted up, loud and boisterous to heaven, he comes in the midst of whoever is lifting his name in this manner. Imagine what God does when praises are at this level, reaching God. He answers

prayers, heals the sick, delivers his people, changes your circumstances, extends his miracle power, opens doors, draws closer to you, and strengthens your faith in him. May I add that sincere, joyful praise lifted to God may very well extend your life's existence beyond seventy years. What many people don't know and realize are the following mood swings: anxiety, depression, gloominess, misery, stress, worrying, doubt, and fear. They can very well shorten people lives as well as ruin the quality of their life too. Whispering-praises is not the purpose of praise because praise is suppose to be boisterous and loud.. The earth has more than enough whispering going around its airways, especially with many of our government officials whispering and conspiring with enemies of the cross of Jesus Christ and enemies of our nation. Let's not forget our own enemies, who are whispering their strategies to destroy our way of life, businesses, churches, job positions, and goals and aspirations. Be not ashamed of the gospel of Jesus Christ (2 Timothy 1:8) (Romans 1:16) with this gospel of Jesus Christ, we will sing hymns and songs. We will testify of his goodness; we will dance with happy feet, for the Lord is good, and his mercy endureth forever. We will praise God with boisterous praise, for there is no other God like Jehovah God. Satan is the king of the whispering ministry. Each night when you sleep, Satan and his dark angels whisper and conspire among themselves about your demise each day you wake to live. Therefore, when you frequently and habitually lift your voice to praise God sincerely for his goodness and mercy, whether you know it or not God shields you. God comes in your presence and dwells with you. Then what happens to all your enemies, who conspire about your demise? God turns their weapons of mass destruction into stepping-stones toward your successful and bountiful future. Give God some praise.

4.   Daydreamers are those in the house of God who witness praise and worship being conducted, but their minds are somewhere else, maybe somewhere more exciting. They are texting a friend during the church services, surfing the Internet, downloading information or pictures, and pondering on yesterday's events; but wherever their minds are, it is clear and evident that their minds aren't on worship and praise. So the end result is that they won't perform any praises, because their thoughts are far from God's goodness. They are in a deep dream, with their eyes fully open to witness praises being offered up by the congregation, yet they won't participate in praise and worship. Are you a daydreamer when it's time to praise God? Wake up, thou that sleepest! Wake up, ye daydreamers to reality, and that reality is God, who deserves all your praise and worship. We salute officers of the armed forces. We celebrate the birthdays of dead presidents. Corporate America celebrates & parties hard just for TGIF (Thank God It's Friday). We watch our favorite teams play sports, and when and if they win, we yell, scream, and dance; we become their biggest cheering corner, and they don't even know our names. And frankly, they don't care to know our names either, but when it comes to the one who created us, we sit down with our lips sealed and hands folded as though we are in a funeral service. The Son of the living God, Jesus Christ, is yet alive. Therefore, we aren't *paying our respects* to God by coming to his house of worship as we do to a funeral service, with folded hands, shut mouths, and minds far from God. Jesus has risen from the dead, and he is very much alive, so we should come into his house of prayer with thanksgiving and praise. Church shouldn't be a

funeral service but a lively and energetic spirit of praise while lifting our voices loudly, exclaiming his name on high. Awake! Daydreamer! Awake! Sleepyhead! Awake ye who are too stoned from the night before and too high from the stuff you've been smoking. Awake thou, dreamer! Dreaming is for those who sleep after being exhausted from working, but when you awake, you should be filled with praise on your lips to the God who woke you up this morning. Sing praises to his name, for he is truly worthy of all the praise. There is nothing wrong with dreaming at night or daydreaming during the day, but this issue presents an obvious disconnect with reality sometimes. Millions of Christians gather as believers to worship God, but most of their time and energy are displayed by sleeping and daydreaming instead of lifting their voices boisterously and sincerely unto God. When you come to the house of prayer, come out of your dreamworld and praise the Lord God and his Son, Jesus Christ, who can *make your dreams come true.*

5. Comatose are those who are extremely exhausted from working hard or aren't getting enough sleep. Whatever the reason is for their extreme fatigue, they still come and sit in the house of the Lord, worn out, and nothing is moving them while worship and praise are in operation because they are in the land of fatigue. They are too tired to lift their hands and worship the God who gave them the strength to work and the energy to get up every morning. So they sit there, angry, exhausted, frustrated, sleepy, tired, and unappreciative of God's goodness, never allowing anything to change their attitude toward not praising God. As they sit there with their eyes halfway open, comatose to their surroundings and feeling empty with no praise flowing from their lips, their only response to praise and worship is to offer yawning from their mouths

and periodic catnapping, never uttering one sound or even whispering praise from their lips. Are you comatose when praises are being conducted in church services? If you knew only how desperately you need the Lord God, you would wake up from your sleep and give your sacrifice of praise because God is worthy of all our praise. Good things happen to those who persevere through fatigue and sleepiness just to glorify God with their lips of praise. Start your morning with praising God, walk through your day with praise on your lips, and before you lay yourself down to sleep, praise God. You should have stored up praise when you arrived at church on Sunday morning, whereby praises become a habitual thing flowing from your lips like waterfalls flow from Niagara Falls in Canada or like waters flow from our oceans and rivers without any hesitation. "Let everything that have breath praise the Lord." Break out of that comatose feeling, lift your voice, and shout, "Glory! Hallelujah!" Anything dead should be what? Should be buried? No! Any dead should be resurrected. Resurrect your praise to the almighty God continuously because he is worthy of all the praise and accolades, we can offer. Why is this necessary? Because God delights in our praise so much that he visits the area where praise is being conducted. Our sincere praise is likened to a beautiful perfume smell filling the area you stand on, and that perfume scent fills the area you dwell in; and when God inhales the fragrance of sincere praise, it becomes so refreshing to God's nostrils that he commands blessings on you. Praise is comely for his people (Psalms 33:1), but the unjust would rather praise and worship idols, false gods, instead of giving accolades to the only God. Awake thou who sleepest, awake thou that sleepiest and arise from the dead and Christ shall give you light (Ephesians 5:14)and lift your voice to praise and worship the God of the universe, Jehovah God, the only true God, for it is a common thing for his people to praise and worship the almighty God and his Son, Jesus Christ.

6. The walking dead/zombies are those who are alive, but they are motionless, frozen, lifeless, unconscious, unmoving. They are similar to mummies when it comes to praising God. They feel it doesn't take all that noise to worship God. They can praise God, but instead of doing so, they would rather remain cold, frozen, noiseless, and dead to praising the Lord God almighty with a loud sound. It would be better if they weren't present in the sanctuary than refusing to participate in worship and praise; instead, they sit there, motionless, callous, stiff, insensitive, numb, ice cold, and bored, refusing to respond to the intensity of the Spirit of God in the sanctuary. And their ultimate goal is to influence and reincarnate others to become zombies and mummies just like them when it's time to praise the Lord God. This is similar to dancing before statues and waiting for a response. Evidently, being in the presence of God doesn't excite the walking dead; they play as zombies, showing no expression or movement. After these same motionless people walk out of the church with no praise on their lips, they will be quickened for the next party mentioned or next upcoming concert; and these same motionless people at church will quickly become vivacious only to prove that people willingly become dead to things they don't want or like to do and swiftly come alive to the things they really like and appreciate. Are you a dead person walking when it comes to praising God in his house of worship? Do you become like a zombie when praise and worship services are being conducted? Everything that is dead should be what? Most people would say, "Buried." No! No. Everything dead should be resurrected back to life, people. So if you have that

testimony of being a "walking zombie" during worship and praise, you need to be resurrected. So in the name of Jesus, I adjure you to rise and lift your voice loudly like a trumpet before the Lord God. Now pull off those dead garments, lift your voice, and praise God. Dance before the Lord God. Stop waiting for others to start praising God; become a praise distributor for the Lord God, which means you praise God so sincerely and vociferously that you make others want to praise God too. Get out of that tomb of doubt, fear, and public opinion. Give God some praise! Anything dead should be resurrected, not buried. Stop burying your praise under your breath. Give God thunderous praise. Let's lift our voices loudly and earnestly to the King of kings and Lords of lords. He deserves all the praise and glory; even if you're not a Christian, you can praise the Lord God. Let everything that has breath praise ye the Lord.

A Personal Note

Did you know it's healthy to exercise? Your body benefits from bodily exercise. The scriptures say that "bodily exercise profits little (1 Timothy 4:8)." It doesn't say exercise profits nothing. So much sickness has invaded people's lives because of the lack of bodily exercise. Many of us have mastered our muscles in our mouth, eating everything in our view which increases our weight and expands our stomach and over time it can possibly weakened our immune system., but fewer of us have tried to exercise our bodies, which, reduces our fatty tissues, strengthens our hearts, keeps our blood circulating properly, reduces sugar levels in our blood, builds our muscles, helps bring down blood pressure, and strengthens our immune systems. Exercise does a lot more. So, in actuality to sit down excessively can be deadly.

I want you to know that it's all right to dance before the Lord.

It's all right to lift your voices and shout, "Hallelujah!" It's okay to jog sometimes while listening to gospel music and music in general. It's okay to get loose and move your body with a dance; you aren't a wall or a tree standing still, because being still is what they were created to do. On the other hand, you and I were never created to be like rocks or tall trees, just sitting there, lifeless, but we were born to be energetic, move, dance, jump, laugh, run, praise, sing, talk, and walk. We were never created to become bumps on a log. Human beings were never created to be motionless, so keep it moving, people. Praise God with a loud shout. Praise God with happy feet. Dance in his presence.

I would never want to be part of a motionless ministry. We were all made to move. If you danced before you came to Jesus, please don't stop dancing; just change partners. And for those who are in that motionless ministry, maybe heaven will be too boring for you because that's not what the angels do in heaven. The Bible says the angels in heaven rejoice and praise God all day (St. Matthew 5;12). We were made to move and conquer. Get out your rocking chair and praise God; dance before the Lord God. He is truly worthy of all the praise we can offer. Praise God every day and let everything that have breath praise God (150:6).

Doctors expect newborn babies to cry and move, and if they don't, these are signs that something is wrong. All those who are in the motionless ministry and carrying on as though they are statues instead of living beings (and the cat got their tongues)— maybe these are signs that something is definitely wrong within them. Only God can deliver them out of this refusal to praise him openly with some bodily exercise. Praising God profits! The Bible says bodily exercise profits little, but the little profit it gives can save your entire life and add days to it. Just that alone is worthy of praising God Almighty. We sit down too much; if you don't believe me, just add all the places where we sit: homes, churches, classrooms, jobs, funerals, doctor's offices, courtrooms, laundry mats, buses and trains, cars, planes, banks, and meetings.

For gracious peace of life, we should grow tired of sitting more than exercising, running, walking, working, and praising God. Certainly life is too enormous to just sit there when, quite frankly, there's so much to be done and accomplished in life. There's a benefit in praising God, but you wouldn't know this because you are using your energy to remain in a zombie world, dead to all the opportunities that await you. Come out of that zombie world and its deadness appeal; you're too valuable for that and worth more than that. Praise your creator loudly. Praises come with many rewards; don't stop praising God.

7. Grave-Diggers The most popular refusal for not praising God aloud in my experience comes from the gravediggers. Gravediggers are Christians who go back to the cemetery where they buried their old habits and sinful pleasures; they dig up those old coffins of depression and worry, cursing and swearing, lying, doubt, fear, addictions, low self-esteem, criminal activity, drugs and alcohol, cigarette smoking, sinful thoughts, stealing, suicidal tendencies, scandalous behavior, deceitful ways, criminal behavior, idol worship, witchcraft, sexual immorality, adultery, fornication, hatred, prejudice, and much more. So while the praise and worship service are being conducted, they feel guilty as charged for digging up those old coffins of sinful habits they participated in. Therefore, they refuse to praise God in this condition, only to become spectators, because how could you come in during the midst of worship and praise service and lift up your voice with praise to God, knowing that you participated in many sinful pleasures? So instead of praising God in the sanctuary, they sit amid to praises and refuse to participate, because they feel like a hypocrite if they take part. So, they become dead to praising God. There are too many Christian spectators in church and not enough praise teams in the sanctuary.

When the refreshing of the Lord (Spirit of God) is in the building, repent of those sinful deeds (Acts 3:19) and ask God to take away the taste and desire for those unclean things; once you do this, you can lift your voice and praise God. Besides, the scriptures don't say only "Christians are to praise ye the Lord." Psalm 150 says, "Let everything that has breath praise the Lord." Is there breath in your body? Then you also qualify to praise God. The scriptures don't say only believers can praise God; they say everything that breathes can praise the Lord. Therefore Lift your voice in the sanctuary and praise the Lord God.

Repent of those sinful actions and turn to God. Turn from your wicked ways so you can freely praise God without any condemnation or guilty conscience. But if you insist not to turn from your wicked ways, God still deserves praise. God is worthy of all the praises, and if we don't praise him, the rocks will (Luke 19:40). The Bible says, "Let everything that have breath praise the Lord"; that's the breath not only of Christians but also of every creature that walks on the earth. Stop with the excuses of why you cannot loudly praise the Lord God. How would you feel if you had a child who never said thank you for anything you did for him or her? The child would be considered ungrateful, unappreciative, and unpleasant to be around. So, we should aspire to be thankful and be filled with praises to the Lord all the days of our lives, for he is the creator of life. Smile and be happy, for God is on your side. Be a cheerful giver, especially when it is time to give praise to God. Give God the highest praise. Did you know that praise is a sacrifice just like a monetary offering is a gift towards God's work? God rewards sincere sacrifices.. Don't you need answers to your prayers expedited? Develop sincere praise to God the Father because God lives amid praises; and when he is present, prayers are answered, and miracles happen.

For those who still refuse to praise God openly, no worries; the sun shall still shine, your heart will still beat, the air you breathe will continue to flow, and you will still have the freedom to govern your life as you wish. God won't force you to do something you refuse to do because he loves you that much. Please remember that the most vital thing in life is the breath of life you possess as well as a right mind, health, and strength. Tell me, what could you do without these vital life components? Absolutely nothing. Amazingly these vital components came from God. I personally have chosen to praise God in the morning and evening because he is worthy of all the praise. *Praise God right where you sit!*

This message was approximately twenty-five minutes long, but it had such an impact on the body of Christ that day. It became breaking news throughout our church circle and many other places too. One example of this was that one of our church members took notes in shorthand and later transposed her notes and used them as a topic in her Bible study during lunch break (the dead cannot praise God), and those who attended her Bible study enjoyed it so much that they shared it with their churches and family members. The topic was hot off the press and straight from God, she quoted. Her audience was overwhelmed and received the word of the Lord intently; as a result of this supernatural event, many publicized this message to various communities, and churches made this message a locally famous sermon, "The Dead Cannot Praise the Lord." Having no idea of the impact this message was having in the church and the surrounding communities, I was very moved by the testimonies people shared with me. Some said that they "never looked at praises like this." Others said that after listening to this sermon, they were going to make some changes."

Once I heard the good news of people sharing this message, I decided to write down all the messages God gave me and save them for a future book. Some years later, I began writing a book comprising short messages God gave me from time to time. I am confident it will uplift, inspire, and strengthen many people. Amazingly, almost forty years later, people still mention that sermon I gave when I was seventeen years old; for this reason, I strongly believe God has given me a sense of urgency to bring forth a book called *Messages of Impact*.

This book is a compilation of messages God has given me to share with the body of Christ and the world at hand. Messages of impact have impacted my life, and it is my earnest prayer that these same messages will influence your life and all who read it. As you read *Messages of Impact* further, please share the messages with other believers and nonbelievers. This book isn't limited to Christians; it is meant for people from all races, creeds, and nationalities. *Messages of Impact* is different from most books; it provides a collection of Sunday-morning sermons, life stories, Bible stories, life experiences, and poems, all together for the enrichment and enlightenment of everyday living, whether you are a church leader or just a curious reader. Its topics can be used in your home or work environment, or in Sunday school lessons and Bible studies; or they can be used as a Sunday-morning sermon selector (and so forth). Reading this book will motivate righteous living, intensify your faith in God, and constantly challenge you to be better, reminding you of how important God is needed in your life and your need to keep open communication with him, because he can impact our lives in ways no one or any book can.

We hope something said in this book will have such an impact on your life that you will surrender all to God. Apparently, God's words (the Holy Bible) alone without any additional help from authors and pastors impact people's lives throughout the world. God's words bring about new beginnings, deliverance, salvation, and resurrection; they give sight to the blind and hope to the hopeless. They heal the sick and hurting, bring joy to the saddened hearts, and encourage the depressed to become giants in the Lord.

It is written, and so let it be said, "There be more with us, than against us" (2 Chronicles 32:7; Romans 8:31). Jehovah God is all you need; if countries are just drops in a bucket to God (Isaiah 40:15), then how small must our problems be to him? Microscopic! So, stop making your problems bigger than they really are. With God all things are possible (Matthew 19:26), but this isn't the case with men, corporations, politics, law enforcement, or the court system; but with God, all things are possible if we believe (St. Mark 10:26).

The Bible is the best example of impacting lives. Billions of people and countless lives have been impacted by the Holy Scriptures. What other book do you know can literally save lives, heal the sick, deliver suicide victims, protect the weak and poor, feed the homeless, instruct the foolish, bring light into darkness, cast out demons, save souls, accurately predict future events, give sight to the blind, give sanity to the insane, raise the dead from the grave, and most importantly, give eternal life? What book can do all of this or even come close? Hallelujah, glory to God! No book can compare; nor will there ever be a book like the Holy Bible, God's living word. The Bible can be found in hotel rooms, churches, libraries, schools, book stores, hospitals, and other countries. The Holy Bible has remained on the best-seller list since BC, even from Moses's time to the twenty-first century. The Holy Bible is our largest reference and resource tool used to write this book, along with Fifty four years of my life experiences; more importantly, God's Spirit is upon me to preach and teach the gospel of Jesus Christ, the soon-coming King.

Look at all the men of God in the Old Testament: Moses, Joshua, Abraham, Jacob, and Joseph. They all served God and were led by God; and the Spirit of God moved on them at different times in history, proving that each had such a great impact on the world, even on our Christian faith today.

All rich, famous, and successful people have one thing in common; they all digested words that motivated and impacted them to soar and prosper. Most likely, it was someone or a book that gave them some encouraging words and caught their complete attention. It made them do something, change something, or even invent something. People of God, don't just sit there and do nothing. Your life matters, and it can positively affect change in others. I want my children's children to one day read this book, and hopefully, it will let them see it's possible to follow their dreams and passions; and maybe it will help them accomplish something great. When you follow your dreams and passions, you automatically impact others.

During the early 1980s, I attended Seward Park High School in New York City, located in the lower Manhattan area. One of my math teachers said something in my class that impacted my life, even to this day. During this time, people were complaining that after graduating from college, they weren't getting jobs. We questioned our teacher that day about why this was happening, and he is quoted as saying, "If finding employment becomes difficult and it seems impossible, create your own job." Today these words have helped me become an independent sales agent for many distribution centers, and they have inspired me to start my own sales agency as well as start my book collection, which will inspire and impact millions of people. So regardless of recessions, depressions, gas hikes, a stock market crash, COVID-19, foreclosures, and bankruptcies, as long as you have health, strength, and God on your side, unemployment won't destroy you. Instead, it will become a launching pad towards your success. There are opportunities in America you won't find anywhere else, and with God on your side, you won't fail but soar. Aren't you and I worth more than dirt? If God can take dirt from the ground and create human beings, then for certain he has installed in us something more valuable, unique, and priceless that will impact not just our families and communities but also the world at hand. Are you ready to impact the world, your communities, and your household?

Joshua said, "As for me and my household we will serve the Lord" (Joshua 24:15). Because of Joshua's commitment to God, in return the Israelites served God as long as Joshua lived. What kind of impact are you leaving with your family, community, church, school, home, and business?

We are on this planet to serve God freely and love our neighbors as ourselves. Yes, we want prestige, expensive toys, companionship, money, respect, and love, but we must first follow God, who can give it all to us. His name is Jesus! When you want a loan, you go to a loan officer at a bank or someone who is rich. When you are sick and need to be cured, you run to the doctor. And when you want to learn music, you go to music school. Then why is it that when you want a better and more prosperous life, you won't go to the creator of life? We will go to a financial consultant first and follow his or her instructions. People of God, stick with the author of the Holy Bible, the creator of the world, universe, and the mind regulator. He's the truth and the way; his name is Jesus, the Son of the living God.

My prayer is that after you have read this book, *Messages of Impact*, your life will be positively impacted, spiritually charged, and infectious throughout your community, church, and city. Once every page has been read and then digested in the city of your soul, you will return to your church with a new outlook and a readiness to work for the Lord; you will also follow the paths of Abraham, Moses, Joshua, and Joseph, all of whom chose to follow God unconditionally. They journeyed through life with a commitment to serve, obey, and walk with God.

Messages of Impact was written for you to study, absorb, share with others, and preach. Live it and teach it to your family and others too, never forgetting that God's word will never return void, because it will always accomplish what it sets out to do

(Isaiah 55:11) "So shall my word be that goeth forth out of my mouth:

it shall not return unto me void,
but it shall accomplish that which I please,
and it shall prosper in the thing whereto I sent it.

God's word comes into the earth to bring about salvation for mankind, heal the soul, give peace to the mind, and bring deliverance from bad habits and addictions. Most importantly, God's word comes to spread love and forgiveness to all people. Regardless of whether we see it, God promised he will finish the work in people's lives. That's not the writer of this book but the author of the Holy Bible, the author and finisher of our faith (Hebrews 12:2), who will complete what is necessary and imperative in people's lives. Only God really knows what each of us needs.

As you read farther, I hope you will get aclear understanding and motivation out of this book. Thank you for your interest in this book. May God richly bless you and your family; please e-mail us at messageofimpact@gmail your testimonies and comments on how this book has impacted your life to the author of this book, Robert James Thomas Sr. also please visit our web-page messagesofimpact.com. Leave your comments on the *Messages of Impact* Facebook page. Although the author of this book cannot answer all your problems, he is connected to the God that created Heaven and Earth and the Universe, who sees and knows the burdens you bear and the path you're on; and he cares about your well-being. Believe this day that God can fix your life and turn your life around for a better out-come, like he did for the author of this book and he can do the same for you.

Now God has inspired me to publish messages of impact to help others escape sin's evil and deadly entrapment from hell. This was created by God's archenemy to annihilate your relationship with God in any capacity and to finally torment you forever with guilty stains of "I wish I could have ." Dear reader, stand for righteousness. Stand for love and salvation, and as you do, God will stand with you; and no weapon, influence, or principality that stands will prosper against you (Isaiah 54:17).

You are uniquely made in the image of God who dares to diminish or down play your extraordinary uniqueness, made from dirt with the hands of a mighty and loving God that thought so highly of us. He created us in the mere image of himself, thereby creating mankind in the image of God and God installed in us his breath of life which comes with many perks, health, oxygen, personality, genius power, thinking power and learning power, creativity and inventive power, smarts and wisdom, vision, discernment, working power and the power to bring life into the world. Wow! We are God's extraordinary prize possession (Master-Piece) made in his image. Certainly, that alone should make us happy each morning we wake. Therefore, don't let no one diminish your great potential, destiny, dreams, and good nature as well as your future.

CHAPTER 1

God Wants More

O ne beautiful Saturday morning, as the sun glistened throughout our living room window, my family and I were preparing our attire for an evening event at church. It was a gospel concert scheduled to start at 7:30 p.m. We wanted to leave and give ample time to arrive promptly at our destination. One of our friends invited my wife to come and sing two selections. We were excited to be performing to a new audience besides our home church. Our entire family is composed of musicians, so we huddled together, discussed our music, and rehearsed our songs and music until we felt they were perfect. We quickly chose songs we would sing and play for the concert, and later that afternoon we did a quick rehearsal for two hours. Then around four o'clock, we started to get cleaned up and dressed to leave around five thirty.

The doors of the concert were to open at seven p.m. We had to travel from Manhattan, where we lived, to Brooklyn, New York, which was a forty-minute drive. As we rushed to this church concert, we struggled through some of the heaviest traffic I ever experienced. We were almost persuaded to turn around and go home. Imagine being on a highway where people were walking around freely because traffic wasn't moving. Horns were blowing, and people were socializing right on the highway; apparently, there was an accident up ahead. Nothing could be done until the tow truck came. So we waited patiently while undergoing almost two hours plus of standstill traffic.

Finally, after much time and desperation, traffic began moving, and within minutes we arrived at our destination, only to find that everyone was seated, eating, laughing, and talking while gospel music echoed throughout the sanctuary. People were sitting at tables, eating. Ushers were serving fried chicken, collard greens, cabbage, candied yams, and macaroni and cheese. The atmosphere was filled with the scent of soul food and hot grease. If you could read my mind that day, it would have said, "What in God's name is this—a concert or a banquet?"

My wife, Marie Della Thomas, wanted to go back home

immediately, exclaiming, "I have seen enough, and I'm ready to go home. I thought we were coming to a concert, not a banquet." One of the ushers approached us and asked whether we would like to sit down and eat. My first response was yes; I definitely never wanted to turn away a free meal, because where there is food, I will partake. But my question to her was, "When will the concert start?"

She responded, "In a few minutes."

Looking at my watch, I saw it was already after eight p.m., so I thought, *The concert will probably start at 8:45 p.m.* Nevertheless, my four children were very hungry because they hadn't eaten lunch and had experienced some of the outlandish gridlock on the highway. I was so frustrated after coming from standstill traffic and seeing that the concert hadn't even begun, but after being delayed from our traffic issues and never stopping for a short snack on the way to the concert, heaven knows we were hungry. I was a little bewildered by the dining issue, but I couldn't deny the aroma of soul food, and its good smell was making my stomach growl. So we dined, and the food was delicious and tasted scrumptious. After dinner, I felt a little sleepy after digesting fried chicken, collard greens, potato salad, candied yams, macaroni and cheese, green salad, and sweet potato pie. I was ready to go home because my stomach was filled and my appetite now was to sleep off this tiredness I felt. Nevertheless, I prevailed through my exhaustion because we were on assignment to minister in song to an audience we had never seen before.

Once everyone finished eating his or her meal, the church ushers approached our tables to put away food and clean up garbage. They removed all tables so the concert could start. The church maintenance crew vacuumed the floors. The entire crowd of guests who had come to hear gospel music moved out of the way to give the maintenance crew clearance. One of the ministers announced on the microphone, "In ten to fifteen minutes, the concert will begin. Please stand by." As we were waiting in anticipation, we made friends with some of the guests and mingled with some of the familiar faces and performing groups. After ten minutes, we were able to find our seats and wait for the concert to begin.

Approaching the center of the church was a middle-aged woman dressed corporately; she sternly looked into the audience's faces and shouted, "Praise the Lord, everybody." Everyone responded, "Praise the Lord." Then she proceeded to open the program with prayer, and another person read a scripture. Someone else sang a hymn, and the musicians were in their places, jamming. They sang. They played. They jammed.

Wow! This concert was jumping, and the atmosphere was filled with joy and the freedom of praise. The musicians played rhythmically, and the audience responded with clapping and dancing feet.

This audience came ready to express and testify of God's goodness, singing songs with melodies of praise and harmonies of love. We felt the excitement, fire, and spirit behind it all. Some people clapped their hands to the rhythm of the beat, and others danced across the floor in the church. Some people ran around the church with their hands lifted and their voices elevated, saying, "Hosanna! Blessed be the rock." Praises did go up, and blessings did come down.

Marie and I both stood up, bouncing from side to side, and our children stood up and moved to the beat. It was as though the house was on fire, leaving no room for spectators. Then suddenly, as the music played loudly and the singing resonated throughout the church atmosphere, the people's voices filled the room with praises from their lips. Some people danced. Others jumped and clapped their hands to the beat of the music, which made us dance. While the room was filled with such enthusiasm, excitement, praise and worship, dancing and thunderous praise and worship, I could hear the voice of God speak to me very clearly and softly in my ear, saying, *"I want more! I want more! I want more than this! You keep giving me your garments, your outer layers, but I want your heart and not your garments*" (Joel 2:3). Rend your hearts and not your garments.

In the middle of all this excitement and enthusiasm in the church, I couldn't ignore that quiet, still voice whispering in my ear. "I want more! I want more than this!" Certainly, God was speaking directly to me. God speaks to his children in many ways, sometimes in a soft and still voice, other times through other people, dreams, threw ministers of the gospel and through life experiences, but he definitely speaks to his children through by many sources.

Finally, at about eleven p.m., they called my wife to sing. We were ready and thrilled to be performing in front of a lively and energetic audience. As we started our first rendition of songs, the audience responded to our songs like they had heard them before. Marie ministered in song to this audience, and she did a wonderful job, but while all this was occurring, along with the high intensity of God's Spirit being demonstrated with great music and rhyming lyrics, I couldn't erase that faint voice of God in my ear, saying to me, "I want more! I want more than this."

After Marie sang a couple of songs, a couple of quartet groups followed her, and the concert ended at about one o'clock in the morning. While we were pushing our way to the door, people complimented my wife for her gift of song. We made some connections with other ministries, and we did network with some of the performers. What a good time we had! Traveling back home, we made a stop to get some soft drinks while discussing the concert that night. We all agreed on the high intensity of God's Spirit in that place while driving back home on the highway. I didn't mention what God had whispered in my ears; it was my secret for now. Along the way back, there was no traffic on the highway, and it took us only twenty-five minutes to arrive home. Everyone was in an excellent mood, and all of us continued to exclaim about our joyful evening as we all departed to our homes.

Yet I couldn't escape from those words whispered in my ears

from the mouth of God. After arriving home, we got comfortable, and later that evening, I went into my personal closet and asked God about what he was saying and why he was saying these things to me. God spoke back to me and gave me the words to say to the world at hand but especially to my family. I definitely wasn't eliminated from this equation. When God speaks to one, he speaks to all. So he spoke to me and said the following:

I'm tired of the simple "Now thou lay me down to sleep" prayers. You are not a child anymore. I want more! You give everyone else your time and heart, and you give me maybe two minutes out of your day. I want more! You come to church, but in your heart, you don't want to be in the house of worship. I want more! All over the country, prayer services, Bible studies, and Sunday schools are nearly empty. I want more! I am tired of your espresso prayers and the short devotions you have with me. I want more! From the beginning of time, I always wanted your heart, but you keep giving me your garments. Imagine a father who deserts his children; he keeps giving them gifts at birthdays and Christmas but never comes to visit them or spend time with them. These children want more. So, it is with you. You do what is expected of a Christian, but where is the personal time between me and you? Just like the father I mentioned earlier, these children would much rather have their dad's presence than the things he purchases for them. So, it is with the Lord God.

You go to church, you pay tithes and offerings, and you talk about me to others. You even sing and dance to gospel music, and you learn about me through the Holy Scriptures. But I want more of you. Stop giving me your garments; I'd rather have you. What are the garments?

They are all the outward things we wrap our time and energy in. More than anything else, God wants our hearts, which are our time, obedience, faith in him, and commitment to him. This includes our constant communication with him, not just church attendance. The phrase "I want more," the Lord God speaks of has everything to do with us Christians and non-Christians spending some time with him in pray and devotion. Other words God wants some of our time and your undivided attention." The question is can we spear some time which he gives us each day we wake?

It doesn't have to be and shouldn't be at the point of death when (and only then) that we give God our absolute attention. Stop the foolishness! The Lord God wants more than this!

Each day you constantly spend your money on things that have no heavenly value. All your time is divided between television time, work and school, hanging out, church programs, movies, Internet, cell phones, iPhones, iPads, sports, music, video games, Facebook, YouTube, Facetime, Instagram, texting time, eating, drinking, and having lots of sex outside of marriage. Your cell phone isn't your god, but if it were your god, you both would be the best of friends because you speak to it every day, carry it everywhere you go, and highly protect your relationship with it. When you're bored, you go to your phone for entertainment; when you're depressed, you search on your phone for something or someone to pick up your spirits; and when you want answers to your problems, you go to your phone. You love your cell phone, but your cell doesn't love you the same way, because when you are slow to pay for your service, your service will be terminated immediately; and when it breaks or malfunctions, you run to get it replaced.

Yes, you love your phone so much that you communicate

with it more than you communicate with your creator. Can you even fit God in your space or schedule? Has artificial intelligence come between you and God? You constantly look for instant gratification. When do you have time for God? "Isn't God our salvation?" You may be satisfied with the five minutes you give him sometimes, if it's even five minutes. God wants more, and you know he does. Lets stop giving the lord all the outward things; give him your heart. Give him your heart!" I have a question for you dear reader have you ever loved someone so much, and in return he or she didn't love you as much or at all, yet the person often verbalized his or her undying love for you, but the person's words were totally empty and amounted to nothing? Their words are just shallow, never measuring up to any expectation. Well, people, imagine how God feels when we outwardly look like we love God in front of people but inwardly we would rather be at an amusement park, or at a ball game, or on a long vacation further away from his presence.

Imagine the God of the universal and earth wants to spend time with me and you? So, I began to write down what God was saying to me. This message was for me first, then for the body of Christ, sinners, people, and backsliders. It's true that our time spent with God is sometimes limited. We spend much of our time with things and people who aren't as important as we make them out to be. Married couples marry because they love each other, and that love comes from the time they spend with each other and nothing else.

Here's a good analogy to get the gist of why God was saying he wants more to me. A husband buys jewelry for his wife, and she loves it; he takes her out to an expensive dinner, and she is impressed. He surprises her with flowers, and because she's feeling very special, now he feels like "Mack daddy," moving his head from side to side. And while his and her emotions are cranked up, his wife slowly leans forward as though she is going to kiss him on the lips, but instead she whispers in his ear, "Do you love me?"

He stares at her with a look of surprise, thinking, *I just brought you jewelry, flowers, and a meal. Those things should prove my feelings for you.* She continues to speak. "I want to know that your thoughts are only for me when we are together. I want your undivided attention so your eyes will never be wandering at other beautiful women while we dine, because it's so important to me that your eyes are only for me when we dine. That makes me feel important and so valuable to you. I need to feel wanted and valuable to you. That's the more I need from you, just as any other married women would want to feel" Other-words, more than anything else God is conveying he wants to spend time with us and when God speaks to one he speaks to all.

So continuing with the story of the couple dinning, she further mentions, "when we are conversing as husband and wife, your eye contact shouldn't be wandering out of space; rather, it should be intensely gazing into my eyes because the eyes are the gate to the heart and soul. Even your wife wants more. Not even the things you buy or give them are enough; they want you. Just as your wife wants more, so does God. Going to church every Sunday doesn't exactly prove your love for God. Church is a good place to hide from God. Churches are sometimes more concerned about the order of services more than about having the presence of God in their midst. So, if this is a reality in your church, you could be guilty of having *artificial worship* services at times. What's artificial worship? It is when your heart isn't in what you're doing.

Let's examine the order of most church services: opening prayer, scripture reading, worship and praise singing, testimonies in some churches, offering, announcements, a song from the choir, and last but not least, the preacher giving his sermon, an altar call, acknowledgments, and then the final benediction. Approximately how much time are you really spending with the Lord worshipping the king of kings? While the services are in process, is your mind on the Lord? Are you praying throughout the service? Is there sincere praise being lifted? Are people being delivered, healed, and saved? Are you speaking to your brother and sister next to you? Are you to dress to get dirty? To bless to smile? Are we promoting Jesus or ourselves? Or is this just a formality we go through to prove we went to church? Or has church become a place to make fashion statements as to who is the best dressed? What are the conversations like after services? Are your conversations about the Lord and his presence or maybe something negative about your brother or sister? You can tell the intensity of any service by the conversations people have after the benediction.

Truthfully, the conversations we tend to participate in after services have nothing to do with being in God's presence. Is this why God speaks to my heart like this and says, "I keep hearing that still voice in my ear I the Lord want more." I must realize and my readers must realize "the lord God is our source of our very existence, and many times we have the nerve to want to distance ourself from him only one that can help us. Many occasions the only time we want to be close to the lord is when we are sick with an uncontrollable disease or when we are on our death bed. The Lord will not tolerate this kind of treatment all the time. He is letting the author of this book and my readers know the Lord, wants more than this. Just think about it, when problems arise beyond our control, then we cry out to the lord, 'Lord, help me!', The Lord, wants more than this. Yes, God is our healer. Yes, God is our deliverer and our salvation, but the question remains after God has done these things for us, will we commune with him? Will we pray to our heavenly Father? Will we read God's holy word, or will we do what most do—walk away from God in your daily routines and devotion but carry on as though we serve the lord in front of others yet we continue to serve another? Do we even worship the lord in sincerity? or do we effortlessly turn to worship our personal idols, which are not real gods but are dead gods, and we freely give them our attention, time, and our life, which God gave us. After hearing the voice of lord speak to my heart I could not erase those sacred words ringing in my ears saying "I want more". *When you think about it, the Lord, gave us, much and we continue to give him less and less of ourselves and our time. Jesus wants more!*

"We read about the Lord, We often sing about him, and we testify about our love for the Lord. We even praise his name in church, and some of us pay tithes and give offerings, but many times we refuse to spend alone time with the lord.. Truthly speaking, what kind of love is this? Sometimes it seems many of us are more concerned about demonstrating our love publicly for the Lord to the world more than doing the very thing the Lord God loves *most*, which is 'spending personal time with him.'Just for one minute think how our creator must feel, when in fact he created us in his own image. He loved us so much he gave us his only begotten Son, Jesus Christ, to die for our sins so we may live without damnation and enjoy eternal life forever. You see after Adam and Eve's disobedience in the garden of Eden, our destination was destined for damnation and hell as a home; instead, Jehovah God made the ultimate sacrifice to give his only begotten Son to be crucified for the redemption of all mankind back to God so we could live forever, which God initially intended from the beginning of time, so you and I would live forever, and yet many of us insist on not spending any time with our creator. The eyes of the Lord God are in every place, beholding the good and the bad, (Proverbs 15:3) even if the doors are closed and the room is darkened. God has night vision that can pick up hidden things and microscopic things. The Lord God, can see in the dark too. So, nothing we do is hidden from God. Yet many of us continue to hide from God as though he cannot see us. News flash, God knows the intentions of our heart, which are to keep our distance from the lord at any- cost. I am reaching out to my readers with loving arms because the wages of sin are death, but the gift of God is eternal life (Roman 6:23). What is that gift? Life and Salvation! But what is salvation without a personal relationship between you and the life giver our Lord Jesus Christ? Many of us relationship with Christ has seemly been *annulled* for some time now, and we are fully aware of it. Some of us know for a fact *our personal relationship with Christ needs to be activated and validated, which will give our relationship with Christ authenticity, and that comes when you spend personal time with Christ in prayer, praise, bible reading and worship. The Lord gave us everything, and many of us continue to give him nothing but distance and our problems. If the shoes were on the other foot whereby you were treated this way you would say; "I want more"!*

"*Your time is all you really have on earth, and, the Lord God, gave you that time. Now give him some time.* the Lord, wants more! Question, what is this thing in which, a mother can love and raise ten children, but not one of them can take care of their mother when she is old and feeble? Everyone is so busy with his or her own life and family that extending additional time for Mom is too much to bear. Apparently, they forgot who gave birth to them, the one who nurtured them and made sacrifices for them so they could one day be able to stand on their own two feet. You simply ignore your mother's plea for help and support, and if she could speak and tell the story, she would say, 'I want more than this. She did without so you could gain. She spent countless hours feeding you, clothing you, reading to you, playing with you, laughing and having fun with you, and teaching you new things. And now you will not even come to mom's rescue or even visit her at the nursing home.

"'If mom could speak, mom would say, I want more than this' is exactly what Mama would say. So it is with us, It's okay to come to church, looking for a wife. It is fine that you come to church to hear your favorite minister preach. It's okay to come to church to support the anniversaries, concerts, revivals, theatrical plays, and so forth, but is anyone coming to church to spend quality time with Jesus by worshiping his holy namce? Because Jesus wants more. He simply wants you, but many of us keep giving him our garments. We involve ourselves and give ourselves to so many things that impede and interfere with our relationship with the Lord God. So, it is obvious that the lord God wants more of us." Therefore we need to Check our daily routine and schedule to see whether or not we can pencil God in our to-do list or daily routine." God wants more!

How do we give God more time? For starters: pray daily in your private closet and read your Bible. *You do other things in the closet. Why not give God a chance to enhance your life? Our closet experiences either put us on top of the world or reward us with many regrets and keep us living beneath our privileges.* The things we do in the closet will eventually surface, whether they are bad or good. Invite God into your closet space, which is your private time. Give him your heart and not your garments. God inhabits the praises of his people; make it a habit to praise God for the obvious things—life, health, shelter, and a right mind and the list keeps going on and on. *The phrase "God wants more" basically means God wants you and your time, and your attention represents you.* You give your time and attention to everyone else. Shall we make a list? I thought so.

If you still do not understand what God is saying, he simply wants you. Not everything else will do because everything else represents your garments, which you can keep, because God wants to spend time with you (on a one-on-one basis). I can still hear the voice of God speaking to my spirit saying:s, "Give me you." God wants to have some daily conversation with you. Trust me, God the Father doesn't bite. As a matter of fact, it is a good and rewarding thing to talk to the Lord God every day. Prayer is our invisible cell phone, which reaches to heaven and touches the heart of God, and the phone number is *"Our father which art in heaven, hallowed be thy name Thy kingdom come. Thy will be done in earth, as it is in heaven. Give us this day our daily bread. And forgive us our debts as we forgive our debtors. And lead us not into temptation, but deliver us from evil: for thine is the kingdom, and the power, and the glory, forever. Amen!" (St. Matthew 6:9)*

That is one of God's phone numbers. Try using it, but after you call that number, don't forget to give him some praise, and some glory. Tell him about your troubles and keep praising his name. Remember to pray for your enemies and friends and family.

Prayer is a two-way conversation in actuality it is literally the first real invisible cell-phone ever to exist in the world. You talk then allow God to speak to your heart and mind. Confess your sins to God, and he will forgive all your sins. Tell the Lord about your concerns, troubles, ideas, and goals. Then praise God with your lips, meditate on his word daily, and God will speak to you.

Spending time with our creator is the missing link in our lives. It is definitely the missing piece of the puzzling things happening in our lives, and that puzzling thing is that we don't spend enough time with our Lord God, and this type of lifestyle results in emptiness. Let us all stop running from the life giver. God doesn't bite. If he did, everyone who committed a horrific sin would be eliminated from planet earth. If God did bite, how many murderers, adulterers, liars, fornicators, false prophets, thieves, con artists, witches and warlocks, child molesters, and hypocrites would instantly drop dead before our eyes? God isn't a harsh God, as many people believe he is. God loves us so much that he gives us chances to get our lives in order; in other words, he wants us to make things right, and the purpose in doing so isn't that we should brag on being righteous but rather that it will be well with our hearts, minds, and souls. He's calling you out. Will you heed his voice? The Lord God wants more. And the more God wants is simply you and your undivided attention.

Joel 2:13 says, "Rend your heart, and not your garments and turn unto the Lord your God: He is gracious and merciful, slow to anger, and great kindness, and repenteth of the evil."

During the time of the prophet Joel, there were many earth-shattering and natural catastrophes, to name a few: rising floods, brutal earthquakes, and death filling the atmosphere. All these events were performed to stimulate fear and trepidation in the house of Judah. These occurrences happened frequently and without warning, just as they do in America and other countries.

Black clouds appeared on the land as though someone had turned the sunlight off, and a legion of locusts dominated the airways, covering all sunlight and destroying all crops. These events were constantly happening to get Judah's attention and inspire them to repent sincerely. God wanted them to recognize their need to come back to their first love, who was Jehovah God, their creator. Apparently, the signs of judgments just weren't turning their hearts toward God, but for some reason, they continued in their ways, forgetting their need for God. So God prepared and sent out his prophet Joel (his name means "the Lord is God"). God sent Joel to preach and call out this nation, Judah, to true repentance so they could once again enjoy the promises God intended for them.

Judah was serving God only through rituals; meanwhile, their hearts and true devotions were far from God. Out of tradition, Judah was going to the temple simply out of habit without any true devotion, all because generation after generation devalued the personal relationship their founding fathers had with God. The stories of their founding fathers were whispered in their ears by their elders, but their own experience with God didn't fully develop or become strengthened by the legacy of their rich past victories from God due to their lack of individual and personal devotion to almighty God. Many of them were heavily involved in their personal agendas. Can you truly worship God when your mind is clouded with lust, hate, witchcraft, anger, jealousies, lying lips, gossip, adultery, murder, stealing, fornication, scandalous behavior, deception, crime, greed, and filth? Joel convinced Judah that God wanted more from them than their *garments and sacrilegious rituals*; he wanted their hearts. This is the message God has been speaking to me about and pressing in my spirit to write about.

Garments represent clothes, robes, or cloaks; they are the

very things we wrap ourselves in just like clothing. The question is, what are you wrapped up in? God wants to be sought after each day, morning, noonday, and evening time. Men should pray always (Luke 18:1). The way to do this is to be in constant prayer mode, give a couple of earnest moments in time, and talk to the Father. You don't need to yell or scream out your prayer, because prayer is sacred and privately between you and God. Most people just pray and never wait to listen intently to the soft, still voice of the Lord speaking back into their ears as Daniel did in the Bible days. Daniel prayed three times a day (Daniel 6:10), pointing his altar in a corner by a window so others could see it was normal for him to pray to the Lord regardless of the king's demand that everyone bow down to the king's music. Yes, this king wanted everyone in the land to bow down to him when they heard the king's music (Daniel 3:10). Daniel later was punished for not obeying this decree, but because of Daniel's refusal to bow to the king's music, God made Daniel second in command to the king; before Daniel's promotion, Pharaoh put Daniel in a lions' den, but God shut the lions' jaws, and the lions became as a soft pillow for Daniel to lie on (Daniel 6:20–22). God will do the same thing for you and me when we give ourselves to the Lord God wholeheartedly. Also when you constantly commune with God in prayer, his holy, bright light begins to shine on your countenance, and people can see you have been with the Lord God.

After the king saw this miracle, this phenomenon, this spectacular moment in history, the king set a new decree that all the people must serve Daniel's God. Hallelujah! God will shut the lions' jaws for you, just like he did for Daniel. All we need to do is give God more of our time. We must establish a concrete relationship with our creator that, like Daniel's, is immovable.

Keep *communication with God continuous*, and no weapon against you will prosper.

After hearing the voice of the lord speaking to my heart saying, "I am tired of your halfway dedication; I am tired of your phony praise, your dishonest prayers. I am tired of those untrue doctrines you spread, making people think they're from God. Your doctrines are pulling people away from God, and I, the Lord, won't tolerate them. I am tired of your man-made laws, which you don't even follow. I'm tired of your filthy communion; you know how you are really living, yet you persist to participate in my Holy Communion without repenting. I am tired of your slack, discontentment, and staleness when entering my house of worship. Instead of entering my gates with praise on your lips, you insist on coming late with your head down to the ground and your lips full of everything else except praise and worship in your hearts. Although you assemble yourself with other Christians in church, you display no love, unity, joy, forgiveness, true worship in your hearts, or praise on your lips. This isn't the church I, the Lord God, built. What is this? I ask for true worship. Stop giving me your garments. It would be better for you to continue in the lifestyle you really want to live than to perpetuate your undying love for me while your heart remains as far from me as the east is from the west (Isaiah 29:13) (St. Matthew 15:8).

"If I cannot have you and you insist on giving me your garments, I will move on. If your heart is not in it, then you aren't truly sincere. I cannot make you love me, but keep living because when turbulence comes to your doorsteps and life hits you with serious issues, you will come to me expediently with such great urgency, begging me for help. Why wait for that? When I am calling you out now! "I, the Lord God, I want more than this"! These are some of the things the author of this book has been hearing in his spirit inspired by our Lord. Can anyone hear the Lord speaks loud and clear to their spirit? It is evident, God Simply wants you and nothing else! The Lord God, have no need or desire to have your money, jewelry, houses, land, business, career, reputation, fame, and fortune. All he wants is you, and you keep giving him your garments. If the lord can't have you, nothing else will do, because everything else will fade away and be obliterated. Without the Lord, we are simply nothing, just like a ship without a sail. It is only God's love and mercy that keeps every breath flowing through our nostrils. Doctors don't give you life, the Lord God, give you life. Your money doesn't wake you up in the morning, the Lord God allows you to rise each morning."

In business, they say to follow your passion, and at the end of the day, you'll be happy, and success will follow you. It is with the heart that men believe that Christ is the Son of the living God, by whom they are saved. If your heart, passion, and lifestyle aren't pointing to Jesus Christ, check yourself. The Lord God won't allow evil men to disgrace his name; nor will he continue to offer you a better life and everlasting life when in fact you continue to make it clear to the Lord God and the world that you want no part of God in your life. If you do walk away from God's salvation, remember that the Lord God has always loved you with no regrets, that's how much he loves you and he's waiting for you to come back to him within your personal time. Come to Jesus!

Tearing one's garments off was a customary way of expressing grief and remorse in the old testament in the Bible (Joshua 7:6; 1 Samuel 4:12). It was a way to show humility and your deep longing for forgiveness. It was common for God's people to tear off their garments, fall on their faces, and pray to God the Father.

However, like most outward acts and rituals, tearing off garments could easily be done without true sorrow or repentance. God requires more than external words and unwilling actions or deeds. He wants more. He wants your heart. Is your motive really to do the will of the Father, or is it to keep up with your peers? What defiles a man isn't what comes out of his mouth; rather, it's what's in his heart, because out of the heart of men proceed evil thoughts, adultery, crime, fornication, murders, thefts, covetousness, wickedness, deceit, lasciviousness, an evil eye, blasphemy, pride, and foolishness. All evil things come from within the heart of man (Matthew 15:18–20). Your thought process is your inward man. Lately what are you thinking about in church?

God is married to the backslider, and he is willing to leave the ninety-nine sheep for one lost one that goes astray (Luke 15:4–7). Always remember that you are important to God. Give him your heart, not your garments. Give God some personal talk time and allow him to speak back to you. Read God's word (Holy Bible) and teach it to your family. Tell your neighbors about his love and kindness. Honor the Lord God, and he will honor you.

Church as we know it can sometimes cloud God out with all our programs, including usher board services, anniversary services, hip hop services, concerts, Christmas services, Easter services, and all our events and schedules. Often we come to church more concerned about who's going to be there instead of making sure God's presence fills the sanctuary. So we carry out and conduct our services, not feeling God's Holy Spirit, being moved by no spirit, singing with no spirit, and sometimes preaching with no inspiration, not realizing we are the church and that it's our job to create a spirit-filled atmosphere while entering his gates with praise and thanksgiving, singing unto the Lord a new song, dancing in the spirit, and inviting our Lord and Savior to be in the midst. This is because when God's presence lives in the sanctuary, God answers prayers, brings deliverance, conducts healings, performs miracles, gives salvation, and does much more. Yet we still come to church, waiting for something to happen instead of making something happen. Get involved! Where are your longing and hunger for God's presence? Are we just spectators, or are we true worshippers? Enter his house with thanksgiving and his courts with praise (Psalm 100:4). God wants more. The most important thing in our services is to fully have the presence of God in the midst, because with God's presence intensely operating within the church, miracles happen, healing happens, deliverance happens, and blessings are dispensed. While you worship God in truth, he's working out your future footsteps. Why wouldn't you do the very thing that causes God's presence to inhabit your dwelling? God loves when his people praise and worship his name. He dwells amid praise(Psalm 22:3). True praises leave a sweet and attractive aroma like a soft but rich perfume fragrance that fills the airways, and when God smells this delightful scent, it makes God come down to that area and reside there.

Despite our shortcomings, lack of dedication, or refusal to truly worship God, God loves people so much that he gave his only begotten Son, Jesus Christ, to be crucified for the remission of sins for all mankind so we may come freely to the throne of grace, be saved, and become true worshippers. It's puzzling that we are more dedicated to so many people and things that cannot give us life, eternal life, health, strength, salvation, healing, and miracles. Many of us complain to God about all the things we need and don't have: more money, more cars, more business, more clothes, and the list goes on. We fail to realize that God has already given us more (life), and the more he has given us, the more we continue to devalue it, diminish its true value, and cheapen its luster and potential; and we frequently look to others as though they have more than we do. God proves to us every day that he gives us more each morning when we awake. Tell me, what could you do or enjoy without life? Yet we persist to give God less and less time each day, showing no appreciation for the obvious of being alive. It is God who shines his sunlight on the just and the unjust. He shows no partiality. God has always wanted a one-on-one relationship with mankind since the beginning of time.

God created man in his image and in his likeness for the purpose of a one-on-one relationship with mankind; having thousands of angels by his side, he chose to create people like himself to become true worshippers. What an awesome God! God created men and women for this purpose, and he expects more from us, so we should stop giving our creator our garments of nothingness. He only wants us.

Are we afraid to lose our fame and fortune if we give God more of us? Really! Or maybe our friends won't accept our patronage toward God. Will we continue to cloud our brains with unimportant things and cram our schedules with everything except God? Stop the madness. Give your creator some time. At the dinner table before you eat, turn off the TV and read a verse in the Bible to your family; and have a short discussion and then prayer. Jesus gave us the perfect example of how to pray by teaching the multitudes the "Our Father" prayer. Jesus was about his Father's business; he walked in love and humility, and he preached the gospel to the multitudes, spreading good news throughout the land. Jesus constantly did the work of his Father: healing, delivering, saving, and building the faith of his disciples. Jesus was tremendously involved in his father's business and vigorously doing the will of his father.

When I grew up during the '70s, when our pastor completed his sermon he would invite whosoever will to the altar. The altar call was about coming to the front of the church and having the pastor pray for their parishioner's: challenges, circumstances, issues and problems. The church altar was filled with people crying, screaming, and boisterously praising God. Some would foam at the mouth, and others would have runny noses. When I asked the minister around the church altar why these people were going through these emotions, he said, "They are trying to get to God." To be honest, from a distance this method seemed to be a bit extreme and difficult. People were tossing themselves on the floor, tumbling side to side; others were repeatedly jumping up and down while the ushers tried to assist these individuals. They told me to get on my knees and say, "Thank you, Jesus" repetitively until God's presence came on me. So, I did as they instructed; at the age of fifteen, I found myself on my knees, yelling, "Thank you, Jesus" over and over again.

My mind wandered to things like, *Who is looking at me? Can God hear me? Why did I come here today? Do I have to be so emotional, and does it take all this?* I must admit that God touched me after I tuned my surroundings out and focused on praising

God. He touched me, and oh, the joy that floods my soul. So, with this experience and conviction, I won't say this was the wrong way to get to God, nor will I say this is the only way to reach God, but I will say that when you are seeking something, you must do something. Please understand that it doesn't take all this to reach God, but in your search to find God, you will do something.

Why do we make things so hard for ourselves and others to come to Jesus when in fact Jesus Christ declared in his scriptures, "Come unto me for my yoke is easy and my burdens are light" (Matthew 11:30)? Who are we to make it so hard for others to come to Jesus? It's by faith that we receive salvation, not by the foaming of the mouth and yelling and screaming but by faith (Ephesians 2:8). Salvation is a gift from God, and gifts are to be received, not hunted down. Who said if you are a drug dealer, you should bring the drugs to the altar? Who said prostitutes should confess all the men they slept with? Who told the adulterer and fornicator to confess all he had slept with? Who told the perverted and lustful person to confess all the sites he or she had visited on his or her computer? If you are a thief, give us the list of names of those you robbed or for the liar to tell us every lie that parted from his or her lips.

No, my friend and dear reader. God already has all that information in his heavenly Rolodex. He sees you on his worldwide universal TV screen beyond those blue skies in heaven. All God really wants is you. He wants your heart, your time, and your attention, which in essence represents you. All you have to do is drop your garments of sin and not pick them up again; rather, you should pick up your Bible and study it, fall on your knees, and spend some time with God, your creator. God wants you more than what you own, and all the money in the world's bank cannot change this, because our currency is of no value to God; it only burns at his presence. That is why we shouldn't worship it. *Money is a tool, not a god.* Those who are handy and crafty with tools (money) become successful, but those who choose to worship money enter worthlessness and emptiness.

The commandments of men are a bunch of rules and regulations set up by self-righteous individuals who make it hard for others to get to God. All the jumping, screaming, and running won't get you closer to God or even move him. Your heart and faith determine the quality of your relationship with God, nothing else. Without these components being demonstrated in your relationship with God, you are wasting your time and energy. Whatever is in your heart will directly affect your daily activities, and believe me, it will point you either to things that will destroy your very life as well as your righteousness and success. Later, I understood clearly that you could yell out Jesus's name ten thousand times, swing on a pole while exclaiming the King had come, dance in the Spirit, and still walk out being a devil, having no desire to change your ways and no yearning to give God more of your time, attention, or prayer time. Whatever is harbored in your heart you will do.

Lucifer, the fallen angel, said in his heart, "I will be like the most high" (Isaiah 14:14). The question today is, what are you saying in your heart? King David was a man after God's own heart. David made it very visible and clear that seeking God was the ultimate thing to do, because he was after God's heart, not the heart of men. He loved God and feared him. David did things God appreciated, and for the wrong things, he entangled himself into until he eventually confessed them to God and repented. He didn't do the same things anymore. God wants more. Simply just you will do. Keep your garments and the exciting things you do, even your offering, because if your heart isn't in it wholeheartedly, your offering is void to God. God wants more! Give him your time, attention, and desires. *Your creator wants to spend more time with you. Imagine the God of all gods and the God of the universe desiring to spend time with us mortal men and women, who are made of clay and dirt. What an honor and tribute to mankind that*

Jehovah God wants our time and not the things we possess. How much time can you spare?

From the beginning of time, *God never meant you and me any harm*, only goodness, kindness, love, peace, eternal life, and a one-to-one relationship between God and man, which he proved throughout history. Give the Lord Jesus Christ more of your time. Every moment in time you live God unselfishly gives to you. God is the time giver and the time keeper for the entire human race, but will we squander each precious moment purposelessly, or will we make an effort to spend some moments of the day with the creator of life while we remain alive on earth? There's not a friend like the Lord Jesus, no not one. He will stick with you through tough times, even unto death. God wants some of your time. Your time here on earth represents you. Will you give God some of your private time? *What God wants is simply you; nothing else will do.*

CHAPTER 2

Don't Forget God

L ooking around my living room, I wondered, *Where have all the years gone, since our children are all grown up now?* No more diapers and infant formula. No more carriages and strollers. Now my children stand tall; some of them can almost look me in the eye. Those earlier years can come back only in memory now. While standing in our living room, my eldest son came to me and said, "Hey, Dad, I'm graduating from high school, and I just received an acceptance letter from the University of Hartford."

"Did you say Harvard University?"

"No, Dad, Hartford University is in Connecticut."

I slowly turned my head to the wall and continued to reminisce about all the things we had done together and the places we had visited. I remembered taking walks in parks, playing catch, swinging on the swings, racing and running, riding our bikes, swimming at the beach, and joyriding through different states. Thank God for all those good times. Our home was filled with laughter and fun and things to do. On Sunday we adorned ourselves for church and sang and played music together. What a time we had bonding with each other. It's all a memory now. My son has become a man now. Wow! He stands in front of me, looking for my support and encouragement. What could I say that would impact his life? What could I say to keep him on the right track? God gave me a word to give to my child, after which this topic became a message for the church at hand.

Don't Forget God

Some of you reading this book may think this was a corny phrase to leave with my child, but it seemed so appropriate and timely because a child cannot take his or her parents with him or her to college, but the child can certainly take God with him or her everywhere. In three months my son would be leaving us to get higher education, and he was looking for some guidance from his parents to show him the way. The Bible says in Proverbs 22:6,

"Train up a child in the way he should go: and when he is old he will not depart from it." God spoke to my heart and said to tell him, "Don't forget God!"

Both Marie and I knew our son Bobby would be faced with peer pressure, drugs, liquor, sex, pornography, and possible gang influences. We didn't want to freely throw our gift from God to the wolves of darkness so quickly. We became extremely concerned parents. So we prayed and invited all our children to the dining room to have a Bible study. They paused for a moment and questioned us. "What's going on, Mom and Dad?"

Marie replied, "Your dad wants to speak with you all."

My six-year-old asked, "Is this a business meeting?"

Everyone exclaimed, "It surely looks like that."

I responded, "Yes, it *is* a business meeting. We will discuss some things that will be paramount to our lives and future endeavors. As you all know, Bobby is leaving for college, and God gave me some words to put in his ears, but everything that will be said will benefit all of us. Everyone, get your Bibles, and then we will begin."

As we opened up in prayer, I felt a little resistance coming from my family as if to say, *When will it all be over?* So I started off with a bunch of questions to open this study and break some of the coldness I felt among my family. So I started with questions like this: How would it feel if people forgot your birthday? What if no one called you, came to see you, or said, "Happy birthday"? How would you feel?

They replied, "Bad, angry, sad but very disappointed."

"What if your boss promised you a promotion or a raise? But as time went by, he forgot, and later you found out he gave raises to other employees in your office and promoted one of your friends. When you reminded him of his promise, he said, 'I might have forgotten. Actually I don't remember.' How would you feel?"

They replied, "I would quit. I would leave without mentioning it."

"When someone owes you money, they promise to pay you back. But if they see you in church and in the neighborhood they simply ignore you, how would you feel?"

They replied, "I would speak to them and tell them off or take them to court."

"What happens if you were sick in the hospital and no one came to see you or even bothered to call you? How would you feel?"

They replied, "I would cut some people off as friends. I would tell some family members off."

You see, everyone wants to be remembered and sometimes thought of by someone. So it is with God the Father. How do you think God feels when we forget him? Yes, you forget God, and we all can admit it. But he never forgets us. The things God has done for us are apparently invisible. The air we breathe is his. He controls our every heart-beat within our chest. The brains in our skulls, which we use to think and comprehend, come from God. Also, the brains in our skulls are the first computers ever known to mankind, created by God. The brain's copycats are (Apple, IBM, Microsoft, and Hewlett-Packard) just to name a few have tried to mimic what God created possibly more than a hundred thousand years ago. They have all tried to create something close to God's great creation, the human brain. No matter how advanced technology becomes, it will always remain artificial intelligence.

Scientists and technology geniuses will never match God's brilliance and elite powers. What about those cloning companies that make human clones from stem cells, human cells, and tissue? You will never match God's brilliance and wisdom. Keep trying, but no one can replace God.

Why do we remember the things people do for us more than what almighty God has done for us? Is it really amnesia? Or is it because it's not that important enough to us because life is freely given to us by God with no strings attached? So we seek other things to gratify our lifestyles more sincerely than the life giver, who asks for very little.

Many of us are guilty of coming to church with no praise, testimony, song, true fellowship, worship, smile, love, personal devotion with God, or love for our neighbors. Are we in church only to be spectators? Is this true? Where is our gratitude? Has success clouded our vision? Is that thing we really want out of life so affecting our memory banks and brainpower that we forget our creator? Are our hearts filled with pride and selfishness? Are we too embarrassed to express our gratitude to the Lord God among the congregation? Our absentmindedness is like a sudden dark cloud of amnesia, which comes over our minds, filling us with the lack of appreciation and ingratitude for our humble beginnings with God. We forget all God's goodness and mercies toward us. It is God who gives us the power to get wealth, and to the working poor, it's God who keeps and protects us. He gives us strength to work and blesses us with family and friends. God watches over the rich and the poor. We all eat from the same farms and animals. To God there are no "big yous and little me's." We are all equal in God's sight.

Ecclesiastes 12:1–2 says, "Remember now thy creator in the days of thy youth, while the, evil days come not, nor the years draw nigh, when thou shalt say I have pleasure in them: while the sun, or the light or the moon or the stars be darkened nor the cloud return after the rain."

Remember your God while you're young, able, and capable to do God's will. When you are very young, your responsibilities are small. Remember God in those good times while your days are full of fun and laughter, while you can jump and run. When you're older, working for the Lord becomes more of an effort, and you also want to create good habits, so when you're old, it will remain.

Everyone wants our youth. The US armed forces want our young. The convincing streets want our young. Drug dealers want our young. Gangs want our young. Different religious groups and cult groups want our children, AIDS and HIV want our young, crime wants our youth, and prisons want our young. Finally, the grave wants our young.

King Solomon wrote the book of Ecclesiastes before his heart turned to other gods. King Solomon didn't forget God in his youth. When Solomon was appointed to be king, he asked God for wisdom instead of riches and fame, and God was so pleased with Solomon's request that he made Solomon the richest king who ever lived on earth. All the combined wealth of Donald Trump, Bill Gates, Jeff Bezos, Mark Zuckerberg, and Michael Bloomberg couldn't compare to what God gave King Solomon. Keep God in your view and watch him lead you and guide your path into peace, happiness, success, and contentment.

In the book of Luke, we find Jesus passing through Samaria and Galilee, and entering a certain village, where some ten men were in exile with a sickness, called leprosy, which was equivalent to AIDS or HIV in our times. Leprosy, an incurable disease, turned one's skin snow white. These men had been cast out of their communities, never allowed to work at any organization. They weren't allowed to enter the doors of the temple to pray. Families disowned any family members who had leprosy. These ten lepers had been totally cast outside the real world; they could hide only in dark places, including alleys, and become beggars for food and money. No one would touch them or come within twenty feet of them because they were afraid they would be contaminated by their disease. Jesus didn't touch them after responding to their cry for help while he traveled through their neighborhood.

When they saw Jesus passing by their area, these ten lepers began to vehemently cry aloud with every breath in their bodies as one voice like a choir. "Jesus of Nazareth!" This made Jesus stop in his tracks, and as Jesus heard their cry, he turned his attention to them and gave them instructions to show themselves to the priest; and as they went on their way to follow his instructions, the disease disappeared from their bodies before they could show themselves to the priest(Saint Luke 17:1-12) .

For one moment, imagine living in a touch-free world: no hugs, kisses, handshakes, tickles, smiles, fun, dancing, or wrestling. Just sitting in a dark place and being scorned by all those who look afar off. Is America becoming a touch-free nation? Don't touch people in the office because you will quickly be charged with sexual harassment. If you hit your child for correction, someone will report you as a child abuser or report you to child protection. If two brothers or two sisters walk down the street, holding hands or putting their arms around each other's shoulders, others may call them gay. If you are a daycare teacher and have an incident in your classroom in which one of your toddlers cannot unzip his or her pants to use the bathroom, you'd better not help unzip his or her pants because that's fondling a child. New York City teenagers are famous for saying, "Don't touch me!" Has New York City truly become a touch-free environment? In a child's life, point of contact is necessary both with eye contact and hugs. There are boundaries we must all respect concerning inappropriately touching children and adults, but we shouldn't be afraid to reach out to help others. Every now and then, we can reach our hands out to help others in need.

These lepers suffered tremendously; they endured a touch-free environment in those days. During these times, no one wanted any physical contact with lepers, and they didn't want to be within twenty feet of them. Many lepers were left for dead because leprosy was a disease leading to death. About 99 percent of the people who had leprosy died. Rumors began to spread of a man claiming to be the Son of the living God; he was going around healing the sick and raising the dead. When these ten lepers received the news that Jesus was passing by, it was their last and only chance to receive complete healing. Now, if they were healed, they could once again re-enter society. So, with such urgency and necessity together, these ten lepers had the same mind, and with one voice in one place, they all lifted their voices like a trumpet and yelled, "Jesus master have mercy on us!"

When Jesus heard them and saw their present state of being, he said, "Go show yourselves to the priest," and as they went on their way, they were healed and cleansed from this disease.

It was a tradition that lepers couldn't reenter society without the priest examining them and proving they were clean. The priest's approval allowed the lepers to live in society again. Jesus completely healed these ten lepers, and now they stood cleansed and were ready to be accepted by their families, friends, workforce, church, arenas, and local community centers.

Jesus gave them their lives back, and he wants to do the same for us too. But sadly enough, only one returned to say thank you to Jesus. Is this the treatment we give God? When we are down and out, Jesus finally lifts us and turns us around. Will we be like the lepers and not make any effort to say thanks to our heavenly Father? This is blatantly the worst sign of being unappreciative these nine lepers could have ever displayed and expressed to the Son of the living God. It's like being stranded on a highway because of car troubles; a perfect stranger comes and helps you get it started, and you just drive off without saying thank you. Better yet, someone lends you money to pay your rent and utility bills, then calls you back and tells you, "Don't pay it back," but you refuse to say thank you to him or her; you just hang up the phone without saying thank you.

This is some cold-blooded stuff. That's how God is being treated in this story. Everything is so more important to us than God, but when trouble flares up and becomes intolerable, that's when we cry out for God's help. God wants more than this. Which of the two are you more apt to help more rapidly? The person who stays in contact with you or the person you haven't seen in years? By far most people will help those they know. Thank God he doesn't operate with amnesia, because God hears the cry of his people, and he responds in his appointed time. God hears the cries of the abused children; he hears the cries of children in sex trafficking. He hears the cry of the innocent. He hears the cries of the millions of aborted babies and those starving children and families in foreign countries and inner cities. He hears them loud and clear, and he sends help.

Jesus asked the one former leper who had returned to say thanks, "What happened to the other nine former lepers? Weren't there ten lepers?" As the former leper stood face-to-face with Jesus, he couldn't answer for the other nine lepers because in his heart he couldn't forget what Jesus had done for him. He couldn't forget the fact that Jesus had given him his life back. He couldn't forget all the doctor bills Jesus had saved him from. He couldn't forget all the begging he had done to survive, and here came Jesus in one day; one moment of time instantly made him cleansed from all leprosy. Hallelujah! Praise God from whom all blessings flow! How could you forget this healer, this deliverer, this forgiving God?

I guarantee you that each out of the nine lepers had a different excuse for not coming back to thank Jesus. These excuses are the same ones some church people use today. The entire nine former lepers forgot God. This is an outrage. Jesus healed ten lepers, and only one returned to say thanks, which mathematically equates to 10 percent. Could this be true that only 10 percent of the church remembers God's goodness? Just one remembers the Lord? After all Jesus did for them, they could display only forgetfulness and ungratefulness? They didn't have the power to change their circumstances or the powers to reverse their sickness; they were destined to die. Who would even bury a leper? These lepers knew Jesus's name so well that they proclaimed it loud and clear to get his attention. Once they got his attention, the healing virtue came from heaven, and they were cleansed while on their way to the priest. It seems to me that they purposely experienced sudden amnesia and didn't bother to mention or remember their miracle from the Son of the living God.

Thank God for not being an Indian giver like many of us, because if it had been us, these lepers would have all been dead. The nine lepers got what they wanted from God and went their own way, never to return to say thanks to Jesus. People, do not forget God because he hasn't forgotten you.

These lepers were destined to die just like we are, but Jesus stepped into the equation, cleansed us from all our sins, and offered us eternal life. Do you want to live? Yes, I want to live. Let's not forget God, because God hasn't forgotten you; nor will he ever forget you. I know God didn't forget me when I was a young lad; he kept me and saved my soul at a young age. He protected me from death on many occasions. He kept me from being addicted to drugs, he watched over me and kept me safe from robbers and murders, and he kept me out of jail and the loony tune sanatorium. Lord Jesus, thank you! So I prayed with my children and wife, and these are the words I spoke. "Now, Lord, look at these your children you gave to me. I ask thee to be their God like you were with me and still are my God."

Children don't run from God or hide; he sees all and is everywhere. Don't reject him. Accept him. It causes you more harm to reject him. So accept Jesus Christ in your heart today and receive life. Simply confess your sins to our Lord Jesus Christ, ask for forgiveness, and accept him as your Lord and Savior in your heart, and you shall be saved. Hallelujah! Glory to the King of kings. Amen! Stop adding up your mistakes and just come to Jesus over time. He will help build your character. God is looking for imperfect people like you and me, not perfect people who brag about how they don't need God right now.

Let's talk about the nine excuses the lepers probably would have used to explain why they didn't return to say thank you, Jesus. Luke 17:11–19 says,

> And it came to pass, as he went to Jerusalem, that he passed through the midst of Vilamaria and Galilee and as he entered into a certain village, there met him ten men that were lepers, which stood afar off; and they lifted up their voices, and said, Jesus, Master, have mercy on us. And when he saw them, he said unto them, Go shew yourselves unto the priest. And it came to pass,

that as they went, they were cleansed. And one of them, when he saw that he was healed, turned back, and with a loud voice glorified God and fell down on his face at his feet, giving him thanks; and he was a Samaritan. And Jesus answering said were not ten cleansed? But where are the nine? There are not found that returned to give glory to God, save this stranger. And he said unto him, Arise go thy way: thy faith hath made thee whole.

The nine missed the whole main idea, which was to be made whole by Christ. All of them received healing, but not all of them were made whole. God isn't an Indian giver; healing them was final. It was so obvious that after their healing, they wanted nothing else from Jesus; he was the furthest thing from their minds. Apparently, their lives went in a different direction, just like some of us in church; church time for some of us is only Christmas and Easter time or when we are in trouble; but when things are good and steady, we choose other things to be involved in. Wholeness is what we need, but we would rather have instant gratification instead of a lifelong relationship with Christ. To be whole takes work and commitment. The miracle was free, but the relationship takes work: spending time in prayer, studying the Bible, witnessing, fasting, praising God, and spreading the gospel. It's easier just to have a form of godliness because it comes without any commitment. That is just like the nine lepers who refused to return and say thanks to Jesus because they wanted nothing more from him but the healing experience without any commitment.

To be made whole is to be content with Jesus alone; no other substitute is needed or required if you desire to spend personal time with Jesus daily. "Give me more of Jesus" is exactly what the one leper purposed in his heart to get, and that was his real rationale for returning to Jesus. He was healed and made whole. The other lepers were healed but not made whole; in other words, their sickness changed for the good, but their lifestyles didn't. They returned to their old ways. When someone makes you whole, the search for another is over. You can be made whole only if you allow it. Return to God in prayer, return to reading God's holy word, return to God in worship and praise, and render your heart and not your garments to God. Never be like the nine forgetful lepers. Return to God.

Let's explore some of the excuses the lepers may have had if the one who returned to thank Jesus had approached them.

One of the nine might of said, "Jesus didn't tell us to return to give him thanks. He said to show ourselves to the priest, and that's it. We did what he instructed us to do. Now we are healed, so why go back when indeed the good master didn't ask us to return? I intend to live my life to the fullest, thank you very much. Next!"

The second former leper probably said, "I was tired after an exhausting day. Our healing presented a lot of excitement for me. I rested and overslept. The next thing I knew, I was summoned to do some more chores and deliveries, which made me forget to personally go back and thank Jesus, but I'm quite sure he knows I am grateful because in my heart I have already thanked him."

The third former leper probably said, "I will write a book about my life as a leper, and I will make mention of Jesus and his healing power in this book; once this book sells millions of copies like the Bible, everyone will know how grateful I am. I will never forget that moment in time."

The fourth former leper might have said, "I've been banned from my community for years. It's time to enjoy life and all the good things it brings. It is time to party because I couldn't do this before. I think Jesus would have wanted me to enjoy life and every moment it brings."

The fifth leper might have said, "I will stay in the temple with the priests and learn their doctrines, and by doing so, I believe this is my way of saying thanks to Jesus."

The sixth leper might have said, "I will study medicine to find a cure for leprosy because if I do, I will be wealthy and help many people get their lives back. There has to be another antidote for leprosy besides miracles."

The seventh leper might have said, "My family hasn't seen me in such a long time. They needed me to stay around to catch up with all the lost time we missed, because connecting with family is very important, just like fellowshipping with other Christians, and I think Jesus would have wanted me to do this."

The eighth leper might have said, "I don't need to travel back to where Jesus was. I can say, 'Thank you, Jesus' right here. 'Thank you, Jesus.' That should please him, right? God sees my heart."

Finally, the ninth leper might have said, "I tried to follow you back to thank Jesus personally, but as I journeyed behind you, there was a terrible sandstorm that fell upon us. I lost track and took cover till the storm ceased, after which time you were nowhere to be found. So I went a different route, and in my searching, I couldn't find Jesus. I tried! My heart was there but not my presence. God knows my heart."

When they all needed to be cleansed, they all were in one place, having one mind, lifting their voices in harmony, crying out loudly to Jesus, and attempting to get his attention: "Master, have mercy on us." Apparently, they were very successful in getting Jesus's attention. From that point on, the lepers' lives changed forever for good. What do most servants do when their master frees them from bondage? Isn't "Thank you" appropriate? How quickly did all nine men forget God's goodness? Are we guilty of treating God the same way? After God heals us, delivers us, protects us, saves us, and gives us the desires of our hearts, why do we forget God? Maybe because we are stuck in our own selfish ways and think we are entitled. Once we get what we want, amnesia falls on us like raindrops; but when things are tough, scarce, and dangerous, and when sickness hits our bodies, we cry aloud to God the Father. After he comes to our rescue and makes a way for us, we forget his goodness and never return to say thank you. Ungrateful people usually experience a cloud of amnesia that conveniently falls over them when they feel things are working in their favor and life gives them a bed of roses, but once this scenario changes for the worse, they come crying out aloud to God almighty.

The nine lepers missed out on being made whole and complete in Jesus. It is true they were healed on the way to the priest, but they weren't all made whole. They received the first-step healing of the deadly disease, but Jesus wanted to complete the work in them. Completion is what many of us need in the body of Christ. We are missing out on the more important stuff, and that's why;

we are broken and discouraged, we often easily drift by every wave and wind, and we often go astray. God wants to plant his people like a tree by the river; the tree never bends or bows to the wind or waves of life. Our hearts and minds are to have a great foundation with Christ. So when trouble comes, we stand strong and courageous as a Christian soldier without falling from the faith. When God completes the work in you, there is no reason to look to others but God.

When God's word and will becomes like meat or nourishment to our bodies and souls, we are made complete in Christ. In other words, your spiritual nourishment comes from God's word, prayer, fellowship, praise, and worship—not from anything else. When your thirst and appetite are for Christ and your hunger is for Christ alone and not material things, God will give you the desire of your heart.

The former leper who returned to say thanks to Jesus received a special touch from him. The leper was made whole! Backsliders slide away from God because they aren't made whole, so they go elsewhere to find wholeness, and to their surprise, they find emptiness and deception because they will get temporary fulfillment only in alcohol, drugs, crime, adultery, fornication, stealing, deception, scandalous behavior, idol worship, perversion, witchcraft, religion, fame, fortune, and riches. Only Christ can fill our empty souls.

Israel was notorious for their refusal to accept God's wholeness; instead, they craved to serve other gods and marry women of other nations who worshipped dead gods. Would you rather live with a dead person for the rest of your life instead of being with a living being? Then why do we serve dead gods? As long as Israel struggled, suffered, and entangled themselves in slavery, they cried out to God for help day and night, but as soon as God prospered them, suddenly amnesia fell on Israel as though they had never known God to be their deliverer. Fortunately, Israel's enemies feared Israel's God more at times than Israel did.

There was a woman in the twenty-first century who was married for fifty years. A news reporter asked her a question about her marriage: Have you ever cheated or desired to cheat on your husband during your fifty years of marriage? She confidently and firmly answered, "Never, because my husband makes me whole and complete." The search is over when you are made complete.

God wants his people to be complete in his presence, never wavering, indecisive, or caught between two opinions but steadfast and unmovable in the things of God because their nourishment is to serve God, not man. We've been digesting, eating, and listening to too much garbage and trash, and the rubbish we entertain in our spirits and minds hinders us from being made whole or complete. So instead of committing ourselves to Lord Jesus Christ and the work of God, we seek another; we are constantly searching for worldly pleasures to fill our empty souls, and the result is that we are never satisfied in ourselves. This is what the nine lepers walked away from: wholeness. Is that your testimony? Are you afraid or not confident of being made whole with Christ alone, or do you seek another?

Many of us give up on God too fast after we have received salvation, miracles, healing, wealth, and deliverance. God desires us to seek his face daily in prayer and in his word; this is what completes us and makes us whole.

Homeowners often find themselves in court due to the fact that their contractor didn't finish the work in their homes, as promised. Unfinished work is so frustrating for homeowners, especially when they paid contractors in advance. So for the contractor to get the job done or complete, they take the contractor responsible for unfinished business to court; if the judge rewards them with monies from their suit, they will begin to search for another efficient contractor, because when something is broken, it needs to be fixed, not played with. Jesus wants to complete the work in you; you come to him for salvation but refuse a day-to-day relationship with him, so you walk away, being an unfinished work, until you bump into an obstacle. Only at that point will you seek God's help. In all actuality, you just want the help, the healing, the miracle, and the blessing, but you reject the day-to-day relationship, which makes you complete and whole. Completeness and wholeness represent loyalty, dedication, faithfulness, steadfastness, and immovableness like a mountain all through our daily devotion with Christ. These are the quality traits you find in people who are complete and whole in Christ Jesus. Are you made whole?

Deuteronomy 6:7–9; 8:11–20 says, "And thou shalt teach them diligently unto thy children, and shalt talk unto them when thou sittest in thine house, and when thou walkest by the way, and when thou liest down and when thou riseth up … And thou shalt bind them for a sign upon thine hand, and they shall be as fronlets between thine eyes, and thou shalt write them upon the posts of thy house, and on the gates."

Waiting and depending only on the preacher on Sunday to give us the word of God aren't enough to keep the word of God in your heart. Gymnasts practice for two to four hours every day. Presidential candidates rehearse countless hours a day just to deliver a convincing speech. Rappers rehearsal their lyrics for many hours each day just to send a powerful message to their fans. If you think being a Christian is just a one-day experience, you are absolutely wrong. The life of a Christian is a daily walk and a continuous dialogue with God. God's Holy Bible instructs us to teach our children the word of God while they remain young. Talk about the word of God as you walk around in your home. Talk about the word of God when you sit down and discuss the word of God before you go to sleep, and when you rise in the morning, you repeat this process all over again. If more Christians did this, maybe our youth wouldn't be so easily attracted to drugs, crime, gangs, fighting, bullying, fornication, killing, prostitution, and cults.

In the Bible days, God's people wore frontlets around their

necks with scriptures on them. They wore these like little signs on their chests to keep the word of God in their minds. Our children forget God when we don't teach and read God's word to our children. Why not put posters with scriptures on the walls in your house, post them on your doors, or place them in your rooms? This could help some people, but more importantly, God's word should be in your heart so you won't sin against him. The only way God's word can penetrate your heart is if you literally plant it there, which means you must read God's word daily in your private times, study the Bible, practice what it says, and teach others about God's Holy Bible; keep a prayer life and fellowship with other believers for the strengthening of your faith. Let God's word be the daily news in your life and allow prayer to be your spiritual I-need-God cordless phone.

God instructed the Israelites to keep his commandments in their ears and minds, and to blatantly keep them near their faces. They were to speak of God's word at home, during leisure time, when they woke up in the morning, and before they went to bed. Even at work, they reminisced about God's goodness. They were to testify of how God brought them out of Egypt, the land of slavery, punishment, beatings, rapings, and dictatorship, the lack of freedom, the lack of food, and excessive work with little rest. He delivered them into "a land he swore to their fathers, Abraham, Isaac, and Jacob, promising them he would give them goodly cities, which they build not, houses filled with good things which they filled not, wells dogged which thou digest not, vineyards and olive trees which you planted not, when thou has eaten and are full: Beware lest thou forget God the Lord which brought you out of the land of Egypt, from the house of bondage" (Deuteronomy 6:10–12).

Deuteronomy 6:15 says, "For the Lord thy God is a Jealous God among you lest the anger of the Lord thy God be kindled against thee, and destroy thee from off the face of the earth."

Wait a minute. Forgetting God can cause you to lose your

life, even your soul? Be careful of your consent complaining, arrogance, and stubbornness toward God. God hears your voice and conversations, and he knows and sees your material motive in all you do. If God has been good to you, it is common courteous to show signs of appreciation toward him. Give him thanks and remember the Lord God.

Here we see in the scriptures a warning for the Israelites not to allow their riches and many blessings to turn their hearts from God. This proves what is true with some people. When they are doing exceptionally well—possessing pockets full of money, having more than one car, living in a mansion, having good credit, or owning their own successful business—all this can cause them to forget who God is. If we entertain worldly things more than we entertain God's word and spirit, we will become naïve, and our hearts for God will wax cold. We are human beings who need to be reminded, or we will forget. That's why we carry planners, calendars, Palm Pilots, iPad, laptops, and smartphones with voice mail and texting; we can't remember so much at a time. That's why we operate these electronic devices—to help us remember. Keeping lots and lots of garbage and unimportant things in the archives of our brain lessens the capabilities and the power of the brain, The power of the brain is: thinking, analyzing, imagining, organizing, managing, solving problems, inventing necessary things, creating solutions, motivating others, mentoring qualified individuals, and so much more. Give God some time, and your life will be abundantly blessed.

Do we keep the Holy Bible as close to us as these electronic devices? We remember civil rights leaders' holidays more than God's Holy Scriptures. There are commercial slogans we remember more than God's Holy Scriptures. There are hip hop songs, rock and roll songs, country songs, and R & B songs we remember better than any church hymns, because they fill the airwaves with their music—from radio shows to television shows.

If we don't keep God's word in our ears, we will eventually forget God and all his goodness.

Keep prayer in your home. Read your Bible and teach it to your children. Watch some religious programs, listen to some Christian songs, e-mail some scripture to your friends and family, and text someone some good news from the scriptures. Flood the airways with Christ-centered dialogue. America has forgotten God, and yes, this country has loudly proclaimed over a hundred years ago and even to this very day that in God we trust, which is on our currency and courthouses, yet slowly but surely America is forgetting God. Family values have been diminishing, and children have no respect for the elders. Gay marriages are legal in many states of America, and adultery is rampant in the church arena. God created marriage, not America; marriage has been called holy matrimony between a man and a woman. Sin corrupts our minds to think America should have a third bathroom besides a men's and women's bathroom; there should be a transgender bathroom too. Seriously! If all our former presidents were alive, they would rebut this sanction for transgender bathrooms. If our great-grandparents heard this news, they would march around the White House and demand that America repent. There are only male and female sexes; if you don't believe this, then talk to your local mortician. It's a mortician's job to pronounce whether a body is in fact a male or female.

Are we trying to create something new? Have we forgotten how we all arrived on earth? Does the law grant everyone his or her wishes? Is that the purpose of our judicial system? Is the land of the free becoming so free that anything goes? People have always gone beyond God's perimeters, especially when they feel they are locked in a box or circle. In the Garden of Eden, God set in place a small perimeter for Adam and Eve; after giving them thousands upon thousands of trees to choose from, God commanded them not to touch one forbidden tree. You know the story. Curiosity kills the cat.

We want things that aren't good for us at times. What formula could I use to prove to my readers how deadly sinful activities are for you and me? Here's one formula for finding the repercussions of sinful acts. There are close to, or more than, five billion people on planet earth. Multiply any sinful act by five billion people, which will equate to probably a dark and dreary world. Now do you understand why sin is a reproach to any people, family, city, state, or country? Sin brings pain, misery, confusion, crime, murder, torture, deception, scandal, evil, pornography, witchcraft, incest, divorce, rape, drunkenness, disease, and death. For centuries we have always distinguished bathrooms by male and female. What has changed? Someone is forgetting God? If animals can detect the difference between a man and woman just by his or her smell, why can't we understand that there are two dominating sexes on earth, male and female? Racial inequalities still exist, and if preachers mention their opinions on some of these issues mentioned earlier, they could be sent to jail or lose their ministries.

Both adults and children have been inundated with gay lifestyles and gay culture on TV sitcoms, soap operas, and Hollywood films. We cannot run from it or escape it. America gives bravery awards to people who decide to change their sexual orientation, but behind the scenes, it is all deception. All these things are indications of America forgetting God, and in my view, this has weakened the fabric of America's strong values. People have their personal agendas, but what about the children in all the things we do? Who is considering the children because they are being forced to live with Mom and Mom and Dad and Dad? They are being inundated with strong sexual content on television shows and in Hollywood movies.

America must come back to God before it is too late. Some of our morals are evil and corrupt. Taking prayer out of public schools was one of the first downfalls of America; meanwhile, we have welcomed drugs, gangs, homosexuality and violence in our schools, giving them applause and high recognition; no wonder our children are faced with such perversion and emptiness. We should remember what our founding fathers said: "America is a nation under God." God loves all mankind—black, white, rich, poor, gay, straight, righteous, and criminals; but it is the sin he hates, and he won't tolerate it. Whether we claim to be Christians or not, sin will eventually be destroyed. A sinful lifestyle brings damnation, but righteous living promises eternal life.

America has forgotten God. America, come back to God. America, what a great nation you are. You have so much potential, America; the entire world watches us, wishing they were in our shoes. Let us not forget God! In every government, there are the do's and don'ts. Having nations without boundaries weakens their justice department, military defense, democracy, family structure, religion, education, politics, and corporate structure. Liberty comes with a weighty responsibility.

What a great nation America is! I love my America, and I pray we will remember God, because I would never want America to be a third-world nation because of her forgetfulness of God. Our founding fathers claim that this nation of these United States of America will be one nation under God, because in God we trust. America, do not ever forget God! Trusting in God does not make us weak but strong. Who dares to stand against a nation that fears the almighty God? There is a remnant of people who stand firm on these values, and only because of this, Americans, hold firmly intact because of God's love, mercy, and unmerited favor for the USA. God bless America!

The power to get wealth comes from God. Deuteronomy 8:18–19 says, "But thus shalt remember the Lord thy God: for it is he that gives thee power to get wealth, which he has establish his covenant which he swore unto thy fathers, as it is this day. And it shall be, if thou forget the Lord thy God, and walk after other gods, and serve them, and worship them, I testify against you this day that ye shall surely perish."

Forgetfulness was a revolving door for Israel. Israel would

have seven years of obedience to God and another seven years of amnesia toward God. God promised Abraham he would bless Abraham's seed (children); he would increase their population and businesses, give them favor with their enemies; as a result, he gave them thousands of acres of land beyond what they could measure, but that's only if they continued to follow God and worship the true God. But if they did the opposite, then Israelites would surely perish—no matter what God did for Israel: open the Red Sea for them to escape from the Egyptians; defeat the Philistines' champion, Goliath, the giant destroyer; tear down the walls of Jericho; and the list goes on. All these episodes were full of God displaying his greatness and proving his great power, yet Israel continued to forget God. King David was committed to remembering the Lord God and keeping his statutes.

Psalm 119:16 says, "I will delight myself in thy precepts, I will not forget thy word."

You need to be like David and be committed to keeping God in your life and on your pathway. It will be easy to forget God if you allow things and people to come between you and God. David sinned before God, entering into adultery and murder almost at the same time. David had so many wives and concubines that he could sleep with a new woman every day out of a year, but he desired one of his soldiers' wives, Bathsheba, the wife of Uriah the Hittite, so bad that he put Uriah on the front line in battle so David could have his way with his wife. David was stunned by Bathsheba's beauty and sexually desired her. The king murdered Uriah.

King David later took this man's wife and married her; soon David fathered her child, Suddenly, God's judgment fell on King David because his actions displeased God, so God sent Nathan, the prophet, to rebuke King David. It took Nathan telling a parable about a rich man and a poor man. The story goes on to say that the rich man had exceeding many flocks and herds, but the poor man had nothing save only one little ewe lamb, which he had brought up and nourished from infancy; and it grew up with his children. It did eat of his own meat, drink of his own cup, lie in his bosom, and was unto him as a daughter. And there came a traveler unto the rich man, and he spared to take of his flock and his own herd, to dress for the wayfaring man who was to come unto him. But he took the poor man's lamb and dressed it for the man who was to come. Before Nathan could finish the story, David's anger was greatly kindled against the rich man's actions, and he said to Nathan, "As the Lord lives, the man that hath done this thing shall surely die; he shall restore the lamb fourfold, because he did this thing and because he had no pity."

Little did David know he was proclaiming his judgment on his life, so Nathan said to David, "Thou art the man, Thus said the Lord God of Israel, I anointed thee king over Israel, and I delivered you out of the hand of Saul; and I gave thee thy master's wives into thy bosom, and gave thee the house of Judah; and if that had been too little; I would moreover have given unto thee such and such things." In other words, David had everything at his disposal; and if he wanted more, God would have given it to him, yet he took another man's wife and killed her husband. Wow!

When we forget God, these are the things we do. Sin always dims our vision, clouds the truth, and gives us a case of amnesia toward God. In my own life, I have wandered into ungodly acts and sinful pleasures, and they cost me dishonor, shame, pain, and a bad name. After confessing my sins to God and others I had hurt and betrayed, I had to get up from feeling sorry for myself and move forward with the constant reminder of what I had done. David lost much for his sins, and when we forget God in those weak moments in our lives, drastic things happen to us. We are no better than David; we all have issues, but David gave his issues to God. He woke up from his forgetfulness and began remembering the God of Israel.

Don't forget God. Keep open communication with your God. Tell others about your God. Don't be ashamed of the gospel of Jesus Christ (2 Samuel 12:1–24).

Although David entangled himself in a web of sins, he came to his senses and was restored to God. His sins were very visible and on the daily news back in those days. He couldn't escape God's judgment. Even though David repented of his sins, he experienced some repercussions. For example, he lost the child from Bathsheba, and his family experienced incest, family killing family members, and the list goes on. Even though David repented of his sins, he never repeated the same sin. God punishes sin.

God was merciful, even with his punishment. He could have taken David's life; instead, he took someone dear to him, David's child. David wept and wept; he fasted and prayed, but God's judgment was final. Then David experienced mayhem within his home as God said he would: brother raping sister, brother killing brother. Wow! David still remained king through all this turmoil. David was the talk of Israel, but he is remembered for all the wars he won and the giant Goliath he destroyed. There are serious repercussions for forgetting God.

Perhaps you are reading this story while living as an undercover sinner while wearing a Christian smile and adorning yourself as a believer but denying the truth and power of God's Holy Scriptures. Maybe you are participating in sinful acts and aimlessly going after things that displease God. Today turn away from this riffraff of hiding your sins and hanging out in dark places; beware that God can see in the dark and knows all that you do. We all must give account to God of what we do with our lives. Keep God in your view and be honest with God and those who really love you. You aren't Superman or Hercules; you are just a man or woman who has weaknesses. Only God can strengthen you. God says to give him your weaknesses, because he will make them into extraordinary pieces of memorable artifacts; and after time, they will become masterpieces that draw people by the story they tell and experiences you have endured.

Who else can take dirt and make human beings out of it? If our God can take dirt from the earth and with his bare hands create a body, mind, and soul of human beings and make them into his image and likeness, imagine what he can do with our dirty sins. Give God your dirt, and he will make it into something of great value. Making the most precious stones like diamonds takes lots of deep cleaning and extreme heat, but when the process is all over, what looked like a dirty rock becomes a bright, shining crystal diamond, which wins the attention of all who behold it. You won't die confessing your sins to God, but in the process of confessing your sins to God, you must turn from your evil ways.

We can't afford to forget God; doing so will cost us too much, even death and optimally our living souls. Confession isn't weakness, but it displays strength and maturity, but the presumption of the same sin is when you need to decide to whom you will serve: sin or God. People most times won't forgive your transgressions, but you can come to Jesus just as you are; confess those ugly sins, and he is faithful and just to forgive them all. Come to Jesus, even if you're caught red-handed in the very sinful act, and it's displayed and broadcasted on news channels and in the gossip in your community and church. God will put your sins in a sea of forgetfulness, never to be remembered anymore, but people will always remember your sinful acts and constantly remind you of them each day. A part of maturity is owning up to your sins and moving forward in a different but better direction.

Who needs peace? Who wants long life? Well, the answer is right in the scriptures. Don't forget God's words of law; you must keep it in your heart for the rest of your days, and it shall give you peace. Read the scriptures with your family, pray together, listen to gospel messages together; and only then will you have some peace. Don't take God lightly; he is the ruler and creator of all things and people. How could you forget God when it was he who woke you up this morning and started you on your way? Your heart beats because of God.

Why does he love us so much? Why does he care? Why did he sacrifice his son's life for us? Amazingly, God finds living beings valuable; being made out of dirt is a plus because God loves dirt. I mean he loves us dearly because all our righteousness to God is as dirty, filthy rags anyway. One day we will return to dirt, but as we remain, God loves us so much, even unto death. God breathed the breath of life into our mortal bodies, and we became living beings; now we can walk, talk, think, love, create, work, sing praises, and so forth. The things we should be forgetting are illegal drugs, lying, adultery, fornication, greed, drugs, murder, stealing, crime, perversion to every degree, hatred, prejudice, racism, and witchcraft. These are some of the things that will send us straight to hell and destroy the fabric of our lives, families and neighbors.

Check yourself to see whether you're in the faith. Saul, the scholar during Bible days, was so hard and evil to Christians during the time Jesus walked on the earth; he gruesomely and mercilessly had hundreds, even thousands, of innocent Christians killed, who claimed their love and allegiance to their King of kings, Jesus Christ, which made them a threat to the Roman Empire. Therefore, Saul used his authority to order countless Christians to be gruesomely murdered in broad daylight. God heard the cry of the murdered Christians, so instead of God instantly killing Saul, he did the unthinkable; God personally knocked Saul off his horse one day and asked him, "Why doth thy persecute me?" Note that God didn't say Christians, but he put himself in the equation to get Saul's undivided attention and let him know that when you hurt the least one of us, you are doing so to God. Wow! God puts himself in our place. He is so awesome!

So the story goes on to say that Saul's encounter with our awesome God literately changed his entire life from a murderer into a Christian and later an apostle of the gospel, but first God had to change his name from Saul, the murderer of Christians, to Paul, a Christian called to be an apostle of the gospel. Although Paul's memory of his previous lifestyle probably haunted him from time to time, the good news and main idea are that Jesus cleansed him from all his sinful actions and changed his name from Saul to Paul, because the old name had too much sinful baggage.

This is the same thing God wants to do with your life. He wants to change the history behind your name for the good so you won't forget God moving forward. After which, Paul remained a dedicated Christian the rest of his days, and later he became an apostle, a pastor of many churches. Paul refused to revisit his past sins.

Why does it seem easier to remember bad things than good things that happen to you? Why is it that one negative word can penetrate, pierce, and devastate our lives, causing a tremendous impact in our lives? And it would take a hundred thousand good words to motivate us in the right direction. Lucifer orchestrated the curse of sin, and then sin entered our atmosphere through Adam and Eve's disobedience to God. Ever since this Garden of Eden experience, forces of darkness seems to pull and magnetize mankind each and every day. That's why we don't need to teach our children to do wrong; they were born in sin. In other words, if sin didn't enter the world, there would be no knowledge of sin at any degree. Always remember, the only remedy for sin is Jesus Christ, the Son of the living God. That is why we should receive his salvation, read his word, praise and exalt his name, and pray to the father. We must create a wholesome and spiritual environment in our homes. Keep God in your view, no matter what status of life you are in. There is a penalty for continuously forgetting God. God loves you, and he wants a one-to-one relationship with you. Don't forget God!

CHAPTER 3

In His Will He Left

R ich and poor people are highly encouraged to have a will in place before death. What is a will? A will is a legal document directing the disposal of one's property to be distributed to the closest kin after one's death. Years ago, only the rich, famous, and wealthy made wills, but these days the middle class and poor take a strong interest in doing their personal wills as well. Why? Because they want no interference with family members when it comes down to who gets what and how much each should have.

It is a proven fact that families need a will set in place before the death of a loved one because families will fight for the deceased's money, jewelry, clothes, vehicles, property and valuables. Also, the government can take every dime if the person doesn't have a will in place, especially for people with over $1.2 million worth of assets. People can't seem to come to a resolve without a will; everyone has his or her own version of what the deceased said or promised a family member. In many cases families go to war because "Mom said I could have her furniture," "Dad said the car goes to his firstborn son," or "My uncle promised me his suits." Everyone has his or her stories and testimonies of what the deceased said he or she could have, and many times it is so far from the truth of what the deceased said, but with a will in place, it keeps all the business of the deceased in place and accurately gives what's due to each family member, as mentioned in the document of a will.

Ladies and gentlemen, family and friends, brothers and sisters, the Lord has left us a written will in the Holy Bible, which we call the "word of God." As we know, God isn't dead but very much alive. The Holy Scriptures tell us what we can have and what God has already given us. God promised us salvation; if we confess our sin and believe Jesus is the Son of the living God, we are saved, and salvation is ours. He promised us power from on high if we seek and receive the Holy Ghost, with the Spirit of God operating within us as a comforter; and this comforter, God's Spirit, will fill us with power and discernment; and the list goes on and on.

People of God, there are so many rubies and gold nuggets in God's word, and it would require you to carefully read his Holy Bible to find all the precious gems God left in his will (the Holy Bible). God has published in his Holy Bible so many valuable benefits for all who believe so we can be successful in life, but we must read his word, believe his word, act on his word, and make claim of all God's promises. God's living will is found in the Holy Bible, and in there are fine jewels that are very valuable to our lifestyles if we use them. There are wisdom, knowledge, righteous living, prayer, faith, God's favor, God's character, and God's love and mercy in those Holy Scriptures. If God can take care of the birds in the air, aren't we more valuable than they? God doesn't want us to worry and lose sleep over our financial problems, relationships, occupations, goals, family issues, sicknesses, business, careers, and education, because God is ultimately in control of our surroundings, and he can make our way clear. We just need to have faith in our creator. God has left us a living testament in his Holy Bible, and it is up to us to read and search the scriptures for these precious jewels, claim them, and put them to use to prosper.

Our topic for today is the will God left; when God says he left a living will, you can count on it being the absolute truth. When God says, "I will," he will surely bring it to pass.

Numbers 23:19 says, "God is not a man, that he should lie; neither the son of man that he should repent; hath he said, and shall he not do it? Or hath he spoken and shall he not make it good?"

The New International Version says it this way: "God is not a man, that he should lie nor son of man he should change his mind, does he speak and then not act? Does he promise and not fulfill?"

Every time God promises to do something, he fulfills it. Oh, yes, he does. Look at your life and see what God has accomplished in your life thus far: healing for your sickness, deliverance from drugs, protection from danger. He keeps your mind sound, blesses you with children, gives you a place to live, gives you employment, and provides food and water for you every day. The mere fact that you are sitting here today, reading this book, is proof God is still taking care of you.

When the earth was just void and empty, God stood in the midst of it all and said, "Let there be light," and light appeared. "God divided the waters from the earth and instructed the water to stay within its realm and the land we walk on God created borders so it would not interfere with the rivers and oceans. Then God created the trees, flowers, vegetations and later created animals of all kind then God gets together with his Son and says, 'Let us make man in our own image' and later created woman from Adam's other rib." When God speaks, it will be done in heaven and in earth; and when God wills it, it shall be done. (Genesis 1-27)

God's hands created life as we know it, and those same hands that created human life once destroyed mankind and the earth with water because of its great wickedness. When God says, "I will," he really means he will do it. Man promises, but he continues to break his promises. So if God has promised you stuff, wait patiently, because in time God will bring it to pass; but if you want to see it come to pass sooner, start praising God daily and watch God come to your rescue. Praises expedite unanswered prayer.

In this chapter, we will discuss "In His Will He Left." There are seven things God promised us, and they should be discussed, preached, taught, remembered, and passed on to the next generation, because these seven topics will benefit each person who reads this book. Please understand that there are many more than seven promises God willed for us to have, especially to those who believe, but we will discuss only seven of his promises today, and maybe if you want to hear more, it will be in our future books upon your request.

1. God Promises Us That He Will Forgive Us

He pardons our sins, dismisses our case, puts our sins in a sea of forgetfulness, and finds us not guilty, even while we are caught red-handed. Only friends and family members will remember your sins each time they see you, but God forgives and forgets, and he doesn't keep reminding you of your dirty deeds, which would be your conscience talking, and the evil one, who takes great pleasure in your wrongdoing. Sometimes people with a multitude of hidden sins always like to put the spotlight on your current evil deeds. When God forgives, the sin is forgiven, never to be remembered, but the enemy of our souls saves and downloads all our wrongdoing, mistakes; he puts sins in his gigantic, invisible database in hell, sort of speak, and every chance he gets, he likes to throw it in your face to discredit and dishonor your good nature, newness of life, and good reputation to destroy your future and destiny. God promises to forgive and forget your sins but not the evil one. Where God inhabits and dwells amid your praises, the evil one inhabits all your sinful deeds and sinful pleasures because they bring glory to Satan and his imps.

Second Chronicles 7:14 says, "If my people, which are called by my name, shall humble themselves and pray, and seek my face, and turn from their wicked ways: then will I hear from heaven and will forgive their sins and heal their land."

The entire Christian foundation is summed up in two words: forgiveness and love. These two are the pillars that support Christianity and God's personality. In my travels, while going from church to church, I've noticed that many Christians don't seem excited enough about God's forgiveness and love anymore. These words *forgiveness* and *love* need to be attached to something materialistic for us to be happy. I have witnessed the enthusiasm on the faces of many church members when they testify of their new jobs, inheritances, houses, cars, and business success, but very few display that same energy and passion about God's forgiveness and loving arms. Jesus forgives us of all our wickedness and sinful living, including prostitution, prejudice, homosexuality, filthiness, deceptions, scandals, perversion, murders, hatred, crime, adultery, stealing, or lying lips. Standing at a distance and looking at some testimony services, you would assume some people value worldly things more than spiritual things. As for me and my house, God's forgiveness and love are more important to me than the car I drive or the house I live in, more than riches and fame.

A SONGWRITER SAID, "I'D RATHER HAVE JESUS THAN ANYTHING."WRITTEN BY Rhea F. Miller in 1922

If someone owed you a million dollars and another person owed you a hundred dollars and you decided to forgive their debts, which would appreciate amnesty more? It would be the one with the most debt. We come to Jesus with a trailer load of sins, being eligible only for damnation, but Jesus washes all our sins away and forgets them so we can live more abundantly. Have many churches abroad lost the true essence behind God's forgiveness and love? That could be why many religious people will be lost. Forgiveness and love are the pinnacles of salvation. Forgiveness is what reunites man back to God, and without it we cannot have a true relationship with God or enter into God's kingdom. Love is so important that God even commands that we love our brother and sister as ourselves(; we should love those who despitefully hate us, use us, and abuse us. It is also recorded in the scriptures that though you have gifts of prophecies, preaching, and miracles, all that is merely nothing if you don't love people. Love is so important to God that he even instructs us to leave our offering in our pockets if we have "an aught" against our brother or sister (Saint Matthew 5:23-24).

Make the offense right with your brother or sister first; then you can participate in the offering. Love is the glue that holds our relationships with God tight. It was God's love that pushed God to create mankind. It was God's love that redeemed man back to God. It was God's love that allowed him to sacrifice his only begotten Son, Jesus Christ, the Son of the living God, to be crucified, nailed to a cross, and tortured for the redemption of mankind. Therefore, no matter how talented and gifted you are or how highly esteemed your job position may be (you may have hundreds of thousands in the bank and in other investments), if you lack love in your heart for your fellow man, heaven won't be in your future, because how could you love a God you don't see and hate your brother and sister whom you see each day? Love is the ingredient needed to achieve a home in the heavens beyond those blue skies.

In America, we pledge allegiance to the American flag. We lift our right hands in court as we swear to tell the truth so help me God. We stand in a courthouse as the judge enters the courtroom. We salute officers in the armed forces; these are all expressions we display in various public settings to show reverence. But where are our excitement, joyful noise, and tribute of praise toward God's love and forgiveness? Please understand that God's forgiveness won't always strive with man. Some people would say, "When I think of the goodness of Jesus and all he has done for me, my soul cries out, 'Hallelujah! Thank God for saving me.'" While we were sinners living our lives our way, Christ came, reached down, and forgave us of all our sins; that alone should make us send up some praise to God. I cannot hold my peace. I must praise God and share his forgiveness with others.

Dear reader, you can do the same; take a moment, confess your sins to God, and ask him to forgive you of your sins right now. Invite him into your heart today. Ask him to cleanse you from all unrighteousness, confess him to be your Lord and Savior, and turn from your wicked ways. If you believe this, you are saved. Hallelujah! Salvation is a heavenly thing, nothing about it is for you to be ashamed or scared of because our Lord and Savior means you no harm only good and a eternal home in heaven after death.

Though your sins are as scarlet, which means though you are

guilty as sin and know you don't deserve to be forgiven, God says, "That's okay. I will make them present you white as snow." Which means purity. Hallelujah! Only Jesus can cleanse our dirty sins and present us pure to our heavenly father Jehovah God.

You should be praising God right there. But he doesn't stop there; he continues, "Though your sins be as crimson they shall be as wool." Glory to God, our Lord and Savior! What this passage means is that even though everyone in your community and the entire world knows about the filth and hidden secrets you have played out for years, causing you to be cast out of society, blackballed in your business, and disowned by family members— and though your personal business has been plastered on every newspaper and radio station—God says, "Your sins shall be as wool to him." What does this represent? Think of the many valuable things made of wool: carpets, baseballs, yarn, mattresses, hats, mittens, pillows, coats, suits, pants, scarves, shirts, shorts, socks, sweaters, pajamas, and so forth. You can't even fathom all the things God can accomplish with your filthy sins. Remember, he took dirt and made me and you into living beings. Now look at us; we are wonderfully made in the image of God. That's what God does when you give him your dirt. Somehow he shapes, molds, and forms it to work for your good in life. I cannot explain, elucidate, or put into words how God almighty does this, but I am a witness when he turns dirt into something more valuable than anyone could ever imagine. Got dirt? Get Jesus! He will wash your sins away.

Only God can take dirt and make human beings. Only God can take dirt and make the most beautiful flowers grow. Some of the healthiest foods like produce grow from dirt and soil. Bring your dirt to God and watch him make you into someone to be reckoned with. Have you ever been guilty of a crime and did some time? Suddenly, you were called to a special review board committee, and they pardoned you for the crimes you had committed and allowed you to reenter society. How would you feel? Wouldn't you be dancing? Wouldn't you be praising God?

Well, my friend, God *has* pardoned you today. You came to court and were pardoned from all your sins by the Judge, our Lord Jesus Christ, the mediator between God and man. He has dismissed your case. Shout, "Hallelujah!" Glory to the most-high God! Honestly, that should be the premise, the reason for our joy, and the reason why we sing. We dance because we have been exonerated, and Jesus presents us innocent to God the Father because the blood of Jesus covers a multitude of sins and presents us guiltless before God. God sees his Son, Jesus, the mediator between God and man, not our sins. So rejoice because God's mercy is everlasting. Thank you, Jesus! God's forgiveness is a heavenly transaction, not an earthly deal. The situation is ultimately between you and God. He left this in his will for all mankind if we accept his promises.

So now that you are forgiven, lift your heads, knowing you are forgiven; move forward into a new direction, with the understanding that God brought you out of a sinful life, and now you have the opportunity to live a Christian life. As you go on in life, never forget that God doesn't discriminate. We are all God's people no matter race, color, or creed. These things aren't an issue with God, no matter our skin tone. God looks at our hearts. Also remember now that since God has forgiven you, you must forgive others, or God won't forgive you. So forgive your neighbor, distant cousin, parents, and spouse. Forgive those who have hurt you or cursed you. Forgive those who even tried to destroy you. When you forgive, this allows you to move forward freely. Forgiveness takes the power out of your accuser's hands and gives you the power to live your life. Life is too short to give anyone the power to seize your mobility or progress. Forgive others and keep moving forward. Maximize your time on earth and never hold onto grief and unforgiveness for excessive time. God says, "I will forgive your sins," "I will pardon your sins,(Isaiah 55-7)" "I will dismiss your sins," and "I will put your sins in a sea of forgetfulness.

(Micah 7:19-19)" Because God willingly forgives us, therefore we must forgive others, but the challenge for some of us is to forgive ourselves. Most suicide cases are based on people refusing to forgive themselves. You have been uncovered, and you're not the first to look in the mirror and not forgive yourself of your past sins, but the good news is that God freely and lovingly gave you life. Who are you to take it on your own? God hasn't promised you that others will forgive you, but he has promised that he will forgive you. Which is more important? If God forgives us, we must forgive ourselves as well; and over time our sins won't be as visible to others. Time will heal the memory of our past sins.

Don't take your life. You have so much to live for.

You didn't create your life. God did. You didn't supply daily oxygen for it. God did. Nor did you keep your heart beating every second of the day. God did. If you want to be rid of your life, give it to God, the almighty, and he will fix you and prosper you. Enjoy God's forgiveness. If God has forgiven you, you must forgive yourself and others too. Amen!

2. God Left in His Will That We Shall Have Victory (1 John 5:4–5)

"For whatsoever is born of God overcometh the world: and this is the victory that overcometh the world, even our faith who is he that overcometh the world, but he that believeth that Jesus is the son of God."

If you are born of God (which means being born again or accepting Jesus as your Lord and Savior), that same faith that believes on the Lord Jesus Christ is the same one that allows us to overcome the world. Our faith in Jesus Christ, the Son of the living God, assures us of victory. This victory extends throughout our entire lives. God wants us to have victory in our lives. Defeat isn't an attribute of God. It has no place in the family of God. If you are feeling defeated, remember, God willed that we will have victory.

Victory means to win (winning wars, battles, struggles, situations) and be successful, triumphant. God knows no defeat. In Christ we are made overcomers. We have overcome sin through Jesus Christ, and the same power that convicted us of our sins also cleansed us from all unrighteousness; it is the same power of the Holy Ghost, who gives us victory in our daily lives. Glory!

There is a scripture I used to hear throughout my teenage life. "Greater is he that is within you than he that's in the world." This verse is the perfect example of why we should have victory; it is because of the greater one (Jesus)(1st.John 4:4) inside us. Winning battles can be difficult and tedious for Christians and people in general, but for our Lord and Savior, Jesus Christ, difficulties tend to disintegrate into thin air in the presence of almighty God. He is the greater one, who wins battles and conquers territories for us and through us. That's why we should constantly build our faith and trust in Jesus because he gives us the victory. Lift up your heads and stop looking downward, because all the help you need is upward; only defeat looks down with a frown. Focus on the creator of the world and move forward with victory. During wartime, battles are won, and many are lost; but what really matters is who wins the war. The war has been won through the death, burial, and resurrection of Jesus Christ. All you and I need to do is to keep our faith in Christ while living on the earth, and we shall have victory.

Many scriptures in the King James Bible confirm that we will have tribulation in this world; even Jesus had tribulation, pain, sufferings, false accusations, and even death penalty; but note that Jesus overcame it all. And because he overcame all this upheaval, he promises us victory. If we believe on him, we can overcome all our obstacles too.

John 16:30 says, "These things I have spoken unto you, that in me ye might have peace. In the world ye shall have tribulation: but be of good cheer; I have overcome the world."

First, before you analyze your problems and circumstances, God wants you to have peace in your heart, and he wants us to be of good cheer about our personal matters. It may seem hard and stressful now, even though some of what we go through we have caused on our own. Nevertheless, Jesus overcame the world with all its pleasures, riches, fame and fortune, filth, witchcraft, and evil. You are his child, and God takes care of his own. You are now born again; you are entitled to have victory through Jesus Christ. Look beyond the mountains of your troubles, from whence your help comes; your help comes from the Lord God (Psalm 121:1-2). Most of your time should be looking upward. God promises victory for your life; you already have victory. Just believe it and receive it. You have the authority to have victory in your life. Victory is yours. Victory is mine. Thus said the Lord God.

The scriptures in the Holy Bible aren't trying to paint a picture that life on earth is a bed of roses or total serenity and tranquility; on the contrary, the scriptures are real with us, warning us that trials and temptations are coming our way, but we have our Lord and Savior Jesus Christ to help us be more than conquerors. We aren't alone; Jesus is intervening on our behalf. Jesus paid for the penalty of sin, so we now can walk in faith and enjoy that blessed victory in Jesus, knowing our sins are forgiven, not taking God's redemption for granted. Rather, we are grateful and confident that we have victory in Jesus to succeed in life and in the life after death. So go to your court date with confidence in the Lord to work on the judge and your case; expect a miracle. Having problems with your marriage and children? Fall down on your knees and ask God to turn things around for the good, and watch God do it. When problems arise in your life, bend your knees and pray to your majesty God, and after you pray, praise God for working it out in advance. There's no power more powerful than the power of God. The victory is already yours; believe this in your heart, and you will witness true victory.

In all these things we are more than conquerors
through him that loved us. (Romans 8:37)

Now thanks be unto God which always causes
us to triumph in Christ, and maketh manifest
the Savior of his knowledge by us in every place.
(2 Corinthians 2:14)

Being more than conquerors consists of more than just winning a battle, but it is winning the war, and sometimes it's winning war on life without much effort of fighting back. Sometimes it's others fighting on your behalf because they feel your battle is their battle too. Well, your battles are the Lord's; he will help you to be victorious. God promises his people victory if we trust and obey him; even when we fall short of God's glory, he is faithful and just to help us be conquerors. God knows no defeat.

However, Satan is the author of defeat, and he could write an entire encyclopedia with twenty million volumes on the subject of defeat, because he is a defeated foe to the human race. Satan had it all in heaven; he was the musical director in heaven, and because of jealousy, greed, and his evil plan, he took one-third of the angels to set up his kingdom to be similar to God and to have a kingdom to lord over, which we call hell. Concealed in Satan heart was to be like the most-high God which was concealed in his heart, so he did just that, which concluded in God's angels warring against former angels. They turned into demons, and they were defeated and sent to hell. Therefore, defeat is in Satan's DNA.

When they crucified Jesus, the Roman Empire and the Jews thought they had really destroyed Jesus's entire life, which they gave him not. The legacy Jesus left for Christians and the world to witness was that just as he conquered death and the grave, with him in our lives we are more than conquerors through Jesus Christ, our Lord. Jesus told the Roman king, "You can't take my life. I will kindly lay down my life for a bigger purpose, which includes the entire human race benefiting from this event." Jesus and his heavenly Father are the Authors of this human race and the world we live in; therefore, who can defeat God? He left in his will that we are more than conquerors through Jesus Christ, who strengthens us. Why are some Christians looking defeated, torn down, depressed, sad, and miserable? It's because they don't realize the power within them to be conquerors. Greater is he who is within us than he who is in the world.

Who is in you? Maybe that's where the problem lies. If Jesus is on the inside of your heart, you are more than a conqueror through Jesus Christ, our Lord and Savior, but you have to believe this to demonstrate your conquering power so you can have victory. Claim your victory! Walk in your victory! Proclaim your victory! Shout for victory! Dance for the victory! Pronounce victory on all the threats of your enemies. Live in victory. Get the victory. You aren't defeated if you are on the Lord's side, so pick yourself up and hold your head up high. Look people in the eye and walk in victory each day you are awake, for God has given you the victory if you would only accept what he has placed in his living will. In his will he left, you shall have the victory. As Jesus rose from the dead with all power in his hand, conquering all the powers of death and darkness, he willed that we do the same. We should rise from those dead things in our lives and live as God intended—living in victory, not defeat.

3.   God Left Healing in His Will

Isaiah 53:5 says, "But he was wounded for our transgressions; he was bruised for our iniquities: the chastisement of our peace was upon him; and with his stripes we are healed."

Jesus was wounded for our transgressions; he was bruised for our sins with every stripe from being beaten with a whip by the Roman guards. Jesus said those stripes were for the healing of his people. When you read the New Testament in the King James Version, you will see that the Gospels (Matthew, Mark, Luke, and John) are full of numerous incidents of Jesus conducting healings and deliverances. Jesus sent his disciples out to conduct healing throughout many regions. Jesus knew sickness paralyzed and tied people down, and it hindered them to live their lives to the fullest, so Jesus set them free to glorify his father in heaven and to give them a new start. Jesus healed thousands of people during his walk on earth. The same people Jesus healed became witnesses for the Lord Jesus Christ, telling all who would listen of the glory and power of the Lord Jesus Christ. Everywhere Jesus went, people were sick, stricken with deadly diseases; they were blind, deaf, dumb, lame, and mentally disordered. As Jesus walked through various townships, people heard the rumors and the great news of his healing power, so they came from far and near to witness Jesus's healing power; Jesus touched some of them, and they were healed instantly. Jesus just spoke a word to others, and people were healed from great distances. Today in our society there are millions of sick people, some unto death; others are learning to live with their sickness. Pharmaceutical corporations are making billions, even trillions, of dollars treating our sicknesses; the reason being is that there are very few profits for corporations to make people totally well. Hallelujah to the King of kings. God gets the glory and praise when he heals his people. Do you want healing? Well, Jesus is the expert at healing. Pray to the Father for your healing and believe he will do it, and it shall be done. Healing is in his will, which he left for those who believe.

Psalm 103:3 says, "Who forgives all thou iniquities; who heals all thy disease."

With such advanced technology and scientific discovery, you would think doctors have all the answers to most sicknesses and diseases, but they don't even know their limitations. It's God who heals people from deadly diseases, including cancer, AIDS, sugar diabetes, heart attacks, and high blood pressure. Healing is here in the twenty-first century, just like it was in AD 528. The power of God never diminishes; it's eternal and will never lose its power. Jesus healed back in AD, and he is healing today. Be healed! Dear reader, be healed in the name of Jesus Christ. No matter what the condition is, your creator knows the number of hairs on your head; therefore, he knows how to heal your body. Every part of you was made not by China but by God. He is your healer. Be healed.

In my church, three members were healed of cancer, and every year they are tested, and there's no trace or evidence of it. Hallelujah! Yes, the doctor removed some of the evidence of cancer, but after the removal procedure, the cancer never returned. Two close family members had major strokes, and after their episodes, they were back to normal as if they had never had strokes. God is a good God, and sickness has no power over him; in fact, sickness must stand still when it hears the voice of God. All sickness answers to God, and God wants us to be healed. Be healed, my dear reader. Be healed! Healing is what God left in his will for you and me. Believe that God can heal you; no matter the sickness you have endured, you can be healed. It's in the Holy Scriptures that God promises to heal our land (2 Chronicles 7:13), which includes you, your family, and all those who call on the Lord. If God said so, who are we to detest what God has declared? Be healed, dear reader, whatever your ailment is. Healing is in his will for his people; therefore, receive it and be ye healed.

4. God Left in His Will That He Will Fight Our Battles

"The Lord shall fight for you and ye shall hold your peace the Lord your God which goeth before you, he shall fight for you, according to all that he did for you in EGYPT before your eyes." (Exodus 14:14)

"The Lord your God which goeth before, he shall fight for you, according to all that he did for you in Egypt before your eyes." (Deuteronomy 1:30)

The Israelites had just been released from their slave masters in Egypt; now they were facing the desert behind them and the Red Sea in front of them, while the Egyptians chased them to recapture them. They had nowhere to go or hide from the Egyptians. The Egyptians pursued them vigorously. The Israelites cried out to Moses for help, and with their lips, they said, "It would be better for us to serve the Egyptians than to die in the wilderness." Can you believe they would even fathom the idea of serving the Egyptians after being enslaved for four hundred years rather than having faith in God's power, which released them from Pharaoh's jail? Just like some of us, we give our lives over to God; as soon as there is the slightest difficulty, complication, or setback, we are ready to leave God's safety net and revisit our old habits, routines, and tendencies, which lead to destruction. Moses says to Israel, "Fear ye not, stand still and see the salvation of the Lord, for the Egyptians whom you see today, ye shall see them again no more forever."(Exodus 14:13) We give up too fast in life, and this give-up attitude comes from two big words, *fear* and *doubt*. You already know who the author of this is: Satan, God's archenemy. Please note that the first thing Moses said to the Israelites was "Fear not." Fear causes you to act swiftly, not leaving room for your faith in God to kick in; we act on impulse, which causes us to give up the riches, rubies, finer things in life, freedom, and peace of mind just to become slaves and debtors to our past. Moses told Israel to "stand still and see the salvation of the Lord." When troubles are in your way, stand still and see the salvation of the Lord prevail. Stand praying and believing because help is on the way; stand trusting, for the King of kings and the Lord of lords will fight your battles. He might not come when you want him, but he is always on time. Moses proceeded to tell Israel, "The Egyptians whom you see today, ye shall see them again no more forever." This was a reward from God, and the Israelites didn't even appreciate it. Their voices should have been lifted in praise and celebration, knowing that the Egyptians who had tortured them, killed their families, raped their women, killed their babies, killed their dreams, and destroyed their hopes and enslaved them for four hundred years for the purpose of building cities for Pharaoh would never be a threat to them again. Where was the rejoicing from Israel? This sounds familiar, complaining about stuff when in fact God already has your situation under control. Doesn't this sound like some of us? Moses said they would never see them again. Now that's fighting your battles, when God destroys your enemies in such a way that you will never face them again.

I would like to do that with my debt! LOL! That's a real fight I caused. The scriptures don't report that Israel lifted their voices with thunderous praises for this great deliverance before it actually happened. God spoke to Moses and said, "The Egyptians whom you see today, ye shall see them again no more forever." Please understand; this means that some of your particular problems you face in life you will never see or deal with ever again. You can rest assured that God has the power to give you amnesty for all things, but the reality of it all is are you willing to endure some things.

The Israelites encountered other obstacles and enemies as they proceeded in life. So it is with us who live in America and all of us in the world; we will also encounter many problems, dilemmas, disasters, failures, catastrophic events, dramas, and even death; but we must stand still and see the salvation of the Lord, especially when we cannot control these various events and episodes. God promises to fight our battles and destroy our foes. All we battle in life aren't our fight, especially when we are living for God. Faith in God literally means we are leaving everything in his hands, because when we do this, be assured that God is going to literally fight for us.

As you wait on the Lord, don't sit and worry; continue to do the work and the necessary things you must but with the attitude that God has got your back. He may not come when you want him to, but he's always on time. Hallelujah! There are some things we cannot battle alone, such as marriage problems, court cases, job issues, children issues, health issues, and church issues. We need divine intervention from God to come down and help us fight our battles. We are born of God, and that entitles us to see God defend us. This should wipe the frown off your face and leave you with a permanent smile each day. God is your defender.

Your boss thinks he's in control. Ha ha! Little does he know that God is controlling him, for the scriptures say, "The king heart is in the hand of the Lord like the river of waters he turns it where ever he wishes" God can turn his heart either way(Proverbs 21:1)." Is there a hallelujah in the building? God has the controls of mankind and humanity, and he controls all leaderships including the government in the USA. Can I preach? God controls the very elements of the air, and the oxygen we breathe belongs to God.

Have you ever been on a plane forty thousand feet in the air? Everything looks microscopic. So it is with God; to him your problems are smaller than a drop of water in a bucket. Who is this God we speak of? He is the creator of the entire world and creator of all human beings of all colors, nationalities, and languages. Your personal issues are minuscule to God. He can handle our issues with ease, but can we handle trusting him totally?

No one can speak to someone's heart like God can. He can use a dream to get his point across. He can take a life to make his point absolutely clear. Our source is God. Let him fight your battles. What are you battling today? God wants to fight your battles. The "I will" God wants to fight your battles. Maybe you are going through a horrible divorce, and your spouse is taking everything from you, leaving you with nothing, and stripping you from your dignity and pride of life. Well, let God fight your battle, stand still, and see the salvation of the Lord. Pray to the Father and see him work it out for you. Sometimes God works speedily; other times he moves in different angles. Other times he uses people to help you out. No one knows all God's strategies. You might think you're not perfect or mature enough in Christianity; neither were the Israelites. They complained, murmured, and spoke treason; and God still fought their battles.

God loved the world, and he gave his only begotten Son, Jesus, to save the world from their sins. God destroyed the Egyptians, and they became a memorial for the Jewish nation to this day; just as God destroyed the Egyptians for the Israelites, he will destroy some things for you too. Are there some things you would like destroyed? Hold your peace and let God do the fighting for you. Praying to the Father and holding your peace are very appropriate, because if you speak too fast, you may incriminate yourself and say things you will regret. "Hold your peace and stand still" and witness the power of God. God doesn't need our help. Don't interfere with the work of God, especially when it is beyond your control.

Finally, God opened the Red Sea so the Israelites could escape from the Egyptians. Is there a Red Sea you need God to open in your life? Open doors of opportunity are what we need. God is the door opener, but we must walk through those doors and work through those opportunities unmistakably presented to us.

The Egyptians put the fear of God into the hearts of the Israelites to the point that the Israelites easily conceded to become slaves for the Egyptians instead of their employees. The Israelites had God's promise of blessings on their lives, but they chose defeat and slavery to be their way of life. Israel outnumbered the Egyptians one hundred to one. Instead of fighting for their freedom and their right to be free, they conceded to the Egyptians without any resistance. So it is with us. We choose to be in debt for the rest of our lives. We choose to be broke, never knowing the true potential we have to change our circumstances. The Israelites outnumbered the Egyptians, yet they couldn't see their advantage. The Egyptians used and depended on weapons and chariots to control Israel, and Israel feared trepidation from the Egyptians. Did they know how powerful God was? Did Israel know that no weapon formed against them would prosper? Dear reader, with God in your life, your enemies are outnumbered, and their weapons formed against you shall not prosper. God will fight your battles. Give God some praise and glory.

5. God Left in His Will "He Will Never Leave You nor Forsake You"

Joshua 1:5 says, "There shall not any man be able to stand before thee all the days of thy life: as I was with Moses, so I will be with thee: I will not fail thee, nor forsake thee."

After the death of Moses, the Lord spoke unto Joshua to encourage him to go to the promised land. It was important for Joshua to hear from God, especially after Israel's hero, Moses, was dead. Moses was and is the most famous Bible character who ever lived besides Jesus Christ, our superstar. Being alone isn't easy, and God knew Joshua needed some encouragement after losing his confidant, Moses. God told Joshua, "As I was with Moses so shall I be with you and I will not fail thee, nor forsake thee." Wow! Can you imagine God saying such a thing to you? Well, in essence, God *is* saying the same thing to us who believe. Joshua was a servant of the Lord, and we are servants of the Lord, so when God speaks to one, he speaks to all. God wants you to know that he will be with you, and he won't fail you or forsake you. Hallelujah!

It might seem lonely at times, and you may not be the most popular person in your family. You might even witness friends and family disappear when things get hard for you. God wants you to know, and be assured he is there for you; even though you cannot see God or feel him at times, know that he's there. When his presence seems void, that's because he is either working things out for you or carrying you through our troubled waters. We cannot see the wind, but we know it's there; we cannot feel or see oxygen through our nostrils, but we know it's there. You must first believe that God exists and that he rewards those who serve him.

Keep serving the Lord, no matter what happens, no matter what is said about you, no matter what people do to you, even when serving God isn't popular, because God is going to reward those who serve him continually.

First Kings 6:13 says, "I will dwell among the children of Israel, and will not forsake my people Israel."

There goes our Lord and Savior again promising to dwell with his people and never forsaking them. Do you realize how important this promise is? Why God loves us so much? "I don't know why" is what most people would say, but the real reason why God loves us so much is that we are valuable to him, yet we run in the opposite direction. This is just like what some of us did to our loving but protective parents; we did the opposite of what they told us, yet they loved us and endured our disobedience because we were valuable enough for them to be patient, waiting for us to come to our senses. Our God isn't a statue or some monument, shrine, or tombstone; he is the only living God in the universe, and he is interested in you, and we shouldn't take him for granted. He wants to dwell with us and have a daily relationship with us, but we would rather rub on a magical lamp, waiting for a genie to appear to make our request known. The God of the universe wants a relationship with you, and the perks that come with that are that he will be with you always, he will never fail you, and he will never forsake you. You should be singing, "Hallelujah!" about now.

Imagine having a god in your life that you had to wake up in the morning. Imagine a god you had to frequently remind about his promises. Imagine a god who could be in only one place at a time; if there were other people's needs, he would have to take a cab or plane to reach them. LOL. Imagine a god who puts you on hold when engaging in prayer. Imagine a god who didn't keep his word. Imagine a god who openly showed favoritism. Imagine a god who killed everyone who committed sin. Imagine a god who gave you no freedom or free will.

If all these things were in God's character, we would be robots and slaves for God. But the God we serve never sleeps; the God we serve knows and sees everyone and everything. He is omnipresent. God never lies, and he so loved the world he gave his only begotten Son so through him the world may be saved (St John 3:16). God dwells with his people. If anyone is leaving this relationship, it would be you, not God, because God promised never to leave you.

Matthew 28:20 says, "Teaching them to observe all things whatsoever I have commanded you: and, Lo I am with you always, even to the end of the world. AMEN."

Jesus at this time died on the cross and rose on the third day. Now Christ was on his way back to the Father in heaven, but he lingered so he could comfort his disciples, letting them know that although he was leaving them for now, he would be with them spiritually and would never leave them, even to the end of their days. Naked we come in this world, and naked we shall leave this world, but the things we do for God will last. They are those heavenly things we invest in that will determine where we end up.

Jesus is the answer for the world today, and it is our job to get connected with God and stay with him. Don't partake in worldly things and unrighteous behavior because it disconnects us from God. Either we are hot or cold. Either we will serve God or serve the devil. Choose the creator. God will be there during your darkest night, and he won't leave you alone, but will you leave him? Just remember God's promise in his living words from the scriptures; he will never leave or forsake you. Stay with God, dear reader. There are so many more benefits when you stick close as glue to the creator of life and the world. He truly rewards all those who serve him.

6. **God Left in His Will That We Should Prosper and Have Good Success**

> Only be thou strong and very courageous, that thou mayest observe to do according to all the law, which Moses my servant command thee: turn not from it to the right hand or to the left, that thou mayest prosper whithersoever thou goest.
>
> This book of Law shall not depart out of thy mouth; but thou shalt meditate therein day and night, that thou mayest observe to do according to all that is written therein: for then thou shalt thy way prosperous, and then thou shalt have good success. (Joshua 1:7–8)

God gave Joshua some instructions for Israel to prosper. Joshua was told to observe all the law, to meditate on it day and night, and not to turn from the right or left but to be strong and courageous. Then he would be prosperous and have good success.

Prosperity and success come with instructions, and those instructions came from God. We must obey God and follow his written word, and he will prosper us; and only then will we have good success. People really think God wants to keep people poor and enslaved, when, in fact, it's the opposite. God wants his people to prosper, but we choose to go after other gods: drugs, sex, pornography, crime, liquor, sexual perversion, homosexuality, violence, witchcraft, and the list goes on and on. So many of us choose money in the fast lane and get rich-quick schemes; we worship worldly possessions and still have no peace, joy, or contentment. When God gives you success, it comes without any sorrow or guilt. If you want to follow a success story, follow the creator of the entire world's wealth. Follow the God who set up government, kings, and presidents. Follow the God who can take dirt from the ground and make a total living being.

Joshua made up his mind that he and his household would serve the Lord. The Lord God promised Joshua that no man would be able to stand before him all the days of his life. Wow! What a promise. Joshua was able to walk fearlessly with God; with a promise from God like this, who wouldn't walk fearlessly? When God is on your side, who can stand against you? Joshua was feared by his enemies and all those who opposed him. People of God walk fearlessly because no one can stand against them, who love the Lord. Demons can't touch you, and when things get out of your control, God will fight your battles, which is another promise he left in his will for all those who believe. This is your reward for keeping a close relationship with your creator.

Third John 2 says, "Beloved, I wish above all things that thou mayest prosper and be in health, even as thy soul prospereth."

Above all things, you may think it is important what John said: "I wish above all things that thou may prosper and be in good health, even as your soul prosper." This is a significant message for a Christian to have a balanced life. God came not only to save us but also to enrich our lives. That's why he healed the sick, changed water into wine, fed the multitudes with two fishes and five loaves of bread, raised the dead, and cured leprosy. He wanted people to prosper while serving God. It wasn't the enemy of our souls or corporate American that invented prosperity; rather, God created it, and it was intended for mankind. God deliberately created mankind to enjoy prosperity and success, but many of us have been blinded by other people's success and riches, not realizing that all the gifts, talents, and greatness he bestowed on us were intended to prosper our endeavors. There are multitudes of imitators who say they are successful but not happy; they are successful, but they refuse to say the success came from God's blessings. God's success comes without sorrow; God proclaimed success and prosperity for mankind. A balanced life is necessary for true success, and it's important that we are never so spiritual that we become of no earthly good. The earth and all the elements it contains belong to God; so if that is the absolute truth, why aren't we spending more time with him instead of chasing emptiness and nothingness and falling into oblivion?

It has been said that to be successful, you must associate with successful people. Who's more successful than God? Trust in the Lord, and he will prosper you, and you shall have great success. Although God gave man *dominion* over the earth, the power to *multiply*, the power to be *fruitful*, the power to *replenish,* and the power to subdue the earth, some may believe that God took these five attributes away from man after Adam and Eve failed in the Garden of Eden. Not so. God didn't take these attributes away from mankind; rather, these five powers exist in all our lives, but we need to activate them. God commanded man to work from the sweat of his brow so everything won't just fall into his hand so easily. We have to work for it; but when we finally realize the greatness God's installed in us and the great powers we have to prosper and have great success, our faith in Christ should blow up like a helium balloon. When you have great success, it isn't just for you but for others who are less fortunate like the next generation, your children, and their offspring.

The purpose of great success is to help others, not to hoard it. Investing in people is the best investment ever. God willed that we be successful. Why? So we can help others succeed and make our world a better place to live in harmony. It's in God's will that we will be successful in life. God doesn't need a bump on a log, who just sits for countless hours with no goals, energy, aspirations, zeal,, work ethic, strategy, planning, or organization. Or one who just sits there, waiting for someone to do it for him or her, leading him or her to the fountain so he or she can drink thereof. What God has left in his will for his children has been placed within you, but you need to work the gifts, ideas, visions, and goals; and as you do so, God will sprinkle his Spirit on you for prosperous endeavors. Get up and be about your father's business.

7. **God Left in His Will That "He Will Reverse Some Things for You" (Numbers 23:1–30)**

There was a king named Balak; he was king of Moab, who happened to witness the Israelites utterly destroy the Amorites. After they defeated the Amorites, they pitched their tents in the plains of Moab, which were on the side of Jordan by Jericho, making themselves neighbors to the Moabites. The entire Moabites countrymen were afraid and distressed that Israel had moved so close. So the king of Moab, feeling threatened, sent messengers to a prophet called Balaam, a strange prophet, who claimed to worship God and also practiced divination and the forbidden arts of darkness. Balaam was famous for cursing nations and blessing nations. King Balak knew the people of Moab couldn't defeat the Israelites, so he sent for this well-known prophet, Balaam. King Balak wanted the prophet Balaam to put a curse on Israel so it would be easy for the Moabites to defeat them. Israel outnumbered the Moabites by the thousands, but if they were cursed by Balaam, the Moabites would have the advantage over Israel and could defeat them. This king, Balak, was jealous of Israel's success and God's blessings on their lives.

God took good care of Israel, and because there were no other gods in the world like Israel's God, there's weren't any gods that could defeat Israel's God; it made king Balak apprehensive of just the sight of Israel living so close. Israel's being neighbors to Moabites made the Moabites threatened by their presence, so they sent for Balaam, the prophet, who had a track record of reversing the odds with his evil and wicked spells on armies. Since Israel prospered and had great success, other nations in their hometown stood afar off, pondering in their minds how they were going to destroy Israel, the great nation. The enemies of Israel intended to cast a spell on them so Moab could manipulate Israel's actions and control the outcome of war. King Balak construed with the prophet Balaam, but because they planned to destroy Israel in secret, God reversed what would have been a curse from the prophet and turned it into a blessing each time he tried to curse Israel. In short, the prophet went to God for permission to curse Israel, and God spoke to Balaam and told him not even to go to Moab; he also told Balaam that God had blessed Israel and that this couldn't be reversed. Hallelujah!

King Balak wouldn't hear this treason, so he asked the prophet to try calling God in a different location, and maybe God would allow it. So the prophet tried several times, and on one occasion, God said to the prophet Balaam, "God is not a man, that he should lie; neither the son of man, that he should repent: hath he said, and shall he not do it? Or hath he spoken and shall he not make it good? Behold, I have received commandments to bless: and he hath blessed; and I cannot reverse it."

People of God, are you listening to this story about people who try to destroy you for no apparent reason? They want to destroy your reputation, business, church, family, and marriage because you and your family are doing well. They are called haters. In most cases, you can't even pinpoint your enemies until you progress in life. So as King Balak set out to destroy Israel using a prophet who had a history of cursing nations and casting spells on them to control them, God spoke to the prophet Balaam. Instead of the prophet Balaam cursing Israel, he had to bless them because Balaam couldn't reverse God's blessing. They intended to curse a blessed nation, a blessed people, but God reversed the scheme of King Balak and Balaam. No devil, warlock, or prince of darkness in hell could reverse God's blessings.

When your life belongs to Jesus Christ, our Lord and Savior, no one can touch you unless God allows it. Are there some things you need God to reverse? Do you have a court case and need God to turn the verdict around? He can do it. Yes, he can! While you sleep at night, evil people are devising mischievous things against you, making it hard for you to flow and be successful, but God said he will reverse it, making those mischievous things against you become stepping-stones toward your success and prosperity. The God we serve can exonerate business owners of millions of dollars owed to the IRS, although this doesn't mean you shouldn't pay Uncle Sam anything; it just means God can reverse a challenging situation in our lives to bring glory to his name and because he loves us and wants to reward and take good of his people.

The God we serve can reverse your foreclosure. The God we serve can reverse your diagnosis of cancer, AIDS, sickle cell, sugar diabetes, or tumors. God can reverse that eviction notice. God can reverse your termination at work. The God we serve can reverse that demotion and make it into a promotion. The God we serve can promote an employee to become the CEO. There is nothing too hard for God. Don't think people aren't conspiring against you, because they are, but God blocks their arsenal of weapons against you, reversing their plots of attacks into ammunition that shoots you to success, prosperity, and victory. Your haters will use weapons like lies, scandals, deceptions, and violence to destroy your reputation and blast your private and personal stuff on social media. They will report false information about you to higher authorities, friends will denounce you, family will betray you, and people will set out to destroy your church, marriage, job, career, business, and friendships; but God uses their weapons of mass destruction as instruments and tools to make your life better. Hallelujah!

God is so powerful, yet we underestimate his power. We gaze with amazement at how Superman, the Hulk, Captain America, and Thor are so powerful; but all the powers of the Justice League, Avengers, and X-men combined cannot even come close to the amazing power of the Lord Jesus Christ; may I add that some of those superhero powers are carbon copies of some of the powers God gave the former prophets in the Bible days. God opened up seas and rivers, held the sun in place for an entire day, and destroyed the earth with a trillion tons of water. The angels of the Lord wiped out nations plotting against Israel in a day. That's not even God in full throttle; that is a taste of God's mercy side. Don't get him angry, because then you will see his judgment side. No one can stand tall when the wrath of God is on him or her. So whatever your problems are today—marriage issues, family issues, employment issues, personal issues, church issues, business issues—all these things appear to make you better, stronger, smarter, and wiser. You are a child of the King, and just because you are a child of God doesn't mean you won't have crises, difficulties, dilemmas, heartbreaks, obstacles, problems, setbacks, and troubles because God takes all that negativity and damaging matter and turns them into a better you, a mature you, and a wiser you.

You are never ambushed when you fully trust in the Lord God, and as for those who would plot traps to destroy you. God will reverse their cunning devices into weapons of mass destruction for themselves. Glory hallelujah! Can God reverse your credit rating, foreclosure, criminal record, and divorce status? Yes, he can! But can you trust in the Lord with all your heart? Can you change your evil ways? God is the only one who can reverse all the works of darkness, all the works of bigotry, chauvinism, discrimination, injustice, corruption, prejudice, and unfairness. In God's will, he promises to reverse the bad things that are beyond your control and will fast-forward you to victory if you have faith in him; and if your faith is weak, my God will still deliver you from evil so you will glorify his name.

God isn't like mankind. They judge you based on your income, looks, clothing, jewelry, personality, history, and, family; God sees your heart, not your suit or tattoo; God sees your heart. If you give Jesus your burdens, he will give you rest; and if you confess your sins, he is faithful and just to forgive you, and he will pardon you for all your transgressions. God said that if you serve and obey him, he will prosper you in all your ways. and you shall have good success. Give up your hypocritical ways, give up your evil ways, and plant your feet on the rock of salvation. That rock is Jesus Christ. In whatever is going on in your life, hang on to the promises of God found in his Holy Bible. The word of God is God's living will. God's living will has been established purposely for his children to declare the promises of God and to benefit from them. More importantly, we should have faith and receive these promises found in the Holy Scriptures.

Jesus documented his living will in the Holy Bible. Only you can activate God's promises in your life; receive your forgiveness, your victory, your healing, your salvation, and the Holy Ghost and power.

Who is your defender? God. He will fight your battles. God will reverse bad things and turn them into good things and useful things, just like he took dirt, which is useless to many. But when God handles it, it becomes and is made into living beings. Remember, no matter how lonely you feel, God said, "Lo, I am always with you; I will never leave you nor forsake you." You must believe this. God promised you and me prosperity and success, and last but not least, he promised to reverse any curse that sets itself against you into a blessing; and when God blesses you, who dares curse what God has blessed? The trap your enemies lay before you to entangle you into their web of evil and destruction will become an instrument and tool that will launch you to blessings and victories, while your enemy's weapons against you seem to appear like weapons of mass destruction. It will turn into their own demise, and they will never again be able to touch you or stop your progress. God will reverse the situation so their instruments of deception will be used for their own folly.

Take a minute to stand up and praise the almighty God. God has given us much, and we continue to give him so little. Praise God! Praise him in the morning, noonday, and evening. Praise him when the sun goes down. I have no more words that could put running in your feet; the only thing I have is Jesus Christ, the soon-coming King. After reading this chapter, I can only lift my hands and voice to praise the almighty God. He is a wonder to my soul, a giver to my life and my family. I will praise the God of my salvation. I am on the winning side, and there's no other God who is more powerful, smarter, wiser, more loving, or more caring than my Jesus. Lift your hands and praise the King of kings, the Lord of lords. It's God who allows us to prosper. God's will for us is more meaningful than any living will a person could ever leave us after death. The will Jesus Christ left for us isn't from a dead man but from a living God. Hallelujah! Praise God, from whom all blessings flow.

CHAPTER 4

God's Mathematics

A ll through my life, my parents, especially my mother, told me how important mathematics was and how much I needed to be good at it to succeed. My father went to high school, but my mother finished only third grade. My mom was forced to work in the fields of Yamesee, South Carolina, at the early age of seven years old. My grandparents, the Bobien family, owned several hundreds of acres of land, and they needed help to till it. Having fifteen children, my grandparents put their children to work in the fields. It was hard working those fields and getting up at five a.m. to feed the pigs, cows, and chickens. She had to endure extreme heat with no shade and long hours for no pay. Their survival as a family depended on the crops from their land. After Mom lived through these rough times and tough conditions, she promised herself that her children were going to be educated and have better jobs and opportunities than she did.

My mother, Katherine Thomas, diligently reminded all her children, "You all must learn to read well and do math well so you can be successful."

The foundation of learning is composed of reading and mathematics. Being able to read, calculate, and compute numbers is so important because you will use these skills for the rest of your life, so why not be good at them? In today's society, some of our children don't see the importance of these values. In every business, mathematics is used, and the ones who tend to go out of business had problems with numbers and finances. Saying all this, let me add that numbers must be important to God, because numbers are displayed countless times throughout the Bible. Chapters and verses are all numbered, and there's even a book in the Bible named Numbers. When God gave Moses the commandments, he numbered them and called them the Ten Commandments. Jesus said, "On the third day I will rise from the grave." Hallelujah!

So numbers are important to God. God is the author of numbers; therefore, he understands numbers a million leap years more than mankind does. God gives mathematics to mankind to calculate, compute, and understand the things God created on earth. God uses mathematics so mankind can figure out problems, comprehend true value, obtain measurements, give solutions to problems, and create formulas that answer problems and so forth. Some of the greatest scientists used mathematical equations to invent electronic devices and to send astronauts to the moon.

Man's mathematics says and proves that zero means nothing and that nothing from nothing is zero; and when zero is added, divided, multiplied, or subtracted by itself, it remains a big, fat zero. On the other hand, in God's mathematics, zeros and nothingness mean a new beginning, a fresh start in the right direction, and an opportunity for greatness. They mean man's extremities or limitations make room for God's opportunity to make greatness. God's best work and miracles are preeminent when there's no answer or solution. Zeros make room for God's provision and God's promotion. Give God voidances; he'll make a world and universe filled with such array and decoration. Give him worthless dirt; he'll make man and woman in his image, not clones. Give God complete darkness; he'll make sunlight, which can light up our world and the galaxy.

Our God is an awesome God, but something about zero equaling nothing attracts God. What is God's attraction to nothingness? Well, it allows him to be God; it gives him the controls to do wonders; most of all he gets glory in taking nothingness and making it into something worth more than anything you can imagine, something that has immeasurable value. Now that God made man in his image, does this make us robots? No way! It's up to us to give the desires of our hearts to him, and as we do, God will lead and direct us to greatness. We have the options to refuse God's directives, which will lead to our destruction, but if you accept and believe his holy word, which is the remedy to your success and victory, your pathway will be abundantly blessed. You must not lean to your own understanding but allow God to direct your pathways to live prosperously. You could be a person with very little education, no business skills, no influence, no credit, no job, no place to live, no food to eat, no family, and no friends; but when God steps into the equation, he will equip you with the very things you need to succeed, and he will bless you to be a winner and a conqueror. Is anything too hard for God? Give God your zeros, and God will use your zeros to make great resources for you; he will build your confidence and give you favor with people who can help you succeed. Finally, God will take all your inconsistencies, shortcomings, weaknesses, and inadequacies and wrap them all together; and somehow after all is said and done, he can create something in you that amazes the entire world. God's mathematics is unexplainable at times.

When God was ready to make Moses into a Deliverer for the Israelites, he spoke to Moses and said, "Moses, Moses," and Moses said, "Here am I," and God said, "Draw not nigh hither": "put off thy shoes from thy feet, for the place where on thou standest is Holy ground" (Exodus 3:4–5). God also said to Moses, "I have also seen the oppression wherein the Egyptians oppress my people. Come now therefore, and I will send thee unto Pharaoh, that thou mayest bring forth my people the children of Israel out of Egypt" (Exodus 4:9–10). Moses replied, "Who am I that I should go to Pharaoh, and that I should bring forth the children of Israel out of Egypt." Later God told Moses that if they asked who had sent him, "tell them I am that I am sent you," and God proceeded to tell Moses to go down from the mountain and tell Pharaoh to "let my people go,"(Exodus 5:1) and Moses replied, "I can't speak well," yet God still used him despite his inadequacies because God doesn't see your frailty or weaknesses on his billboard or big-screen television set. What he does see and look for is your heart, your true character. That's what God is concerned about. Moses asked God, "Whom shall I say sent me?" And God responded and said, "Tell them that I am that I am sent you." I am that I am is the only God in the universe(Exodus 3:14).

I sit here and write this book under the influence of the mighty God to encourage readers to give God all their zeros in their lives, because, just like God used Moses to lead thousands of Israelites out of Egypt, God wants to use you to do something great in your family, church, job, neighborhood, city, state, and country. God loves glory and praise, so when you give your life to him and worship him, he rewards you with miracles, prosperity, good health, a sound mind, and great success. Who am I talking about? The great "I am" God. God takes the unqualified and qualifies them to do the job.

Let's go to the beginning of the Bible, in Genesis 1:5. "And the evening and morning was the first day." Here we see God counting the days; as you read this chapter, there was a second day, third day, fourth day, fifth day, sixth day, and finally a seventh day. It was on the sixth day that God created man, and on the seventh day, God rested. These seven days represent the first week that ever existed and recurs each time, even in this twenty-first century. God created the first week for mankind, which represents the beginning of time.

Genesis 1:28 says, "God said; let us make man in our image and God blessed them, and God said unto them, be fruitful and multiply." Stop!

Multiply is a mathematical terminology. To multiply means to increase in number or degrees or to double in number. Men say one times itself is one, God says, "Give me one man and one woman and I'll make them one flesh, and together they will produce generations of people by the seed of one man." That's what it means to "be fruitful and multiply." God made one man and one woman to populate the entire world. That's God's mathematics.

Before we go any further, we must realize some of God's characteristics to understand how our creator works.

Isaiah 55:8–9 says, "For my thoughts are not your thoughts neither are your ways my ways saith the Lord; for as the heavens are higher than the earth, so are my ways higher than your ways and my thoughts than your thoughts."

Look into the sky. The sun is close to 92.96 million miles from the earth, and the moon is close to 238,900 million miles from the earth, so it is with God's thoughts and knowledge, and his ways are as far as the sun is to the earth; that's how much more advanced God is in comparison to our mortal soul; in other words, we on this planet are a hundred million light-years behind God's intellect, creative powers, technology, mathematics, methods, and formulas. Neither you nor I can outwit or outthink God. He is the omnipotent one, the all-knowing God. He knows your inner thoughts and those secret things you do. We cannot fathom God's ways. We all have limitations, but with God, all things are possible, and because we know this, we should be totally dependent on Jesus Christ. If you are having some serious issues, problems, heartaches, trials, temptations, and circumstances going wrong in your life, stop trying to figure it out by asking yourself, "Why me?" "Why now?" "Why this?" Just give your issues to the God who turned water into wine, and he will take your problems and turn them into solutions. Give your burdens to the Lord, and he will give you rest, peace, and victory while others lose their minds trying to figure things out.

The world's biggest issues aren't cancer, AIDS, kidney failure, sugar diabetes, high hypertension, and heart failure, but it is stress (worrying), which can cause high blood pressure, heart attacks, cancer, brain tumors, ulcers, nervous breakdowns, and much more. Stress breaks down our immune system, allowing foreign agents to invade our bloodstream and cause deadly sicknesses.

Trust in the Lord, because he is the only one who will take our zeros and make something out of them; he'll take your one talent and multiply it. You may have a thousand enemies attempting to ambush you, and you don't know what to do; but the same God who delivered the Israelites from Egypt will deliver you from your enemies' hands, and he will give you the power and authority to put your enemies under your feet(Malachi 4:3) . Can someone say, "Glory hallelujah"?

Let's measure the percentage rate of your personal relationship with God; are you 10 percent in this relationship with God? Are you 20 percent, 30 percent, 40 percent, 50 percent, 60 percent, 70, percent, 80 percent, 90 percent? Or are you 100 percent in your relationship with God? It has been proven that when youngsters join a gang in the street or in jail, gang leaders require 100 percent loyalty from their members, so it is with soldiers of the US Army. They want 100 percent from their soldiers.

The Lord God has always desired man to give him 100 percent. The percentages above represent the quality levels of your relationship with God. In other words, how much involvement is your heart in serving, worshipping, praising, working, and living for God? Is it 100 percent dedication? God won't tolerate indecisiveness from his people, people who can't make up their minds on whether to serve the Lord God almighty or to serve worldly pleasures? In Revelations 3:16) "I know thy works, that thou art neither cold nor hot: I would thou wert cold or hot. So then because thou art lukewarm, and neither cold nor hot, I will spue thee out of my mouth" " these types of people as warm-blooded people (indecisive) God would rather you were hot or cold. Seemingly most people decide and prefer tangible things the world has to offer. Why? For anything you want to be exceptionally good at, you must give it your all. Serving the invisible God isn't popular or on the best-seller list, and serving God requires commitment. The word *commitment* is a scary word for many people because people want options. Marriages fail because of no real commitment. People embezzle money from their jobs and church because of no commitment. Commitment is spending time with your creator in praying and reading his word.

There was an old axiom that said, "Marriage is a fifty-fifty relationship," and many who followed that credo are divorced now. True marriage is when both couples bring 100 percent to the relationship. In other words, both spouses should know the dirt and the good stuff, dumb stuff, and smart stuff of their spouses.

They should know the debt and wealth each other possesses so together they can work on solutions to create a successful marriage. Once the information is shared, couples should make each other better, and with their commitment and determination to stay together through tough times and good times, they will prove each is giving the marriage 100 percent. There are some extreme cases only God can tackle to keep marriages in operation, but when coming into a relationship with the mentality of 50 percent psychologically, emotionally, spiritually and romantically, there is no way you will be totally committed through rough times, and you won't honor those vows you repeated to each other when you said, "For better or worst … in sickness and in health … for richer or poorer … unto death do us part."

God wants your commitment to serve and worship him just like in a marriage. Only his request won't interfere with your earthly marriage; as a matter of fact, it will enhance your marriage when you put him first in your life. That's the spiritual part that everyone leaves out. God created marriage between a man and a woman, and God wants to be part of the union between man and woman, for once we can get over these new interpretations of what marriage is, we should understand that marriage didn't start yesterday, but it goes back since the beginning of time, and woe to those who have made progress to change and redefined marriage in this twenty-first century. Marriage was instituted for companionship and for the purpose of creating generations and generations from a man and woman. Marriage isn't a selfish act but an open commitment between a man and a woman to live together for companionship and to have children and serve God. God so loved the world that he gave his Son to be hung on the cross as a living sacrifice to redeem man from sin. That's a 100 percent commitment from God! What level is your commitment to God?

All Jesus is asking us to do is to come unto him and follow him and lean not on our own understanding, because he loves us with a great love more than we can imagine, but if we choose not to commit to him, we will commit to something or someone else either way. Choose God's way! Mathematically, where is your relationship with God? Is it 100 percent good, or is it a much lower percentage? Only you can personally answer this question, but whatever your answer is, God already knows your heart. The same formula applies to marriage or friendships. Where does your commitment lie? How do you make calculations or assumptions to where your 100 percent commitment is?

Use this simple questionnaire. Where is most of your time spent? Where and to whom do most of your energy go? Where are your thoughts most of the day? What do you read most of the time? What things do you make a great effort for? How often do you communicate with your God? When it comes down to commitment, there's no secret where a man's heart is, because it shows in his actions.

Noah was an upright and perfect man of God, and his relationship was a true 100 percent with God—so much so that God decided to destroy the world because every thought of mankind was evil, and God chose Noah to warn the people about this destruction to come. While Noah preached his heart out to the people for one hundred years that a storm was coming, God gave Noah the technology, mathematical solutions, and architectural design to make a ship large enough for Noah and his family and various animals to escape this soon-to-come destructive flood. Obviously, Noah spent lots of time with God and used all his energy to preach about God's mercy and his decision to destroy the world with rain for forty days and forty nights; Noah endured ridicule, scorn, and mockery because of his efforts to convince others that it was going to tragically rain like never before; nor would any future floods compare to its catastrophic effect. For one hundred years, Noah preached, but no one repented; no one believed. After one hundred years of preaching, no one else tried to build his boat, but Noah kept building and building the boat until it was finished; and suddenly, a drop of rain fell, and the people looked astonished, surprised, and dumbfounded. They all ran to Noah's boat, but it was too late. The doors were tightly shut.

Genesis 6:14–16 says, "Make thee an ark of gopher wood; rooms shalt thou make in the ark, and shalt pitch it within and without with pitch, and this is the fashion which thou shalt make it of: the length of the ark shall be three hundred cubits, the breadth of it fifty cubits and the height of it thirty cubits, a window shalt thou make to the ark, and in a cubit shalt thou finished it above; and the door of the ark shalt thou set in the side thereof; with lower second and third stories shalt thou make it."

In the above scripture, we see God instructing Noah to build an ark, which would be an instrument of safety for Noah's family and a few select animals. This is very similar to the extended salvation plan Jesus gave mankind; without God's salvation, men and women would be lost because after death, there will be only two destinations; we all end up in either heaven or hell.

Let's examine three elements in the story of Noah. First, God's warned the people for one hundred years. Second, while God warned the people, he prepared a safety boat that would act as salvation for Noah's family and animals. Third, God's warning became reality. Now there was nowhere to hide, nowhere to run, and no time to make a boat. The only thing was to drown; without Christ in your life, you will drown.

Let's get back to the point at hand. God gave Noah mathematical measurements to build a large boat equivalent to a small football field; it was surely an awesome sight to see. The length of the ark was three hundred cubits; a cubit was an ancient way to measure length using a man's forearm, which was eighteen to twenty-two inches long. So when we do calculations using the forearm technique (22 inches times 300 cubits = 6,600 ; divide this into twelve inches = 550 feet), this is approximate .125 of a mile long.

So our great God gave Noah some geometry and a physics lesson in BC times. Can you comprehend how much more advanced God is over men? God knew exactly how high the water levels would be and how high the waves would be, so God helped Noah build the ark very long and wide to accommodate their travels while protecting them from drowning. This is a perfect example that God knows what's ahead, and only he can accurately take you through without any scratches and without drowning you in your troubles and problems. Stop trying to figure out the solution and making false predictions, because if you trust in the Lord, he will strategically and mathematically arrange for your success. Please lift your hung-down heads because God is in control. God has calculated your victory, and there is another thing: God desires to build our lives like the ark: big hearted toward God, wide and spacious to help save others, sealing all the holes in our lives to keep trouble out. Then God tightly shuts and seals the doors of our hearts from going astray so easily. He completes us so much so we won't turn to the left or right, nor drown but our faith in Christ remains unmovable. We can reach our destiny and walk on dry land like Noah did. Living this life, we must wait patiently with faith in God to lift us above the water waves of life, looking forward to the rainbow of God's promise of eternal life. Hallelujah!

Matthew 10:30 says, "But the very hairs on your head are all numbered."

God knows the number of hairs on your head. Ever tried counting the strands of hair on your head? It's almost impossible, and if possible, there would be tens of thousands of hair strands to count. If God knows every strand of hair we have on our heads, that means he really knows us better than we know ourselves, which really means we are obviously very important to him and more valuable than the sparrows, which he takes care of for food and shelter. They never worry like we do; instead, they continue to fly high. Fly high, people; don't let your worries keep you down.

Fear not therefore, ye are of more value than many sparrows. (Matthew 10:31)

And he commanded the multitude to sit down on the grass, and took the five loaves, and two fishes, and looking up to heaven, he blessed, and brake and gave them loaves to his disciples, and the disciples to the multitude. And they did all eat and were filled, and they took up of the fragments that remained twelve baskets full. (Matthew 14:19–20)

Explain this to me mathematically. How did Jesus feed a multitude of five thousand people with only five loaves and two fish? Being in the food service business for twenty-five years, I can attest that five loaves and two fish could feed up to thirty or fifty people, depending on the size of the fish; in no way could five loaves and two fishes feed five thousand people at one sitting. This kind of mathematics you see throughout the entire Bible, where God defies the law of mathematics; he defies the law of gravity and science. God takes a very little substance and makes it into a monument of value. Hallelujah! Let me ask those elite math technicians this. Can you figure out how God does these things? His name is Jesus Christ, the Son of the living God. Mathematics can't explain these phenomenon, sorcery can't duplicate it, religion can't believe it, scientists can't comprehend it, and our government can't seem to understand it; this is what makes God great; he does the impossible, unimaginable, indescribable, unbelievable, incredible, unthinkable, and inconceivable. Can the church say, "Hallelujah"? He is God alone, and he defies all the powers of the earth: physics, geometry, calculus, and statistics. God defies all earthly technology and intelligence; there's no greater one than God. Who dares to challenge him?

Jesus lifted the food to God and blessed it; by lifting the food to God, he changed the entire equation. Putting God first makes the difference. God changes man's formula, methods, and problems into success stories. That's God's mathematical way; we cannot explain how God does things like this; rather, we need to believe and have faith in the creator of all. Jesus asked the Father to bless the food, and something miraculous happened. Just to think that many of us don't even ask God's blessings over our food. Maybe the lack of blessing our food before we eat is causing sickness and disease. Only God really knows.

The odds might be against you, and the probability of your success may look dim, but if God is for you, tell me who can be against you (Isaiah 54:17). In other words, even if the entire human race were against you, who are they compared to your creator? They are as grass to God and will wither away. Jesus fed the five thousand with only enough food to feed thirty to fifty people. People of God, you don't need to be rich to do great things; you need only a great God to do great things; your little becomes much when you put it in God's hands. You might have very few resources, a little money, and a little food to eat; but if you lift your limitations and shortcomings to God, he will bless you and give you an increase. God's blessings add no sorrow(Proverbs 10:22). In other words, when God blesses you, there's no need to lose sleep at bedtime. His blessings come with no stress, no debt, no material motive, no bait and switch; they are totally free without any pressure. If God can take care of the sparrows and pigeons all over the world in order for them to live stress free, surely he will keep you, clothe you, feed you, employ you, educate you, and bless your ideas and business ventures. God is all knowing, a very present help in time of need (Psalm 46:1). I personally cannot pray to a dead God or statue are you serious we are more than they. The God I pray to must be alive first and able to respond to my prayer and supplications. He must be vibrant, resourceful, loving, unselfish, merciful, kind, and able to defy gravity and do beyond what we can ever ask for. Now that's a real and very powerful God. Let the church say, "Amen!" What's his name? Jesus Christ the son of God!

If we wanted to spread some good throughout the world, how many people do you think it would take? Some corporations would hire hundreds, even thousands, of people to start a promotion campaign state by state to reach the seven continents of the world. Jesus chose only twelve disciples to spread the gospel, and they were very successful at making the Holy Bible the best seller of all time, even in this twenty-first century. Hallelujah! And amen!

Jesus called the twelve disciples (Matthew 10:1–5).

As you read Matthew 14:19–20, you will find that Jesus used twelve disciples to be the foundation of his evangelistic ministry. Jesus and the disciples turned the world upside down. Here again we see God using a small number to do great exploits. Give God your small problems and watch him turn them into stepping-stones toward your success and victory. Your financial affairs could be in the hot red zone; give them to God and watch him give you financial freedom. Do you believe?

> And the lord said unto Joshua; see I have given into thine hand Jericho, and the king thereof, and the mighty men of valour. And ye shall compass the city all ye men of war and go round about the city once. Thus shalt thou do six days and seven priest shall bear before the ark seven trumpets of rams' horns: and the seventh and when ye hear the sound of the trumpet, all the people shall shout with a great shout: and the walls of the city shall fall flat and the people shall ascend up every man straight before him. (Joshua 6:2–5)

God already gave the city of Jericho to Joshua but with instructions, and those instructions dealt with numbers. Why? So only God would get the glory and because God said so! Israel was to march around Jericho for six days with seven priests carrying trumpets of rams, and on the seventh day, they were to march around the city seven times. Although God gave Joshua the city, it came with instructions that thoroughly needed to be followed through. Some of God's greatest blessings come with explicit instructions, which must be followed through 100 percent; and then comes the blessing and victory.

After Israel carried out God's assignment, the walls of Jericho instantly fell down flat. If God didn't give complete instructions to Israel, Israel's ego would have risen higher than the tallest mountain, and they would have taken the credit for this miracle. So God made them prepare for this miracle. God wanted praises from his people; he wanted a great shout from his people. Did you notice the mention of the number seven—seven priests, seven trumpets, and seven days? Apparently, God's favorite number is seven.

Numbers are important to God but not necessary for him, because he defies mathematics and science anytime he desires. Men and women must understand measurements, equations, methods, and value to obtain the knowledge of how to solve problems and build things. Jericho had walls around its city, and the walls were extremely high; there were no enemies able to defeat them because of their massive walls. The people in Jericho had no need to go beyond their walls because all their provisions were met within their walls. This fact made it hard for their enemies to invade or capture them.

God spoke to Joshua and told him the city was his, but he gave Joshua instructions to follow, and after Joshua followed God's instructions, Jericho's walls fell down like Goliath the giant fell when a little boy named David used a slingshot to bring the giant down to the ground. The city of Jericho was never defeated until God's people put their trust in the Lord and followed his instructions. The city is yours for the taking; just believe God and follow his instructions. Stop the struggle. God can give you victory; just begin to praise God right now because God wants you to conquer. Stop complaining! Trust the Lord. March around your problems in prayer and begin praising God, read his word, attend church, and spread his word abroad. And as you do, watch those walls fall flat.

Walls are used to separate people; they could also keep truth and sincerity out. Walls separate darkness from the light. Racism is a wall. Prejudice is a wall. Slavery is a wall, and they all close the doors to freedom. Whatever walls you face today, they are going to fall. Satan's kingdom is going to fall, and everything that exalts itself will fall. Those walls of deceptions and hidden secrets that damage relationships, churches, families, businesses, marriages, and friendships must fall flat in the name of Jesus, our deliverer. Rid yourself of doubt and unbelief. God will tear down these walls so you can live again and enjoy the good things in life. Please recognize that God didn't build these walls; you did, and others did it deliberately. March around these walls with a praying heart and praise on your lips. Praise God like a trumpet; lift your voice loud, dance before the Lord God, and watch those walls fall.

How do praying, praising God, and spreading his gospel tear down walls? That's God's mathematics. You can't explain it. You need to believe it. You just rest in God's promises, and he works it all out for you. Hopefully, it's all adding up for you and you are dividing the truth correctly, subtracting the bad, and adding the good along the way. Incredibly enough, things happen when you trust in the Lord with all your heart. God is 100 percent the real deal. Give him a chance in your life today.

The purpose of speaking about God's mathematics isn't to promote playing numbers, astrology, lotto, or off-track betting; instead, it is to show you where mathematics comes from. Its origin comes from God, not from your math teacher or math book. God often takes our carnal things on earth to illustrate a spiritual point of view.

Jesus spoke in parables so Jewish rabbis and gentiles would understand the will of God. God used numbers only as a tool, but he loves you more and wants the best for you and your family; also, God would much rather desire the relationship between you and him than a math lesson. Numbers don't impress God, but what moves God are righteousness, faith, love, compassion, praises, and sincere prayer. God searches man's heart and thoughts. God has a way of doing things that astonish us, and at times he uses math to bring forth his glory. Examine each story presented to you through the scriptures, and you will find that each episode brought glory to God almighty. Righteousness exalts a nation, but sin is a reproach to any people(Proverbs14:34). God's mathematics is more than numbers. God can do the impossible, so ask him for the impossible. Ask God for the incredible. Ask God for the unimaginable. God defies mathematics, science, technology, the medical industry, computers hackers, the politics, government, the Supreme Court, Wall Street, the stock market, banking systems, the board of education, religion, and so forth.

Mathematics limits God, so God defies it whenever he chooses. And as for all the earthly powers of the world, they remain just drops of water in a basket to God. That's God's mathematics. Who dares to defy Jehovah God?

So give God your zeros and nothingness, and he will make your nothing grow into something, and your zeros will become a million times bigger than what you started with. That's what a real God does. God's mathematics is absolutely so much different than man's mathematics and equation for life. Men fail every day of the week, but God fails no day of the week. Men trust in the stock market, banking system, and world economy, but those who trust in the Lord God trust in a heavenly system far beyond those blue skies, and he hasn't failed yet. When all are said and done, God's mathematics leads us back to the greatest love story ever told of a father sacrificing his Son's life for the redemption of mankind, for the improvement of man's life, so man can hold his head up with the confidence in knowing God loves him dearly and has prepared a special place in heaven for all who believe. Glory hallelujah! Praise God from whom all blessings flow.

CHAPTER 5

God's Much

od has given us much, and we have given him so little, but with the much he has given us, we care so little of. He has given us life, but we choose death; he has given us light, but we choose darkness. He has given us health, but we much rather have wealth. God has given us ears to hear, brains to think with, and hearts to love with. God has given us arms and hands to write with, touch with, and hug with; God has given us legs and feet to walk, dance, and run with. God has given us lips and a mouth with which to speak, taste, smile, and eat.

Finally, God gave us a nose to breathe and smell with; tell me, how much did we pay for this? For one moment take a deep breath and then exhale. That is free, dear reader. No strings attached. Whether you are a Jew or a gentile, black or white, small or tall, fat or slim, you can't beat that. What God has given us is priceless. Tell me, what we can do without God's gift of life. The answer is simply nothing.

If you can pay for something very valuable, then it's worth nothing much, but there are those things you can't pay for that have the most value. The air we breathe has no dollar value, but it is a vital element for human beings on earth to live. Try living without this air we breathe. Please understand that God gives us valuable freebies: health, oxygen, eyesight, ears to hear, and a brain to think. These are all God's gifts to mankind called life, and we ought to appreciate this prize called life. Every day we should praise God for his freebies. Stop taking God's freebies for granted; you and I should be grateful and excited about God's freebies because life didn't have to be this way. Handle God's freebies with the utmost care; be fragile with them. Don't pollute his temple or desecrate his temple. Our bodies are the temples of the Holy Ghost, so as we live our lives handling God's freebies with the utmost care because without his freebies, it would be impossible to live. Period. Even the most wicked, immoral, and treacherous people have God's breath of life in them, they yet live by God's mercy.

Try being successful without God's freebies. It just can't be done; all the gold and money in the world, including those in the Vatican, cannot compensate for God's freebies. We ought to be grateful every morning we rise from our beds. We should sing praises and give glory to his name. What God has given us is more than a Christmas gift; it is eternal gift.

But that's not all of God's much. God has given us something more valuable than fame and fortune; more precious than gold, silver, and rubies; and more significant than this current life, and that would be eternal life. Unfortunately, eternal life doesn't excite the church anymore. Back in the day where I grew up, folks were happy about eternal life. We danced about it. We cried about it. We praised God about it. Not anymore. It's all just a cliché now! Just like during the day of Noah. People made jokes about it. "It's really going to rain?" "Sure, sure, it's goin' to rain!" "Why, of course, it's going to rain!" "I'm good with the fact that it will rain! Rain, rain, rain! Come again another day!"

If we believe on him, we can live forever, but this fact doesn't motivate church folks anymore, because in today's society, people would much rather have the bling, which are the mansions, luxury cars, fame, and green paper, called "cash." Who's talking or preaching about eternal life anyway? I'm not afraid to say eternal life isn't on the best-seller list anymore; it's a forgotten cliché; people care less and less about the here and hereafter, but most of us would rather live for the moment. Christians are following the fads. "Live for the now and the present." The value of eternal life has diminished maybe because many people are becoming millionaires at an alarming and startling rate.

Heaven on earth is the popular lifestyle for society now, and some people willingly deny the Lord Jesus Christ for it. This is the lifestyle many daydreamers dream about, but life on earth is temporal.

The Bible says, "Lay not your treasures on this earth." (St. Matthew 6:19) It will all perish. Earthly treasure can be stolen and will corrode. On the other hand, your heavenly treasure lasts forever. On that note, I guarantee that you won't witness anyone shouting and dancing on that note. But if you won the lotto, somebody would be dancing in the Spirit; the church would dance the night away. Am I talking right?

What would you choose over $50 million? In most cases, many people would choose the money instead of eternal life because of many reasons. One reason may be instant gratification. The second reason may be tangible ownership and never having to work a nine-to-five job. A third reason may be being able to purchase anything you lay your eyes on without being in debt, and the list goes on. Some people need to admit they don't want heaven as bad as they claim; we just want heaven when we are old and our youthfulness is gone. Then we talk about heaven and how we want to be ready. In our golden years, we are ready to give our lives to Christ; it's then that we appreciate life. Family becomes more important, and relationships are built; we find time for people, and we start doing things we enjoy and visit other places we dream of.

Don't wait until you're old and feeble; come to Jesus just as you are. Give him your heart and believe on him that he can save you from your sins and give you eternal life. Salvation is a gift to the world from God so men and women could come to the knowledge of the truth.

God isn't seemingly good enough for some people; most choose the empty things in life instead of the things that fulfill our lives. His name is Jesus. God says to choose life. Eternal life isn't on the front page of Christian magazines or secular magazines, because it doesn't sell. People want the splendor of it all. One rich man came to Jesus and asked, "What shall I do that I may inherit eternal life?" (Mark 10:17–25).

> Thou knowest the commandments, do not commit adultery, do not kill, do not steal, do not

bare false witness, defraud not, honor thy father and mother and he answered and said unto him, master all these have I observed from my youth.

Then Jesus beholding him loved him and said unto him, one thing thou lackest; go thy way, sell whatsoever thou hast and give to the poor and thou shalt have treasure in heaven: and come take up the cross, and follow me.

And he was sad at that saying, and went away grieved: for he had great possessions; He was rich. "He was loaded."

Jesus looked around about and saith unto his disciples: how hardly shall they that have riches enter into the kingdom of God and the disciples were astonished at these words. But Jesus answered, saith unto to them children, how hard it is for them that trust in riches to enter into the kingdom of God. It is easier for a camel to go through the eye of a needle than for a rich man to enter into the kingdom of God. (Mark 10:19–25)

Jesus said, "Sell all your riches" The rich man was puzzled and totally stuck to his riches—so much so that he chose to walk away from Jesus to enjoy the pleasures of life; his walking away from Jesus came by four things Jesus said: (1) sell, (2) give, (3) take up your cross, and (4) follow Jesus. Before we discuss the four things that probably made the rich man walk away, let's discuss this.

First, Jesus didn't tell him to give all his possessions away. He said to sell what he had and then give to the poor. And may I add that Jesus didn't tell him how much to give to the poor; he just said to give to the poor. If the rich man had sold what he had, there would have been profit to claim; and if there had been a profit made, giving to the poor would have been an honor. But the rich man took this as a hard saying, and he couldn't handle losing his wealth. He honestly thought he had wealth. Didn't he know whom he was talking to? Jesus and his heavenly father created the heaven, the earth, and human beings. No one is richer than Jesus, the Son of the living God. The rich man didn't realize that selling what he had and giving to the poor would have resulted in him gaining much more. Jesus said some powerful things after he told the rich man to sell what he had and give to the poor. After Jesus said, "Sell all that you have and give to the poor," the rich man probably thought, *What's in it for me?*

Giving to the poor should be easy for the rich because they have more to share; evidently, the rich man refused to share. Giving is a principle in God's kingdom. Giving is a spiritual thing to do, and God rewards those who give. Third, Jesus asked the rich man to take up his cross; the taking up of your cross represents taking the burden of your sins and carrying them to Jesus, because he is the only one who can transform your sins into a working mechanism that will be used to glorify God. This task isn't as easy as it sounds, but you need to be committed to the transformation of your life after giving your life to Jesus.

Fourth, Jesus asked him to follow him, and the rich man just walked away. I am puzzled by this response; didn't the rich man just say, "I have followed the Ten Commandments ever since I was a little lad"? If the Ten Commandments were what he followed all his life, he still didn't recognize that the author of the Ten Commandments was standing in front of him, asking him to follow him. The Ten Commandments are just rules to follow, but to follow Jesus is more than a rule book; it is an intimate relationship, whereby there is daily dialogue and open communication, which this rich man didn't want any part of. He wanted something to tickle his ear, something easy with no commitment, no involvement; does this attitude sound familiar? We want a born-again experience, but we don't want the one-on-one relationship with Jesus or any commitment to serve and worship him forever. This rich man would have felt better depositing his money in a bank or an investment fund instead of depositing it into someone's life. The biggest investment is to invest in people. People are who make and break companies.

Jesus didn't ask him to give up all his stuff; instead, Jesus asked him to sell and give to the poor. Nevertheless, this rich man was convinced that he would rather serve his riches than the Lord Jesus Christ. This rich man wanted no part of selling or giving back to the poor. He only wanted profit. So Jesus warned the disciples about how difficult it would be for rich people to enter God's kingdom. It is easier for a camel to go through the eye of a needle than for a rich man to enter the kingdom of God; this means that rich people who worship their riches more than God cannot enter the kingdom of God. Do yourself a favor; add all the things you can take with you when you die. Nothing! So why do we immerse ourselves in things that fade away? And for the things that last forever, we care so little.

So, rich people, beware. Worship the King of kings and Lord of lords, Jesus, the Son of the living God. Don't fall for the trap of riches over God. Does this mean rich people can't go to heaven? No. Worship God, not money. Love your neighbor. Give from your heart and never give grudgingly.

There's a new breed of Christians who are roaming the earth and say we can have the world's pleasures and the treasures of the kingdom too. They call them God's blessings and increase. God's blessings add no sorrow. The children of Israel were always blessed as long as they worshipped God and obeyed his commandments. Nations would fall at Israel's feet because God was their King and Ruler. Israel had all the gold jewelry and silver, fine linens, precious rubies, milk, and honey; but as soon as they turned to other gods, God allowed their enemies to take every single crumb of wealth from them, and they ended up enslaved. You see, when you worship things more than the creator, the situation never works in your favor.

You cannot serve two masters; either you will love one or hate the other. If these earthly things are overpowering your heart, you will eventually follow after them and lose sight of God and his heavenly treasures. Seek first the kingdom of God, and all these things shall be added unto you(St.Matthew 6:33). Easy money changes people. Look at King Solomon, the richest king who ever lived. In the beginning of King Solomon's reign, he focused on leading and serving God's people, but after being lured by foreign women from other nations, who served other gods, slowly but surely King Solomon's heart was turned to other gods because of the constant convincing of his wives from other nations, who worshipped other gods while under Solomon roof.

We are people of habits, so if we do something often enough, it will become our way of life. If you keep driving with those old friends, who do drugs and liquor, soon it will be easy for you to try some of that stuff too. Most sins are committed gradually, and as time goes by, we find ourselves far from God. Sin enters the mind through the eyes and then is rehearsed over and over until it enters the heart; only then do we follow its command, just like sheep following its shepherd. Don't get it twisted. God wants you to be blessed, and he commands a blessing for you to have increase, promotions, and harvest in your life; but once you get these things, will you still worship the creator? Will you give to the poor? First, be content in whatever state you're in, knowing God can turn things around for you. Learn to appreciate some of the finer things in life, such as your health, strength, ability to work, vocal cords, the friendships you have, the family you have, where you live, what you drive, where you work, and the church you attend. Stop measuring your blessings and success against what others have and accomplish, because if you do, you will always be miserable. Life itself is a gift and a blessing.

Take vacations and enjoy God's earthly wonders. Do good

things for others and be content with your current income, and if you need more, work harder and smarter. Be happy in whatever state you are in. Envy no one's wealth, create your own wealth, and stop measuring your life based on others because everyone is different. The gold and silver we fight about down on earth; in heaven the angels walk on streets paved with pure gold. God walks on the most valuable things on earth.

God's much seems to be too little for some of us and not enough to turn away from earthly treasures. Does this mean we shouldn't have our heart's desire? No! It simply means we should choose to worship God, the creator, above all things. Regardless of being rich and famous or destitute and poor, we still choose to worship God whether we are on the mountaintop or in the valley of life. Naked we arrived in this world, and for sure naked we will leave this world. So while we have our being, let us serve the Lord God and enjoy his much. Appreciate each new day and new experience, for life is precious and delicate, and we must handle it with care. But most of all, we should be exhilarated, vivacious, ecstatic, and excited about life, knowing that every day above ground is a blessed day; remember that life is a gift from God, so while you live on this planet, keep your eyes on Jesus so you may obtain eternal life, which is the much God offers to those who believe and serve him.

CHAPTER 6

Open Your Blinded Eyes

O pen Your Blinded Eyes, Isaiah 42:7 to open the blind eyes, to bring out the prisoners from the prison, and them that sit in darkness out of the prison house

Our church, Mission of Hope Evangelistic Ministry, sponsored a crusade in Anderson, South Carolina, during summer 2007. The first night, our youth department was in charge, and they asked me to be one of the speakers for the evening. God gave me a message right before entering the tour bus; the message was titled "Open Thou Blinded Eyes." Amid all the joyous noise on the bus coming from our youth department, I couldn't dismiss the message God had laid on my heart to speak for the evening. It stayed on my mind and wouldn't leave, even while the youth department sang songs, watched videos, laughed, and played games. It was a great trip.

I rehearsed in my mind whether this message would be appropriate for youth night, and the Lord spoke to my heart and said, "Open Thou Blinded Eyes." I could hear this message title all along the way from New York City to Anderson, South Carolina. It was a good opening message to get the audience ready for the other speakers and teachers, who were expected to speak as well.

Our eyes are vital to our way of life, and it would be extremely difficult to conduct our lives efficiently without eyesight. Being handicapped in our society is just another stumbling block for mankind, but it can be conquered. Psalm 146:8 says, "The Lord openeth the eyes of the blind: the Lord raiseth them that are bowed down: the Lord the righteous."

The Lord opens the eyes of the blind and lifts the hung-down head. God wants you to see clearly, and he wants your head to be lifted. People can experience great accomplishments and still feel depressed and discouraged, so it is with people who have twenty-twenty vision. They can be blind to a whole host of things staring them in the face.

Psalm 119:18 says, "Open thou mine eyes, that I may behold wondrous things out of thy law."

David asked the Lord to open his eyes to behold the *value* and treasures found in his book of the law (Holy Bible). What a wonderful thing to ask God for, a better understanding of his holy word, because it is God's Spirit who gives us the insight to rightly divide his Holy Scriptures. Yes, we have eyes to read God's words and a mind to make some sense of what the scriptures are trying to convey, but to get a true understanding, we need God's Spirit to really break it down so even a child can comprehend, and that's what we need to ask God for on a daily basis. "Open our eyes" daily because every day we have many things in our view, but we cannot see the true value or message behind it all, so we need insight from God.

I have always been in amazement that two people can look at the same picture and walk away with different perceptions of the same picture. One sees circles and squares; the other sees life forms, and both create a theory behind each other's perception. It's the same picture with two different perceptions. So it is with two men who work at a job for the same number of years. Finally, at the end of the week, they both receive pink slips (they are fired). One goes home and has a nervous breakdown, and the other starts a small business. Both men face the same situation, but each reacts to the same circumstances differently. So it was with two women facing a horrible divorce. One drives to a nearby bridge and jumps to her death; the other lady writes a song about the experience and months later receives a royalty check for two hundred and fifty thousand dollars. I'm quite sure that with that kind of money, the pain of divorce could become a little less agonizing. Don't you think? Now she has a reason to celebrate. Last but not least, two men go to jail for the same crime and do the same time. Both are released. One repeats the same crime, and the other finds a job and eventually starts a nonprofit business to reach out to ex-convicts. Two men face the same circumstances, but each reacts to his situations differently.

You are currently facing issues in your life, but what do you see while engaging in your life circumstances? Are you depressed about them? Or are you optimistic about them? Do you believe God is going to give you the power to handle and conquer them? Or are you ready to give up on yourself and call it quits forever? Jumping ahead of my point, I must say that God installed in us dominion power to rule over our circumstances in a way that doesn't make us fall to pieces. Let's get back to the message at hand!

It's amazing to me that in the above examples of people facing similar situations, each had different perceptions of how to handle the same situation; therefore, each handled and saw his or her situation differently. So it is with us as believers; we are all in the same church, singing the same songs and listening to the same sermons. All of us are in the same place for different reasons. Some people are in church because of family connections and because "Mama and them" told us to come; others come to meet someone special. Others are sitting and waiting for the show to begin and for something unusual to happen; maybe they are waiting for a famous and prolific speaker to stand behind the podium and speak words of wisdom into their ears. Consider the purpose of the church Jesus established. He said it was his bride, and he said it shall be called the "house of prayer," whereby we should pray to our heavenly father and praise and worship him more than anything else we do. Then the next thing is to point people to Jesus, the Son of the living God. Hallelujah! Glory to God! We come to fellowship, worship God, and are reminded that the Kings of kings is coming soon. Say, "Hallelujah," somebody. The purpose of church as we know it is to make us better Christians, increase our faith, and extend and spread the gospel and the plan of salvation to all who will listen. As we do these things, God will heal our land, sickness, and diseases. God will regulate our bodies, minds, and souls so we can help others who are less fortunate.

Can't you see the signs on the walls as well as signs in the earth, signs in our government, signs in the atmosphere, and signs with nations to nations? God wants us, his people, to open our blinded eyes so we can see the day of the Lord is soon to come. Without Christ in our lives, we are like a ship without a sail, drifting nowhere. We need to see that with God on our side, there is nothing impossible. God is our deliverer, healer, protector, defender, salvation, comforter, miracle maker, and business partner; and we must always keep him in view so when we are ambushed from the stress of life and difficult circumstances that appear in our lives, we can have victory. Let the church say, "Amen!"

Open your eyes, people of God.

Mark 8:18 says, "Having eyes, see ye not? And having ears, hear not? And do not remember?"

Just because a person is physically blind doesn't mean he or she cannot see, so it is with people with twenty-twenty vision. It doesn't validate that they see or visualize the signs of the end times. The above scriptures speak about having eyes, and yet you can't see the things to come, nor the things at hand; having ears, you cannot hear. Let's go a little further.

Mark 8:1–2 says, "In those days the multitude being very great and having nothing to eat, Jesus called his disciples unto him and saith unto them, I have compassion on the multitude because they have now been with me three days and have nothing to eat. And if I send them away fasting to their own houses, they will faint by the way: for divers of them came from far."

Jesus wanted to feed the weary multitude for their patience and efforts to come listen to him speak for three days. So Jesus commanded the multitude to sit down on the ground, and he took seven loaves of bread and two fishes; he gave thanks to the father and, breaking it, gave the food to the disciples to distribute it to the multitude. Please understand that Jesus fed the multitude, which was five thousand people, with only five loaves of bread and two fish. God multiplied the food because the multitudes ate and were full; after this phenomenon, Jesus entered a ship with his disciples and went into the parts of Dalmanutha (St.Mark 8:10) Pharisees followed him and began to question Jesus, seeking of him a sign from heaven. The Bible says they were tempting him. Jesus was annoyed with these Pharisees, so he left them, entered the ship again, and departed to the other side. -- So finally Jesus moved forward with his journey along with his disciples, Jesus charged them, saying, "Take heed, of the leaven of the Pharisees, and of the leaven of King Herod"; the disciples began to reason among themselves, blaming themselves that Jesus made this comment only because they didn't bring any leftover bread for their journey. When Jesus knew this, he said to them, "Why reason ye among yourselves because ye have no bread? Perceive ye not yet, neither understand? Have ye your heart yet hardened?" Here Jesus asked them a bunch of questions to get them to understand what he really meant about the leaven. Then Jesus said, "Having eyes, see ye not? And having ears, hear not? And do not remember?(St. Mark 8:19" You get it?

They were worried about not having enough bread for their journey when Jesus was and is the Bread of Life. Did they not see and witness this great phenomenon of Jesus feeding a multitudes of people with only two fish and five loaves of bread? And their eyes were wide open and yet they did not get the gist of what our lord did in front of their eyes. So why did the disciples start murmuring among themselves about not bringing enough food for their journey on the ship when Jesus had clearly proved to them and the multitude that he was the ultimate provider for food? They didn't see, hear, or understand that the same God who had fed the five thousand with five fishes and two loaves of bread was the same person dwelling among them, and he had the power to feed them in the desert.

More importantly, Jesus tried to tell the disciples to beware of the Pharisees and King Herod's wickedness, corruption, and their evil dealings because of their wickedness, which is referred to as leaven. Leaven is like yeast; it swells and grows like cancer, spreading throughout the body. So Jesus told his disciples to distance themselves from the Pharisees, because the Pharisees' evil would spread like cancer in them and on them. Although Jesus said this elaborately, his disciples couldn't see, hear, or understand what Jesus was telling them at first because of their blinders.

Billions of citizens on the earth can see but not spiritually discern or see the truth if it was pushed in their faces. Open your blinded eyes, people of God, and see that it is better to live for Christ and gain eternal life than to have all the earthly treasures of life and your soul be forever lost and destroyed. Come to the light and walk not in darkness, because you will end up with nothingness, emptiness, and worthlessness.

This reminds me of the true story of a former employer of mine who was driving by a shopping center and noticed a gentleman selling a fifty-inch TV for $200. The demo was working perfectly—so much so that he doubled park and dashed out to purchase his big-screen TV. He was full of smiles and desperation on his way back to his wife and family. Finally, he arrived home with his big-screen TV. He plugged it in, but nothing happened. He looked in the back of his TV, and there were only a big screen and rocks inside the television set. He had paid $200 for nothing. His eyes saw only the demo and didn't observe the con artist; nor did he check out what he was purchasing. If we entertain witchcraft, perversion, hatred, jealousy, lust, stealing, lying, corruption, pride, gossiping, and violence, we will eventually become not only participants of these things, but these things will become part of our character. Evil communication corrupts your good manners (1Corinthians 15:33). Beware of walking around with your blinders on; it could cost you your life and soul. Open, thou blinded eyes.

Jesus came to the world to open the blinded eyes, heal the sick, raise the dead, feed the hungry, deliver the imprisoned, clothe the naked, and give sanity to the insane. Who is this we speak of? Jesus! Open your eyes and see God working on your behalf.

Each day you wake up, remember it was God who opened your eyes. Check today's obituary, and you will not see your name listed, because God woke you up this morning and started you on your way. Life comes from God, and that's priceless. Stop purposely walking in darkness. Open those blinded eyes and see God making you righteous, seeing your circumstances change for the better. Faith in God changes what you physically visualize, and it revolutionizes things supernaturally for God's glory. Open those blinded eyes and face the reality of life and what life hands you. Put it in God's hands, and your pathway will be clear and successful. God is in control of all the elements, political powers, legal powers, Wall Street powers, employment powers, higher education powers, religious powers, and all the powers of the world. So when you put your faith in him, you are entitled to enjoy prosperity, wholeness, freedom, love, peace, and happiness.

Faith in God changes things and circumstances. Who said we can't be happy? Who said you will always be broke? Who said you will always be sick? Who told you your business will never be successful? Who said your church will never grow? Who said your children will never amount to anything? These are the things men and women verbalize in secret about others. Are they God? Do they have the last say in your life? Did they create you? Do they keep your heart beating? Stop losing sleep and worrying about everything you can't control. Just rest in the Lord today and open your eyes, because what you don't see is the invisible God working in your favor while you sleep. So when you wake up in the morning, take off your blinders and trust in the Lord God so you can witness God turning your situation around for the good. Hallelujah!

Mark 8:222 says, "And he cometh to Bethsaida; and they bring a blind man unto him and besought him to touch him. And he took the blind man by the hand and led him out of the town; and when he had spit on his eyes and put his hands on him, he asked him if he saw ought and he looked up and said I see man as trees walking. After that he put his hand again upon his eyes and made him look up; and he was restored and saw every man clearly."

Is your vision blurred today? You can't seem to see clearly, just like the blind man in the above scriptures. Maybe you need a second touch from Jesus just like the blind man received a second touch from Jesus. Repent and ask the Lord to open your eyes and give you a clear vision. Without a vision people perish (Proverbs 29:18); anything you want to accomplish in life starts with a vision. Visualize yourself walking tall and strong in the Lord, owning businesses and your church becoming a megachurch. Open your eyes and see the salvation of the Lord while working the strategies from the scriptures. God is with you, and there is nothing that can stop you but yourself. I know you may wonder why God can't just do everything for us if he is God. No, my dear reader, God isn't in the mind control business, but Satan is. Nor is God a magical genie hidden in a bottle and waiting for you to rub it so at your command he will grant you all your wishes. Instead, God has dispensed in you hidden powers, which you must discover, develop, and utilize. You have freedom of choice. What a wonderful gift from God! Thank you, Jesus.

I heard of a great songwriter blind from birth whom God gifted to sing and write songs, and with his gift of song, he consecutively became a Grammy Award recipient, and his songs impacted the world, causing the earth to shatter with positive results. If someone had told this young man he couldn't see, he would have given you a look of disbelief, because he had visualized his entire career; he visualized his albums selling millions of copies, and his eyes were focused on his vision. Though physically blind, he used his inner vision to pave a successful career. If a blind man can see and pave a successful career, what about you and me?

Later, this blind man became very involved in social and community affairs. How did a blind man accomplish so many things? The answer is having a vision that's bigger than what may be in front of you. It's a vision bigger than that of all your enemies, who try to hinder you, a vision bigger than your handicap issues, a vision bigger than your debt, a vision bigger than your education, a vision bigger than your limitations, a vision bigger than your nine-to-five job, a vision bigger than your storefront church, and a vision bigger than your apartment. What's stopping you from having a vision for your life? Nothing! You are the only entity that can stop your progress in life. A vision is the road map to prosperity and success. Open your eyes!

Stop pronouncing failure because of temporary episodes that appear in your life. We can learn a lot from our handicapped brothers and sister because they purposely allow their vision to be enlarged one thousand times larger than the handicap appearing in their lives. Their handicap becomes only a stepping-stone for their success. When you can look beyond your personal handicaps and see greatness in your life, you have truly opened your blind eyes.

Do you remember the song "Amazing Grace"? It starts like this:

> Amazing grace how sweet the sound
> That saved a wretch like me.
> I once was lost but now I'm found
> Was blind, but now I see.

Can you see now? What do you see? You were blind, but now you see.

If blind and crippled people created a better life for themselves and their families, even the world, clearly we must be able to create a better life for our families and communities with God's help. But first, we must open our blinded eyes.

Open your venetian blinds, which cloud your mind with your present condition so heavily that they darken your true potential and stop you from being focused. Confess your sins to God and turn from your evil ways so you can see again. God never uses our sins as ammunition to shoot us down, but he uses our sins to build us up and create a new us. Come to Jesus and give him your sickness, past mistakes, job issues, marriage problems, church issues, financial troubles, addictions, sexual misconduct, lying lips, and criminal activities. Jesus will pardon you from all your sins so you can see and focus on the gift of life God gave you and begin to do things to help others.

Let me tell you what I see.

I see God solving our problems. I see God healing our sicknesses and diseases. I see him saving the lost souls and delivering his people out of captivity and poverty. I see God washing our dirty laundry. Do you have any dirty laundry? I see God giving us health and wealth with a purpose. I see God opening our blind eyes and taking away our addictions. Are you addicted to anything? I see God moving mountains in our lives so we don't need to climb them. I see God connecting distant families back together. I see God reversing court decisions from guilty to not guilty. I see God changing eviction notices to home ownership. I see God giving his people promotions and business ideas that will change the world. Can you see now? The enemy of our souls enjoys putting blinders on God's people *because the quickest way to defeat your foe is to blindfold them. Then it becomes easy to defeat them. Open your blinded eyes.*

Samson, the strongest man who ever lived in the world, was a triple threat to the Philistines. His purpose in life was to defend God's people, "Judah," from their enemies. God chose one man to be the protector of Israel's one hundred thousand foes. Samson's enemies sought to kill him daily, but he was too strong and mighty for his adversaries. Did you hear what I just said? They sent armies after Samson, and those armies of thousands of soldiers couldn't defeat Samson. They searched, explored, hunted, and investigated Samson for weakness but couldn't find anything that would weaken him.

With God on your side, you are undefeated. As long as Samson kept his integrity and his eyes on the Lord God, he was invincible. Did you just hear what I said? He was invincible. We are invincible with God almighty. They used Delilah to find Samson's weakness. After being in Delilah's company often, Samson was amused by this attractive woman when she was so desperate to spend time with him and eager to lie with him. He saw her beauty but didn't see (or maybe didn't want to see) the ugliness, evilness, and scandalous intentions behind her desperateness to destroy him. So it is with us. We are amused, fascinated, and engrossed by what the world has to offer us; and within the process, we fail to realize or see its wicked intentions for our lives. Our enemies' mission is to make us powerless and under their control. Delilah's only reason or purpose was to find Samson's weakness and then surrender him to his enemies so they could crush him into a weak and feeble warrior.

So after Delilah's many attempts to use her soft voice, beauty, poise, sexual advances, and tender, loving touches, Samson finally weakened and disclosed where his strength and power came from. And he told her that "if you cut my long hair, I will become just like most men." So when she obtained this information, she waited until Samson fell asleep and cut his hair completely off. When she was done, she consulted with the officers of the Philistines and said she had found his weakness and would give a signal when it was time to entrap Samson in her chambers. So as Samson slept, Delilah said with a loud voice, "Samson, the Philistines are upon you," so the Philistine soldiers came into her chambers to capture Samson. As Samson awoke, he had no strength to defeat them. He was captured by the Philistines, but the Philistines' enemies weren't satisfied with just finding his weakness; they wanted to burn his eyes out of his sockets so he could never see again. Then they put shackles on his feet, threw him in prison, and made a mockery of him.

Ladies and gentlemen, that's what the enemy of our souls wants to do to you and me. He wants to find our weakness and blind us forever like he did to Samson. He wants to put us in a prison of feeling sorrow for ourselves so we will eventually consider committing suicide or being followers of darkness. But first, he wants to blind us so we never see the light again and remain in darkness forever. Understand that if we fall from grace, as long as we can look up while being down, we can get up. Open your eyes and see how much God loves you and cares for you, even when you have done something wrong. God is concerned only that you will come to him with all your heart, and he will forgive you and place your feet on hind's feet so you can do the work of the kingdom and spread the gospel.

I hope you see now.

We need to get it through our thick skulls that the enemies of our souls want to destroy our lives, reputations, children, friendships, marriages, careers, businesses, vision, and churches by leading us to self-destruct with bad behavior, bad decisions, and things that are opposite of what a child of God should be doing. Samson knew Judah and the Israelites weren't to intermingle with the Philistines. They were enemies of God's people; therefore, for what reason Samson heeded her advances. Evidently, Delilah was some beautiful and curvaceous silhouette, who made Samson weak in the knees and made Samson heed her advances because he found Delilah to be irresistible.

Is this the problem with us? Do we find this world irresistible? So it is with most men. We are tempted by women, but this doesn't give us the right to lose it all for a one-night fling. We are all worth more than this. Well, you know the story; the cost was that Samson was defeated by the Philistines, permanently blinded at their hands, and jailed. This is what the enemies of our souls want. They desire for all of us to endure this kind of situation, whereby we lose it all and are blinded so we cannot see our way out. Open your eyes and see the scandal set before you to destroy your life, your relationship with God, and your family. Most of the time, anything that seems too good to be true is a hidden lie that keeps luring you into a trap designed to ensnare you into your own demise. Sometimes things and people closest to you could be draining God out of you each moment you are with them, and you are slightly unaware of this until you lose everything; then you can reminiscence only on the entire scandalous scheme saved in our memory banks forever.

Let me be the first to encourage you today, dear reader; we all have had some type of Samson experience to some degree, but losing a couple of battles doesn't necessarily mean you have to lose the war on life. If you fall down, as long as you can look up, you can get up; I know that's what I had to do. Get up and come to Jesus now. You've got some junk in your trunk; give it to the Lord in prayer. You really think Jesus died on the cross for the well, rich, perfect society and famous people? No! I must laugh at that question. Jesus died for the weak, undeserving, poor, downtrodden, backsliding, ungodly, hopeless, sick, and weary. He died for the forgotten and all who, like Samson, have had a hard fall from grace.

You have to take off your blinders today, because if God hated you so much for the sin you committed in the past, why didn't he take your breath of life from you? Why are you still able to see, walk, and make your own decisions, even though many of your past decision were horrible? Yet you remain alive and able to live your life. This is called God's mercy, God's forgiveness, and God's unconditional love for mankind. So wherever you are in life today, God loves you so much that he wants you to live and have your own being; but he wants to be part of your life only to enhance it, not to destroy it, if you will allow him. Open your eyes, but first take off your blinders so you can clearly see. God never meant you and me any harm; all he only wanted since the beginning of time was a one-to-one relationship with mankind. Is that so much to ask for when quite honestly God gave you this life to live? Can you spare any time to talk to the one who created time and you? Open your blinded eyes and see that if God be for you, who can be against you?

Greater is he who is in you than he who is in the world.

Let God arise and our enemies be scattered (Psalms 68:1).

So when you feel alone, ambushed, or overwhelmed, just remember that there are more with us than those who are against us.(2Kings 6:16-18)

Second Chronicles 32:7–8) says, "Be strong and courageous, be not afraid, nor dismayed for the king of Assyria, nor for the entire multitude that is with him: for there be more with us that with him is an arm of flesh but with us is the Lord our God to help us, and to fight our battles and the people rested themselves upon the words of Hezekiah, king of Judah."

The Assyrians purposely wanted to put tremendous fear and trepidation in the hearts of the people of Judah, so they got up early in the morning before the battle, threatened Judah, and said how they were going to destroy them into pieces. In our times, we would call this bullying, but the people of Judah rested on the words King Hezekiah had said: "That there is more with us than with them." The Assyrians had the arm of the flesh, but Judah had the arm of the Lord Almighty to help them defeat their enemies and fight their battles. Judah rested on these words.

When was the last time you rested on the promises of God's word? Assyria encamped round and about their fortress, preparing for a surprise attack on Judah; instead of preparing for war, Judah rested on God's words, and to their surprise, while they rested and slept the night away, their enemies stirred up threats and intimidation all night long as Judah rested in the Lord's protection. To the surprise of the Assyrian army, God sent an angel to the Assyrian camp at night to destroy all the men of mighty valor in their camp along with their leaders and captains. God wiped out the Assyrian army during the late evening; Israel didn't need to fight or use one single blade to conquer their enemies. All they did was rest in the Lord God. Wow! It pays to rest in the Lord. Hallelujah!

God is a loving God, but don't mess with his people, because although your threats may be frightening to many people, when God sends his angels to fight our battles, we better watch out. When Judah woke up, their enemies were all slaughtered. Hallelujah! Glory to the King of kings! Trust in God, and he will direct your path; and as for your enemies, who purposely set out to destroy your reputation, job position, ministry, marriage, family ties, peaceful home, and peace of mind, God says, "Rest on these words: 'There be more with you than with them.'" Who is with you? Jesus, the King of kings? So rest and be of good cheer. God is working it out while you sleep. Open your eyes and see the Lord working in your favor.

God will move people and things out of your way if they hinder you from moving forward into your destiny. Rest in the Lord! What do you see now? God is the same yesterday, today, and forevermore. God changes not. At times it may seem like the world is against you, but open those big eyes of yours and know that if God is for you, who can be against you(Romans 8:31)?

Second Corinthians 3:13–16 says, "And not as Moses, which put a veil over his face, that the children of Israel could not steadfastly look to the end of that which is abolished. But their minds were blinded: for until this day remains the same veil untaken away during the reading of the Old Testament: which veil is done away with through Christ. But even unto this day when the story of Moses and God's commandments is read out loud in some churches with the veil upon their hearts, never the less, when it shall turn to the Lord and the veil shall be taken away."

To this day, the veil remains in some religious sects, where the priest and other men of the cloth put a veil over their faces when reading the Ten Commandments. But in Bible days, the veil kept Israelites from seeing the glory of God on Moses's face, as recorded in scriptures (Exodus 34:27–35). Because of religion and tradition, the veil prevented and prevents men from seeing the glory of God; the new covenant of God set up for mankind through Jesus Christ gives us insight and power to see that the new covenant has transcended and fulfilled the Old Testament because of its greater glory. It is evident and clear that man loves darkness more than light; as you know, light exposes hidden secrets, sinful acts, and all the works of darkness. The veil exists, not on the face but in the heart of mankind, and its purpose is to keep man from coming to the truth, which is accepting the Lord Jesus Christ as Lord and Savior. The veil on our hearts is to keep us blind from coming to the truth. Jesus wants his children to come back to prayer, worship, reading his word, and their first love. Jesus Christ loves us so; take the veil off your eyes and heart, and see the hand of the Lord reaching out to you with loving arms. Don't reject his call; instead, repent and accept the Lord Jesus Christ as your Savior today. Start living without the blinders.

Second Corinthians 4:18 says, "While we look not at the things which are seen but at the things which are not seen: for the things which are seen are temporal; but the things which are not seen are eternal."

Stop judging everything by what you see. because visible things will perish, disappear, and fade as time goes by, because they are all temporal. Set your eyes, focus, and affections on those invisible things from God, like salvation. Salvation is invisible because it is by faith that you are saved, and God's gift to the world is salvation and eternal life. Faith is invisible, but when it is exercised, you can move mountains, heal sickness, live righteously, be victorious, overcome weakness, and become worry free. Faith builds your confidence. It helps you to walk over your enemies' devices planted against you. Faith will help you win legal battles, start a profitable business, and find forgiveness for all your debts. Open your spiritual eyes and see the Lord, who is great and mighty. What do you see now?

Many of us worry ourselves sick until we wind up being admitted to the hospital after losing our cars, apartments, marriages, churches, jewelry, furniture, jobs, promotions, money, friendships—and the list goes on. Yes, these things can hurt us dearly, but we cannot wear our hearts on our chests because the invisible things are more important. You can rebound from all losses. Not one of these problems mentioned above is more valuable than your life or missing out on eternal life. Do you believe this?

Open your eyes and give your burdens to the Lord in prayer.

Here we see in 1 Samuel 17:8–26 that the Philistines gathered together around the mountains, and below them was a valley, and in that valley their champion Goliath appeared, standing close to ten feet tall with a wide stature. He walked out, fully armored ready for battle, and he began bullying, intimidating, and threatening Israel's army, saying things like, "I defy the armies of Israel this day; give me a man whom we may fight together." This was said morning and evening for forty days, presented by Goliath. King Saul was dismayed and greatly afraid; so was Israel's army. Many of them fled and hid in ditches because Goliath's stature was larger than any man they had ever seen. They were extremely frightened. Clearly, they saw a giant monster. It was already sanctioned in their minds that Goliath was invincible, unbeatable, and unconquerable. Clearly, they had allowed that veil of fear and disbelief to cover their eyes, minds, and hearts. So the world's strongest army in history, the Israelites, ran scared and hid in ditches like little ants.

Are you running scared? Well, you are running in the wrong direction. Who dares to defy the armies of the Lord God?

There is no supreme being but God, and if you make anyone supreme in your mindset, it is like putting him or her above the creator of all human flesh. Why was the army of Israel running scared? Did they not know God had delivered them from worse conditions before Goliath? What happened to Israel's memory? Israel was full of trepidation, terror, fright, and panic. Their eyes were blind to the powers of our great God, and they could see only the threats of this undefeated giant of the Philistines. Evidently, Israeli parents talked about the popularity of God delivering the

Israelites out of many terrors and threats from massive armies. No one thought to check their history of countless victories. Also, if Goliath was such a great threat, why didn't the Philistines attack while Israel ran scared? I'll tell you why. The Philistines sent this giant out to Israel to put the fear of God in Israel's hearts and minds, because Israel had already won the war, which made the Philistines quickly retreat to recover the damage done to them by Israel's army.

Goliath was a ploy, scheme, and trick which the Philistine army strategized to stop Israel's army's pursuit and ambushing the entire Philistine army base because they were already beaten to a pulp. Israel's army had the Philistines running like little girls back to their parents. When the Israelites beheld Goliath, they quickly retreated to their camp so they could regroup and behold this great monster of a man as he made his threats to Israel. For some reason, the Israelites allowed terror and fright to enter their hearts, which made Israel stop their vicious and violent attack on the Philistines. Israel had won the battle already, but instead of conquering the element of surprise, they ran and hid in ditches.

My theory is that obviously, Goliath heard about the great reputation Israel had of conquering territories and destroying nations. In actuality, the real champions were running scared as though they had forgotten the powers of their God. Why didn't King Saul roll back the clock of time of all Israel victories throughout their rich history? Instead, Israel's armies ran into ditches like little blind mice, hiding from one tall man. That's what fear does to all of us; it blinds us from clearly seeing conquests, accomplishments, triumphs, and successes. Fear keeps you from looking beyond obstacles; it keeps you from planning and preparing for winning. Fear darkens your vision and makes you panic into oblivion; fear makes you give up. It keeps you running until you can't run anymore; then everything you learned about war tactics goes down the drain, all because your eyes are blinded from the threats of the world. And you can't see that they are more with you than they are against you. Am I talking right?

When you read the story of the Philistine's champion, called Goliath, which happened to be their visible secret weapon, why didn't the Israel's army brag about their invisible secret weapon? Was it the Lord God almighty? Instead, they fled. My theory is that if the Philistines needed a champion like Goliath to intimidate Israel, they felt some intimidation from Israel's army already, but Israel's army was too blind to see this. Israel saw only an unbeatable giant; they saw Goliath's extreme height, body mass, and weapons of mass destruction. Israel saw defeat, and lastly, they didn't see God at all. Just like us on earth, we see only the visible things that come to destroy us, and we run like flash in the DC superhero comic book. When we are guided by fear and doubt, we crumble at the sight of challenges, threats, and circumstances. Later, we crawl into a fetal position and become slaves to people and things we are supposed to overpower. The Philistines did a lot of threatening, lot of cheap talk, that surprisingly really worked up a type of hypnotism in Israel's army. Israel admitted that Goliath was a giant; they confessed that he was a champion, and they acknowledged in their hearts that he was unbeatable. This is what we do before we even fight. We complain about what we don't have and how much more someone else has, and we cower down instead of standing up for our lives and livelihoods.

But let us read the text correctly. When young teenage David heard the rumors of Goliath daring God's chosen generation Israel, he didn't at any time call Goliath by his actual name; nor did he admit that Goliath was a giant. David didn't voice Goliath's name or call him a champion. At no point in the scriptures did David declare Goliath was unbeatable; instead David laughed at Goliath's accusation. David gave Goliath no respect, accolades, title, or credit. David's words about Goliath were, "Who is this uncircumcised Philistine that defies the armies of the living God?" David's neighbors in his community heard about David's feelings toward Israel's foe, Goliath, and they spread this rumor about young David to all who would listen. David exclaimed his strong desire to go to battle with this uncircumcised Philistine, so much so that others told King Saul about David's earnest desire to fight Goliath for Israel, because not one soldier dared to stand up to Goliath.

Can you believe no trained soldier offered to fight Goliath? Only a twelve-year-old boy did. What a travesty! These soldiers were lost and needed faith in God. Why didn't Israel's entire army jump this giant like the New York City gangs do in the twenty-first century to people who threaten them? Israel had thousands of men, who had just made the Philistines retreat in defeat, so when Goliath initially stood before them with threats from hell, they should have surrounded Goliath and faced him, fearlessly looking him dead in the eyes. I'm quite sure Goliath would have run like a little toddler does when he or she is scared. How do I know this to be true? Because Goliath threatened to battle only one of Israel's soldiers, not the thousands who hid in ditches. Who dares to give options to his or her overpowering opponent when dealing with war tactics? Goliath was probably a ploy and a distraction to give the Philistines time to retreat and recover so they could resume warring, because when armies win battles and wars, it's because they got the best of their enemies, and the enemies had no other choice but to surrender. They dared to insult God's people by threatening his army with one tall soldier among Israel's thousands of soldiers, who had stood up to your weak army and beat them so bad that they ran scared. Now one tall man stood between Israel and their pursuit of total annihilation of the Philistines.

Fear gripped the heart of all Israel's army, including their king. So it is with us. We go to church, do Bible study, and attend prayer services; and we still walk in fear. Fear darkens our eyesight, and we continue to run from our bill collectors, opportunities, and marriages. We abandon our families. We run from the truth. We hide in ditches of secret societies. We hide behind walls of addictions, perverted habits, and sinful acts. We become unreachable and untouchable, and we escape reality because of fear. We stand afar off from commitment to God and others dear to us while becoming open and dedicated to false gods. These gods cannot move, nor are they alive but dead. King Saul and Israel definitely were in a backsliding state of mind. Of all those generals, captains, and sergeants in Israel's army, not one of them offered to fight this giant; instead, they entertained the thought of sending a child to fight a grown man's battle. And when did the losing team get to choose how things are done on the battlefield? The king should have been arrested for child abuse and endangerment. Israel was already in battle with the Philistines and winning, but when they saw Goliath, they all ran and hid in ditches like that move was going to stop Goliath.

This story proves that children can fight the good fight of faith with the help of the Lord God. Let us not give up on our millennial generation(1980-1994), nor generation Z (1995-2012), or Generation Alpha (2013-2025) although these generations are born within the same years; many of them have gotten a bad rap in our inner cities, but there are many David characters and Moses characters in these generations waiting for the opportunity to stand up for something great. Please let us not forget that these generations learned from the elders of their day.

David had a strong relationship with the unbeatable God, the living God, and the God who created the heavens and the earth and Goliath too. This is the God who sent angels to destroy Israel's enemies and the God who delivered Israel from the Egyptians. David refused to call Goliath a champion. Ha ha! The only champion David knew was God almighty. Israel called him Goliath, the giant and champion of the Philistines; none of these words came from David's lips. He called Goliath the uncircumcised Philistine dog. The worst thing you can do to a champion is to send a kid to fight him, which is the biggest insult you could ever give a champion. Goliath's response to Israel's rudeness was, "Am I a dog that thou come to me with staves?" And

Goliath cursed David by his gods. He cursed David by his dead gods. Shall we all laugh aloud? Not everything in life is funny, but we need to learn to laugh at our seemingly tough opponents, who came to put fear in our hearts to doubt the almighty God. No statue can come to anyone's rescue. Goliath opened his big mouth and said, "Come to me and I will give thy flesh unto the fowls of the air and to the beast of the fields." Sounds like Goliath prophesied his own fate. Wow!

At this point, most people would have run like a cheetah, one of the fastest animals on four legs. Instead, David stood his ground and didn't budge with his eyes wide open; the only thing David smelled was victory. The only thing David saw was victory, and it was obvious that David could taste victory, so he did.

David approached Goliath, not with his head hung down and knees shaking; instead, he stood tall, unwavering, and said some powerful words that blew Goliath away. "Thou comest to me with a sword and with a spear and with a shield but I come to thee in the name of the Lord of host, the God of the armies of Israel whom thou has defied(1Samuel 17-45-50)." David set the premise of why Goliath would be defeated.

David continued to speak and said, "This day will the Lord deliver thee into mine hand; and I will of smite thee and take thine head from thee; and I will give thine carcasses of the host of the Philistines this day unto the fowls of the air and the wild beast of the earth, that all the earth may know that there is a God of Israel and all this assembly shall know that the Lord saveth not with sword and spear: for the battle is the Lord's and he will give you into our hands." This sounds like a warning for Goliath to surrender to Israel and just maybe find mercy instead of a death sentence.

After which, David didn't walk toward the Philistine, but he ran toward the Philistine's camp, reaching for a rock to put in his sling; and once he swung his sling at Goliath, Goliath was history, and he fell to his death. Close your eyes and reminisce on the undefeated Goliaths in your life. Stand up to your foes, because if God be for you, tell me, who can be against you? The instruments David used were used in the name of the Lord. That's what makes the difference because Goliath had more updated artillery, and it was more suited for war; but the difference was that God was on David's side, and his instruments of warfare obeyed God.

Open your eyes and see that in whatever you're going through in life, if you include God in your life, his presence will make the difference in whether you will be victorious or defeated. Feel like winning? Include God in your life and daily devotion, and winning will be a way of life for you. Stop bragging about your enemies, limited powers, and business tactics, influence, and political connections; the King of kings is on your side. Stop talking about your enemies' strengths, titles, success stories, and the people they have influenced over the years. Approach your enemies as defeated foes, beatable enemies, and those you must conquer.

When Israel saw Goliath, they saw defeat, fear, a giant, and an unbeatable champion. They saw the Philistines' advantage over them, and they forgot God's almighty power and superiority over all people and things; whereas David saw an uncircumcised Philistine dog, he saw someone who was tall and needed to fall. He saw a man who was no match for God. David never called Goliath a champion; nor did he admit Goliath was a giant. David considered Goliath an enemy of the Lord of hosts, and he handled him like a real dog with a loud bark.

What do you see while facing your issues and circumstances?

Is God bigger than your troubles and health issues? Is he bigger than your diagnosis? Can God help overturn the judge's decision? Open your blinded eyes. Your problems and extreme complexities aren't as big as they seem, for the Lord God is greater than every one of them.

And Caleb stilled the people before Moses and said let us go at once and possess; for we are well able to overcome it. But the men that went up with him said, we are not able to go up against the people; for they are stronger than we.

And they brought up an evil report of the land which they had searched unto the children of Israel, saying the land, through which we have gone to search it is a land that eateth up the inhabitants thereof; and all the people that we saw in it are men of great stature and there we saw the giants, the sons of Anak, which come of the giants: and we were in our own sight as grasshoppers, and so we were in their sight. (Numbers 13:30–33; 14:6–9)

Here we go again, speaking about two groups of men seeing the same thing, but both came up with two different reports. It was the norm that before an army invaded a country, they sent scouts to view the land and people they planned to invade; afterward, they strategized a plan to overtake a new territory. So it was important that the scouts were thorough with their details and information. Joshua and Caleb gave a good report to Israel and Moses. Their report was, "Let us go up at once and possess it for we are well able to overcome it." They didn't even mention the giants to the people of Israel. Did you hear about any giants in the land? Did you hear about men of great stature? Did you hear anything about Israel looking like grasshoppers compared to the giants? No! Both men knew a bigger God than the giants, and they were confident that the giants would fall to the ground. So why mention that giants existed and stir up fear in the hearts of Israel, especially when the battle was already won?

Joshua and Caleb mentioned victory, but the other scouts who went up with Joshua and Caleb announced a bad report and said, "We are not able to go up against the people for they are stronger than we." These men saw giants and felt it was impossible to defeat them. They saw their limitations and couldn't see any way of escape from their negative report; even if you're outnumbered, you can never motivate soldiers with such a negative report. "They are stronger than we." And the people digested those words and were gripped with fear and terror. They continue to look at the threats of their enemy and quickly mentioned how much stronger the giant was than they.

Always remember that when God is in the equation, he changes the outcome into victory for you. Line up all your giants in your life and compare them to God's power. God is more powerful than the entire world's armed forces. He moves faster than lightning; he's supernaturally strong enough to handle any situation that appears deadly, because he holds the entire world in the palms of his hands, and he can reach down from heaven into man's heart. So do the math. What can a giant do compared to Lord Jehovah God? If you have giants in your life threatening your life, health, and success, whose report will you believe today? God is bigger than every one of your problems. Second, he is well able to give you the victory in every situation.

Ponder not the size of the problem but rather, worship and praise the problem solver, God the Father. The Lord is good, and his mercy endures forever and ever (1Chronicles 16:34). Who can understand the mysteries of God? The earth is the Lord's and the fullness thereof. If God be for you, tell me, who can be against you (1John 4:4)? Greater is he who is within you than he who is in the world. Open your eyes and see that if God is on your side, he is more than all that is in the world and the rulers of darkness combined. The world depends on the arms of the flesh, but we trust in the Lord of hosts, creator of all, way maker, our solid rock; and when he speaks, things happen, and the earth shatters. God moves by his Spirit, and he holds salvation in his hands.

What really troubles me personally is that when the people of Israel heard the first good report from Joshua and Caleb, there was no applause, no one cheering for the victory, no dancing or singing praises to God the Father. Weren't they all waiting for a good report? Or is this just my imagination? Maybe they just didn't want to fight because they thought that if God gave them the city, all they had to do was walk into the city without fighting. *Victory always comes with a battle; without a battle, there can be no victory.*

After hearing the first report, Israel seemingly refused to celebrate; instead, they anxiously waited to hear the second bad report from the other men. Misery loves company. The other men gave a bad report, announcing how much weaker they were in comparison to the giants and boldly admitted that Israel couldn't defeat the giants, and the people began to make a roaring sound— not against the men who gave a bad report but against Joshua and Caleb, who gave a good report. Now they raised their voices loud and clear against Joshua and Caleb and planned to kill them both, not realizing the men who gave the bad report had *insulted God* and his people by saying, "We are weaker than they. We cannot defeat them." These men should have been stoned to death; instead, Israel stood there, being persuaded by these evil men's report, and they took their rage out on Joshua and Caleb, thereby committing mutiny against Joshua and Caleb and God's people. God had already destroyed all Israel's enemies and giants up to this point, so why did they think he would do differently? These people were blind and knew not the God of Joshua and Caleb. All their energies went to rioting against Joshua and Caleb instead of praising God for the victory. They believed a bad report that was developed and orchestrated by the enemy of their souls; it wouldn't surprise me if these spies had been working for their enemies, because the God of Abraham, Isaac, and Jacob always delivered his people out of the hands of their enemies. These same scouts were probably spies for Israel's enemies. There is no true warrior that goes to battle with defeat in his mind; rather, he tastes and smells victory, and he fights for it. Their rage should have been pointed at the men with the bad report. Men rather have darkness than light (St. John 3:19). When you live in darkness for a long period, it becomes comfortable and tolerable, so when someone is trying to point you to the light, it's uncomfortable at first because your vision is dimmed; and it takes some time to adjust your vision to the light, but when your vision is finally clear, you can enjoy victory.

It's amazing to me that you can speak a thousand words full of triumph and optimism to help someone and others march forward, but one negative word can make them all abort their missions, visions, and goals; and they begin to move backward and hide in ditches. Seemingly negative words carry so much weight; they throw people off track, sets people back, and blind their eyes from seeing victory. We see only defeat. Joshua and Caleb did nothing wrong, but they only tried to illuminate their minds and open their eyes to clearly see victory and not worry about obstacles, because in every victorious battle, you will encounter difficulties. That is why you must continue to push forward to victory.

David didn't see Goliath as a giant, but Israel did. David saw Goliath as only an uncircumcised Philistine dog barking at Israel. You see, the difference between champions, doubters, and haters is that they don't see what champions see. As I said before, Israel saw Goliath as a giant, unbeatable and strong in stature, but David denounced any such accolades given to Goliath; all David saw was a defeated foe, an uncircumcised Philistine, who must be defeated by a child who had the power of God on his side. David was terribly angered by the threats and the mentioning of how Goliath dared to defy or challenge the armies of the Lord God. Goliath's bragging pumped up fury inside David—so much so that he was determined to behead Goliath. Israel's response to Goliath's so-called threats and intimidations so annoyed and irritated David. David wanted to know what Israel's armies were going to do about this uncircumcised Philistine dog; instead of fighting and strategizing a plan for victory, Israel was running scared and hiding in ditches. David immediately saw victory, but Israel saw only an unbeatable foe.

God, please help us to see the victory in our circumstances with our medical diagnosis, unemployment, business ownership, and education; victory in our marriages; victory in our churches; and victory with our children. Open your eyes; even if you don't see the victory, believe God for the victory. Who dares to defy the power of God? Who dares to promote and boast about the giants in your life over the God in your life, who happens to be the great giant destroyer? God crushes giants every day of the week. Who dares to defy my God in heaven?

Numbers 14:6–9 says, "And Joshua the son of Nun, and Caleb the son of Jephun which were of them that searched the land, rent their clothes: And they spoke unto all the company of the children of Israel saying, the land, which we passed through to search it, is an exceeding good land. If the Lord delight in us then he will bring us into this land which flows milk and honey."

After the people heard the good report from Caleb and Joshua, they sought to kill Caleb and Joshua. Israel believed the bad report more than the good report. Where was Israel's faith? Did they backslide into darkness without their leaders knowing? Israel couldn't see victory because they focused on and believed in only defeat. They focused on the strength and great stature of their enemies, not on the power of God. God is bigger than your credit score. He is bigger than any bank account or lending source. He is bigger than any doctor's diagnosis. He's bigger than your boss and the CEO of any company, and he's bigger than Internal Revenue Service. Who dares to defy the armies of the Lord God? All this being said, the giants we all face day to day threaten us just like they did in the days of Joshua and Caleb, but Joshua and Caleb opened their eyes and saw victory before the battle had begun, and they saw strategies that could defeat the giants; but more importantly, they knew God was with them, and because God was with them, victory was theirs for the taking, not for the asking.

It's time for God's people to take our enemies' territories. We've been scared too long. We've been procrastinating too long. We've been holding back too long. We've been believing our enemies' report too much. We've been waiting for someone else to do what we dare not do. We've been complaining too long, and we've been fighting among ourselves much too long. How long? Much too long! It's time to take back what our enemies stole from us. Can the church say, "Amen"? Can I get a "Hallelujah!" in the building? Whose report will you believe? You can see now!

Don't be like cattle with eyes wide open; they are counted, then driven to a trap and slaughtered. They willingly enter the dungeon of massacre. We act as cattle sometimes if we were to admit it. We carry out our days and lives without including God in any of our activities; then later, when things get spooky and uncontrollable and dangerous, we find ourselves on a road to devastation. Only then do we realize we need God, but in the meantime, enthusiastically and sneakily we continue in our sinful behavior, understanding that it could destroy our lives and reputations, but we rather continue, thinking, *Maybe we won't get caught, or no one will ever know until the tables turn, and suddenly we are exposed and later destroyed.*

Run when you see trouble. Ask for help, because sin grows like cancer and AIDS. Run from wickedness, run from stress, run from immorality, run from sexual perversion, run from adultery, run from deception, run from greed and selfishness, run from crime, and run from lying lips and stealing what doesn't belong to you. Let your affections and emotions point to Christ, our Lord and Savior. Keep your eyes on Jesus, or you will fall hard. Jesus destroys sin. Before God shines light on your filthiness, come to the light so Jesus can cleanse you from all unrighteousness. Jesus is the light of the world, and he promises to give you a better life, which leads to eternal life.

Open your blinded eyes and see God trying to guide your footsteps so you won't fall for everything. Open your eyes and see that God alone wants to help you, save you, bless you, and keep you.

God wants to give you a better life with less stress and minimal worries. Life brings many options to choose from, and these choices later become our habitual way of living (being in poverty, lying, cheating, constantly worrying, gossiping, doing scandalous behavior, and so forth). So if you are very comfortable and satisfied with your lifestyle of living in darkness, living in defeat, living in depression, living in oppression, living in poverty, or living in the limelight of your peers, no one can make you turn away from these choices in life, because if you're happy with your current choices, God is merciful and loving enough that he allows all of us to make our own decisions; but if you open your blind eyes, you will see the almighty hands of God pulling you toward him, the Spirit of God drawing you near to him, and the voice of God, which is his Holy Scriptures, calling you out to serve him. Turn to the Lord, and he will rearrange your life so it will glorify the living God. That's living without blinders on. Open your blinded eyes!

CHAPTER 7

There's Greatness within You

will never forget the love and support I received from my church family after losing my eldest sister, Ruby Melton. Ruby had a gift of writing poems. She would call me late at night to read a poem to me; sometimes I listened intently, and other times I held the phone away from my ear. I suggested to Ruby that she copyright her poems. She never ventured to do so; instead, she just wanted to encourage people through her writings, whether it was over the phone or in churches.

Now look at her baby brother writing a book, which my sister Ruby also inspired me to do so. I must add that English wasn't my major, nor was grammar my best friend, but I continued to move forward with this project and write *Messages of Impact* regardless of my limitations; I always said to myself, "I can do this." If I had listened to my fears, doubts, limitations, and shortcomings, this book would have never come into existence. To my dear readers, you also can do the same as I did. Oh yes, you can. Look beyond your limitations and handicaps. Push forward toward your goals, aspirations, and purpose; and see something greater to strive for because there's greatness within all of us, but most people either ignore it or don't have a clue of its existing in their lives. Never give up on you. Fight the good fight of faith to accomplish your dreams. Ruby Melton will be greatly missed and remembered for the impact she left on her baby brother's life.

During the time of my sister's death, I felt sort of lonely and did much grieving; and while I was dealing with my bereavement, God spoke to me and gave me a message: "There's greatness within you." When God speaks, it's such a warm feeling, and it cannot be erased from your mind. I have heard thousands of messages from ministers in the pulpit over the fifty-four years of being on this earth. Most of their messages covered topics about our sinful natures, bad things we entangle ourselves in, and bad decisions we make, including serving other gods, our lack of stewardship, our friendship with darkness, our disobedience to God, our stinginess to tithes and offerings, our poor dress codes in the house of the Lord, and so forth. Rarely did I hear ministers speak and drill in the ears of the congregation a message about the greatness within them. It is understood that we are sinners saved by grace (Ephesians 2:8), and all our righteousness is as dirty as filthy rags toward God (Isaiah 64:6); but when was the last time someone told you there was greatness in you? Looking at your past sins and current sins, your possible involvement in criminal activity, and all sorts of ungodly deeds you've committed, you may question having greatness within you and doubt that the great breath of God, installed in your nostrils, causes you to have greatness within. Although you cannot seemingly erase the sins you committed, make no mistake that sin is what God hates—not you. They are the sinful acts we digest in our hearts and display with our actions that God hates, not you. The only eraser of sins in our lives is Jesus Christ, the Son of the living God; only he can erase your truckload of sins; but even with sin present in our lives and in the world today, it cannot diminish the fact that you and I have greatness within us and that these sinful actions are evil barricades to keep us from seeing our true greatness within us. So let's first talk about the greatness of God first, and after we have explored God's greatness, we will discuss the greatness God installed in you and me. Amen.

Psalm 48:1 says, "Great is the Lord, and greatly to be praised in the city of our God, in the mountains of his holiness."

The word *great* means "something or someone immense, large, vast enormous, noble, grand, extremely important and powerful." Great is the Lord God! You may ask, "How great art thou, O Lord?" Here is a great example of how great God is. God created the universe centuries ago, and the greatest scientists in the world today, with all their formulas, metric systems, and abstract mathematics, cannot measure the universe; nor can they find its beginning or ending, and every one of their attempts to find the universe's dimensions has failed. Wow! This fact alone should have all humanity standing in awe of God almighty. How great is our God to have built an entire galaxy that fits billions, even trillions, of stars! These stars happen to be twice the size of earth, and they outnumber all the population on earth, including its dead and living people, too.

This universe holds within its capacity nine planets, not including the ever-so-bright sun and moon, which we care so little about. God is the greatest God and the only God who lives. Wouldn't you want to serve a great God like this? Why worship a weak and small god, like a statue that can't talk, speak, or walk? You assassinate your true potential when you serve dead gods. Who would want to serve a dead god, who can't be moved but has to stay stationed and as stiff as a statue? It can't talk or walk, and you have to rebuild it when it breaks. If you serve a god like this, shame on you. You should want to serve a living and real God who loves you; after all, you are a living being. Why do you need to worship the dead? Life begat life, and the life of another could be taken by another; but nothing dead can fight back, can resurrect itself, so stop talking to the dead. Jesus rose from the dead and remains alive. We will worship him. Another thing is, if you worship a god that doesn't speak back to you, let me introduce you to Jesus Christ, the Son of the living God; and when you pray to him, he will answer your prayer. That's a sign that he's alive and well. There are thousands upon thousands of fake gods in the world, and I don't want to insult anyone by naming them; but truthfully speaking, there's only one real God. Jehovah God is the only God.

So our problems compared to God's awesomeness must be so minuscule compared to the elements of the universe. Our immense troubles and colossal issues cause us to have heart attacks, nervous breakdowns, high blood pressure, brain aneurisms, and strokes, all because we choose to carry so many things inside our hearts and minds instead of giving them to the great God of the universe, who makes our problems look like a walk in the park. That's how great God is!

Genesis 15:5 says, "And he brought him forth abroad, and said look now toward heaven, and tell the stars, if thou be able to number them; and he said unto him, so shall thy seed be."

God was speaking with Abraham, asking him to number the stars if he could; they are innumerable just like the grains of sand on land. God promised Abraham that he would bless his seed like this. Ever try counting grains of sand? The creation cannot be greater than the creator. We have a portion of God's greatness. God installed creativity in mankind, and because of it, we have transcended from riding chariots to high-level jet planes traveling at the speed of light. We enjoy advanced technology communicating with people through iPhones, iPads, laptops, smartphones, and traveling to the moon with rocket ships; but with all our great developments, all of it is still a million leap years behind God's technology.

Deuteronomy 1:10 says, "The Lord your God hath multiplied you and behold ye are this day as the stars in heaven for multitude."

God was telling Abraham, "Behold, this day as the stars in heaven for multitude." That was said in BC time. Right now the nation of Israel is probably ten times the size of their population since then. This was a promise God gave to Abraham because of his strong faith in God; God gave him much land and an uncountable population including the Arab nations, too. Some people may not agree, but if you do the research, you will see that the Israelis and Arabs came from the same seed through Abraham. If we can't agree on this issue, we should agree that our God is great, great, great! And we aren't talking about Tony the Tiger from Kellogg's. We speak of the great "I am that I am" God, the bright and morning star. Jehovah God is his name.

Isaiah 40:15 says, "Behold the nations are as a drop of a bucket and are counted as small dust of the balance: behold he takes up the isles as very little thing."

All the nations of the world are just a drop in the bucket to God; he counts them like dust particles. We sing, "He's got the whole world in his hands," but do we really believe what we sing, because if we did, we would stop worrying about our world leaders, nuclear warfare, terrorist attacks, health care, the stock market, presidential candidates, congress, foreign nations, wars, and rumors of war, because our great God has it all in control. God holds the world in the palm of his hand, and he shines his sunlight on the righteous and unrighteous. God sees all the evil in the world, including deceptions, countless murders, hatred, violence, prejudice, rapes, child molestations, scandals, and corruption throughout nations, yet he still remains merciful, waiting for mankind to come to the knowledge of the truth. God isn't just sitting back behind the curtains, watching mankind do whatever he desires. God is very much alive and is ultimately in control, but he is calling mankind to come to Jesus before it's too late. Although Satan is the prince of the air (Ephesians 2:2), as the Bible records, we must understand that wherever there's a prince, there must be a king. God is King and the true Kings of kings, and one day God will flip the script on the doubters of the world, because every knee shall bow and confess that Jesus is Lord (Romans 14:11). Finally, everyone will know God is the only God, and all earthly gods, statues, monuments, shrines, witches, warlocks, and evil men in high places will crumble, collapse, and deteriorate into oblivion.

Psalm 19:1 says, "The heavens declare the glory of God; and the firmament shows his handy work."

Look up into the sky or the heavens. That's God's beauty, honor, majesty, and adoration. The firmament is the sky and all its glory; the blue sky, white clouds, and sunlight are God's handiwork. It amazes me every morning to see the glory of God; he gives the world such a great and beautiful, picture-perfect, radiant atmosphere. His glory is so great and adored. If you don't think God's handiwork is good enough, imagine if we didn't have these elements in our world; it would be a very dark and dull place. It would be like hell—pitch black, dreary, empty, and full of nothingness.

Psalms 24:1 says, "The earth is the Lord's and the fullness thereof; the world and they that dwell therein."

It's good to know the owner of the earth. God owns this planet along with the universe and everything in it. The trees belong to God along with the birds, all animals, the ocean with its fish, and everything that creeps on the earth. Are we all losing our minds over dollars and cents when God owns all the gold in the world? Are we worrying about gas hikes when God made the oil, placed it in the earth, and alone knows where the hidden oil is? Are we worrying about our unemployment status when God owns all the land that all fortune 100 companies, such as IBM, Microsoft, Wall Street, Nestle, Prudential, Citibank, Fidelity, Google, Facebook, AOL, Disney, Sony, and Apple, occupy. They all operate on borrowed space from our creator; they are tenants of God's property. Do you remember that song "This Land Is My Land"? Well, this land is God's land; we are just tenants on it; we answer to a higher authority. If you don't believe this, just observe the earthquakes in California and other states and countries, and hurricanes like Hurricane Sandy in 2012, which ripped houses into shreds and had cars, trucks, and buildings floating downstream. How about the tornadoes that come every now and then, demolishing our homes and businesses? How about the tidal wave of waters, like in a tsunami, that wipe out thousands of people?

My friend, someone else is in charge, and it's definitely not us. These are things we cannot control or even stop; God is in control and no other. Sin is what makes God turn his face from us to shake us up and bring glory or his wrath to nations of people. Unfortunately, sometimes tragedy isn't enough to turn the hearts of unbelievers toward God, yet God remains the God of the universe and all the elements of the earth. The Bible mentions that Satan is the prince of the air (Ephesians 2-2), who manipulates the weather conditions and causes havoc in the atmosphere, but even he cannot do these things without God's permission. The earth is the Lord's and all that is in it. The earth belongs to God. That's how great our God is.

Proverbs 21:1 says, "The King's heart is in the hand of the Lord as the river of waters: he turns it whithersoever he will."

Glory to God our employers, bank loan officers, presidents, congressmen, government officials, mayors, governors, district attorneys, pastors, media organizations, and many more make decisions that help shape our world, but little do they know they all rest in the hand of the Lord God. Did you just read the above scripture? It says, "The King's heart is in the hand of the Lord and he turns it whithersoever he will." Wow! If this doesn't make a believer out of you, I don't know what will.

Who is in control? Men and women may hold the office, but God ultimately controls their decisions when he wants. Our God is great! God speaks to people in different ways, sometimes through dreams, our children; other times God speaks through certain circumstances and nature. In whichever way God chooses to speak to men in power, they must heed his voice. God wants to change your sentence from the death penalty to eternal life. With God you don't necessarily need to be qualified as some are because God qualifies the unqualified. If Jesus can change water into wine, he can change an unemployed individual into a CEO of a corporation. If you're sick until death, God can heal you and add years to your life. Are your children acting up, desiring drugs, going to late-night sleepovers, drinking like fish, and hanging out in clubs and dark places? Just release them into God's hands, and God will take control and change their appetite to sin. Put them in the hands of the Lord God almighty, and over time God will bring them back to their senses. Trust in the Lord, people. If he is the great God the ancient scriptures repeatedly say he is, giving your children to him is clearly the right thing to do. Amen! God is great and greatly to be praised.

Praise him for his majesty, praise him from the heavens above, and praise him in the earth below and its fullness. Praise him for health and strength; without them, we could do nothing. God deserves praise from his people, but if you decide not to praise him, don't worry. The very rocks will cry out praises to the almighty God; that's how great God is. In any country it is normal and traditional to give praise to a king, emperor, or president; when people see him or her coming, they respond with applause, cheer, ovation, tribute, reverence, bravos, "Hip hip hurrahs," and big handclaps. We celebrate their office, position, and authority. They are just mortal men, which we have such high regards for, but we are ashamed to lift the name of the Lord God. God created man to praise and worship him. Greatness demands applause, ovation, and accolades. God is great, and we should praise him freely. You ought to praise him. Shout, "Hallelujah!"

> Great is the Lord and greatly to be praised; and his greatness is unsearchable. (Psalm 145:3)

> For the Lord the most high is terrible; he is a great king over all the earth. (Psalm 47:2)

Words cannot explain in total how great God really is. Be thankful God is on our side to guide, lead, and protect us. Salvation is God's solution for man's redemption. When God speaks, thunder roars, and lightning glistens throughout the atmosphere. No man has ever seen God anytime. Moses saw the shadow of God; he was the only man to see a glimpse of God's back. No man in our mortal bodies can see God and live; that's how great God is. No man can outthink or trick God, because he reads our hearts and minds very well. No one has more wisdom than God because God is all knowing. He is the creator of all.

Listen very carefully. God is great, and everything about God is great. After creating the earth and the universe, he said they were very good (Genesis 1:31). When God says something is very good, you better believe it is. But when he formed men into living beings and breathed his breath of life into men's carcasses, we became living souls. God's breath is his greatness, which was transmitted into our mortal bodies through our nostrils, after which we instantaneously became living souls with intelligence, mobility, vision, spirit, sense of humor, and personality. Our bodies are the temple of God. He made us in his image, and this is the greatness I speak of. The breath of God in our living souls makes us great. We are made in the image of God. Greatness begets greatness. Greatness has been prematurely installed in us. Children of God, please hear me loud and clear; you have greatness within you, and mankind didn't deposit greatness in you. The almighty God did.

This greatness within us should be preached about and continually glued to our hearts and minds because life is filled with tons of obstacles we encounter every day that would make us question God's greatness in us. We have the power to defeat every obstacle life brings our way. We struggle and are hindered by difficult circumstances, because we don't believe there's greatness within us that wants to be exposed to the world, but the enemy of our soul and our personal enemies want to keep it hidden. Your greatness must come alive. God's people are great people, and they have great power; their greatness comes from within, and God put it there.

God the Father used his hands to form people into human beings; Adam was the first man God touched and formed. God took time making men and women, but with women, God did something unique; he created in them the nest so they could birth babies, who would turn into generations of men and women. Therefore, believing a fetus isn't a living being is a lie. A fetus was created by a sperm from a man and was joined together with an egg from a woman. Apples grow from apple trees, but destroying apple seeds will annihilate future apples. Killing a fetus purposely is murdering a person. Are we that naïve? Giving birth is a heavenly process done on earth, so much so that John the Baptist and Jesus Christ used the same process of being born into the world except without sex. Certainly, if there's any argument about this issue, let me ask you a question: how did we all arrive on the planet? We exist today because a sperm met an egg and together formed a fetus, which later became a child. Who dares to defy God's process for the creation of human life? God has installed greatness within you, but what are you going to do with it? Shall you live in darkness? Shall you continue to destroy your temple (life) with drugs, excessive alcohol, violence, crime, corruption, political scandals, adultery, sexual perversion, lying lips, racism, hatred, false doctrine, obesity, abuse, and fighting?

Oh, how dangerous you would be if you only knew about the greatness harbored inside you. What greatness do we speak of? That is greatness to invent, create, lead, and evaluate; it is the ability to change your surroundings, the power to build and design, the knack to analyze and compute, the ability to diagnose problems and create solutions, and the ability to make products and services that help employ people, open churches, and create music (and the list goes on). There's enough greatness in your life to slay the Goliaths in your life and walk through the burning furnace without being burned. You can conquer those Egyptians in your life, destroy those Canaanites, tear down those walls of Jericho, and victoriously cross the Red Seas in your life. You can lay hands on the sick so they can recover, raise the dead like Jesus did, witness to the lost and found, feed the homeless, and preach the gospel. Jesus said, "The works I've done ye shall do greater works." (St. John 14:12)

Jesus confirmed that you've got the power to do great things, because his Father installed greatness within you. Who told you that you were worthless? Who told you that you would never amount to anything? Who said your life was a waste? Who said you're nobody? Who said you're sick and can't get well? Who said your children will never come to Jesus? Who said your marriage will always be on the rocks? Who told you your financial troubles will never end? Tell your accusers there's greatness within you and that God put it there; because of this, you will win these battles. You don't have to feel the power, nor do you need to see the power. Just believe the power exists within you to do great things. God installed in us his greatness which we call the breath of life which comes with God's spirit, his genius power, creative power, thinking power, invention power, wisdom, character and so much more. We were wonderfully made (Psalm 139:14) I will praise thee; for I am fearfully and wonderfully made: marvellous are thy works;and that my soul knoweth right well.

God makes no mistakes. You can be a trailblazer for others to follow in your footsteps or a horrible influence for generations to come. Status quo isn't for God's people; mediocrity isn't merely enough either. Christians should strive for excellence in the things of God and in our daily duties. We are neither robots nor some type of mechanical device controlled by the government or world leaders; we are made in the image of God, and that alone grants us greatness status. Your take on others should be that all men are made in the image of God whether they are black, brown, yellow, purple, or white. They are all God's children. Prejudice is ignorance. Why would the color of a person's skin tone matter if he or she rescued you from drowning in the ocean? Really! *So it shouldn't matter if you had to join forces with other races to obtain something greater in life than our obvious differences.*

Once you recognize the greatness within you, which God placed there for you to eventually recognize, then you must access it by using your faith in God, putting your faith to work. Then you can have dominion and be fruitful and multiply, replenishing the earth and subduing it.

> And God said; let us make man in our image, after our likeness; and let them have dominion over the fish of the sea, and over the fowl in the air, and over the cattle and over all creeping thing

that creeps upon the earth. So God created man
in his own image, in the image of God created he
him; male and female created he them. And God
bless them, and God said unto them, be fruitful,
and multiply and replenish the earth, and subdue
it, and have dominion over the fish of the sea and
the fowl of the air and over every living thing that
move on the earth. (Genesis 1:26–28)

These verses have some of the most powerful words in them
than any other scripture I have ever read. Do you hear God speak?
He gives us dominion over the air, sea, and the earth; he blesses us,
and he commands us to be fruitful (not just to have babies) and to
be productive with our lives and livelihoods. We should multiply
and replenish the earth and subdue it.

Start taking control of your life. Get it together, repent, and
start fresh and new. If you need special help, take it to the Lord in
prayer; he will guide you and direct your path.

It is important to know who you are. Lift those hung-down
heads, look up, and see the great almighty. He has given you the
power to get wealth and to live a better life. Open your mouth,
speak those things you want to accomplish, and conquer it. There
is greatness within you, and the only way to discover this is to
become a doer of the word of God; open your mouth and speak
words of life. Be fruitful and productive in everything you do,
multiply yourself (train others to do what you do), and replenish
the earth with your ideas and creativity.

Do you ever wonder why millions of thoughts go through
your mind each moment of the day? It's because God allows fresh
thoughts to flow through your mind each day. Try using some of
them because many of them could be possible opportunities for
great success. Subdue the earth; take control of your situations
and circumstances in life. Diminish some of the intensified stress
and worries in your life. Take control over the traumatic issues in

your life. *Dominion* means to rule over and govern a particular territory. So when you are faced with some crucial things and elements of darkness, remember there's greatness within you to destroy any workings of the evil one. Face your problems with God on your side; take control of territories and terrorists assigned to destroy your mission in life. God freely and unselfishly gave you your greatness, and it's your job to put it in motion and work what the good Lord gave you. And with the measure of faith you have, God will bless your endeavors. Hallelujah!

First John 4:4 says, "Ye are of God little children and have overcome them: because greater is he that is in you than he that is in the world."

Wow! Did you just read that verse? After reading this verse, you should now believe. If you didn't believe before, there is greatness within you; here's proof for the children of God of the greater one, who is Jesus, inside you. These words came straight from the mouth of Jesus, the Son of the living God. Because Jesus lives inside you, there's greatness in you. Hallelujah to the Kings of kings and Lord of Lords. Glory! What's in you is greater than all you face and all that is offered to you. You may live in the ghetto or in the projects or maybe in a group home or a shelter and detention home; this still doesn't diminish the fact that you have greatness within you. Remember, God's Son, Jesus, was born in a stable, a farmhouse with horses, cows, and sheep; it was neither a palace nor a mansion, but in his birth, he came to the earth and took the form of man. He became the Son of God, literally walking among us, and it all started in a stable.

The purpose of Jesus's birth was much more superior than the place he was born in. His entire plan was to redeem man from sin, darkness, and the penalty of death. It all came from a farmhouse, not a fortress. It makes no difference where you live, what you own, what you drive, or what your family tree is. All that matters is that you are God's creation formed by God, and the breath of God flows within you. That's the greatness of God. Don't hide it, don't be ashamed of it, and don't give it up for the pleasure of this world. So write that book, become that preacher, witness to the unsaved, start your business, create your own product, invent something for the world to use, open that church, get your degree, and become that doctor or lawyer. It is all in your hands. What will you do with God's greatness within you? Please don't waste your greatness with procrastination.

If God is so great like the scriptures say, then why is he so interested in and concerned about mankind, who is made out of dirt? Isn't dirt worthless? Yet he loves us! As you know, we were formed from dust, which is dirt, and we will return to dust when we die. Yet God loves us so dearly. Why? God's interest in us must be because he installed his greatness in us, which is God's Spirit, who cannot be denied or erased. God loves us so much that he invites us to be part of his royal priesthood, which isn't a normal practice for royal families, because royalty keeps their distance from peasants but are closely surrounded and engaged with other royal people. But God, our King, is interested in us, because we have something God wants (our hearts, attention, time, and faith in him), and these are all the things God really wants from us; but many people refuse to give God their *hearts, attention, time, and faith in him. This is the struggle this human race has, and God is so aware of it that he purposely doesn't like to intrude in people's lives unless there's a strong purpose that brings much glory to his kingdom.*

You are valuable to God. That's why suicide and murder aren't an option for us because it is God who gives life, and it is he who takes life. Although you are valuable to God, you may not be as valuable to others as you may think, but who cares because God is the ultimate one with whom you want to be in good standing. Others might throw you away and favor another. Family may discontinue all communications with you, your employer may overlook your promotion, and your church may keep you in a box, but that can't stop the greatness of God in your life unless you allow it. Pick your head up, lift your voice, and praise God from whom all blessings flow. God made you the head and not the tail(Deuteromony 28:13).

You've been the tail end of things too long, and God is ready to turn things around for you so you will be running things. Shout, "Hallelujah!" Shout, "Glory to the King of kings!"

When Christians demonstrate their greatness, one can put a thousand to flight(Deuteromony 32:30)," which means you may be faced with a thousand threats, but with God's greatness within, it shall protect you from the threats of your enemies. They will run away from your mere presence, and if you thought that wasn't good enough, start associating with other great people, who believe the same as you. Scripture says, "Two of you can put ten thousand to flight." Hallelujah! That's why the enemies of our souls don't want us to recognize the greatness within us and the enormous power when we join forces with other believers. Two believers would be a superpower and a threat to any foe. Can you imagine how powerful it would be if ten of us were in one accord with our endeavors? Good God almighty, we could take the city and make it our own. Our faith in God should be highly elevated above any doubts, helping us to jump over hurdles in our lives; and if we stumble, we can bounce back with a vengeance. Our flesh wars with our spirits to diminish our greatness. The flesh wants us to use other means to get by in life, such as an illegal apparatus instead of God tools, which are prayers, praises, the Holy Scriptures, fellowship with other Christians, witnessing to non-Christians, loving our enemies, giving to the poor, visiting the sick, having strong faith in God, having peace amid turmoil, and demonstrating longsuffering instead of all the words that represent the opposite of longsuffering. These would include being impatient, contrary, defiant, intolerant, carefree, happy-go-lucky, weary, resistant, unmanageable, unruly, cranky, and ill tempered (and the list goes on); instead, the enemy of our soul would much desire you to exclude God out of everything you do just to live in emptiness and a fantasy world, which will make you end up destroying your character, family and marriage, friendships, churches, companies, your career, your children, and finally your soul without repentance. May God have mercy on us all!

You would think human beings had gold and diamonds in our bodies because of the way God searches for our attention, but the real reason is this. God loves us, and we are more valuable to him than gold, silver, diamonds, rubies, cars, property, and money; so that's why we shouldn't take life so lightly. You are awesomely made and connected to a royal family, and you possess something within that's so great, and there's more waiting to be revealed. Give God some praise right where you stand. How dare you deny the greatness within you? You and I were worth Jesus Christ dying on the cross for our salvation. Don't dare underestimate the value of your life! Your value and greatness don't come from your fame, fortune, money, or reputation, but they come from a God who so loved the world that he gave his only begotten Son (St. John 3:16). Then whosoever believeth on him shall not perish but have eternal life. If someone is willing to die on your behalf, that means you are more valuable than you could ever imagine. Jesus died for us! So we can live forever after death. God sees your greatness within, and he put it there, but it's you who has to work the greatness within you. God gave you greatness within, but it's you who has to work it. *God is the gift giver, but you must work the gifts he gives you, because God will not do both. Give it and work it.* We were destined to work!

Joshua 17:17–18 says, "And Joshua spoke unto the house of Joseph, even to Ephraim and to Manasseh, saying thou a great people and hast great power; thou shall not have one lot only: But the mountain shall be thine; for it is a wood, and thou shall cut it down; and the outgoing of it shall be thine; for thou shall drive out the Canaanites, though they have iron chariots and though they are strong. Manasseh was one of Joseph's eldest sons and Ephriam was the youngest son."

Manasseh was one of the tribes of Israel, which amounted

to thirty thousand strong. They were neighbors to Ephraim and shared territory together with Manasseh. As they were blessed, their population began to increase to fifty thousand in population. Joshua gave both Manasseh and Ephraim an area to occupy, but they complained about the area being too small for two tribes. Beside them was much land, but it belonged to the Canaanites. For them to acquire this territory, they would have to fight the Canaanites, who had iron chariots, which Israel didn't have, and the Canaanites appeared to be stronger than they. So Joshua, being the man of God, began encouraging Israel and making them aware of their greatness. Joshua spoke and said, "Thou art a great people and hast great power."

When was the last time someone in your church told you that you were great and possessed great powers? Some ministers would rather put you down, others want to judge you, and some may say you have a long way to go, but Joshua said none of the above. Joshua spoke life and truth to the house of Israel. Aren't we tired of being talked down to? There's greatness within you. You have great powers and can conquer your enemies. Joshua also spoke and said, "You will not just have only one lot, but the entire mountains shall be thine."

Israel responded very doubtfully and said, "Our enemies are stronger than we." Joshua reminded them of their greatness and their great powers, but most importantly, he reminded them of their great God. I love the way Joshua handled God's people. He never talked down to them or focused on their complaints, weaknesses, or doubt-filled attitude. Instead, Joshua gave them an example of what they would do to the Canaanites. He said, "Just like we cut wood down to size we will cut down those Canaanites to size, and just by moving forward to take the Canaanites territory God will give you the mountain too. Although they have chariots and appear to be stronger, you have greater power to move and drive them off the mountain. So, with this greatness face your fear and confront your enemies head on. What your enemies do not have is the God of Abraham, Isaac, and Jacob on their side(Exodus 3:6)"

We aren't born into this world to live in misery, pain, doubt, and fear. God wants us to live victoriously without any regrets. Stop beating yourself up, and if you are around people who continue to make you feel unexceptional and unextraordinary, minimize your time with these kinds of folks. Just because you don't have what others have, money, good credit many friends and family like others do, none of this diminishes your greatness within; in fact, it should maximize the greatness within you.

You can expose your greatness or destroy it. How many people have died without ever discovering their greatness within them, living a life filled with regrets for not ever trying to accomplish anything? Countless people went to their graves with this kind of mindset and way of life. They said, "I wish I could have," "I would if I could," "I should have," and "I will get to it when I can." Get out of that procrastination mode of "Maybe I could, and I almost did it." These words of procrastination and nothingness coming out of your mouth will get you nowhere fast, and you will never accomplish anything.

When I speak of the greatness in you, I speak of those hidden gifts and talents God has installed in you since your conception. You see, Joshua witnessed God do more than destroy Canaanites; he saw God the Father keep the sun still for a day. He saw the Red Sea open up and allow Israel to pass through while the Egyptians were swallowed in the Red Sea. Joshua saw the mighty walls of Jericho fall flat like a pancake. So now Joshua saw challenges as small obstacles and motivated Israel to fight because they had the same champion Moses had, God the Father.

Being depressed and having low self esteem and being in a lowly bar state of mind isn't for God's people; victory is our testimony. It is high time for changing our status quo lives and thinking capacity into excellence, triumph, virtuosity, achievement, nobility, dominion, dignity, accomplishment, integrity, and righteousness. Run this race called life as an athlete, knowing that the race isn't given to the swift or the strongest but to the one who endures (Ecclesiastes 9:11). The one who endures to the end is one who recognizes the greatness within them. Great people last! My mother, Katherine Thomas, was a great woman of God who believed in prayer, and she started a prayer band in our church. She sang in the prayer band choir, and often she preached a sermon in church. My mom had many gifts, and one of them was good communication with people in general. She knew how to make a living without having a nine-to-five job due to her sickness. Instead of complaining about her shortcomings, mom catered events. She was a seamstress for big wedding parties and a fund-raising coordinator for her church, but with all her God-given talents, she really loved God with all her heart.

My mom, Katherine Thomas, had only a second-grade education, but she accomplished much and more than some people who had a college degree and a master's degree. My mother even opened a soul food restaurant back in the '70s, and it was in operation for twelve years. My mother tapped into her greatness regardless of her shortcoming, and I am so much like her. Oh, how I wish I could see her again! But I *will* see her again in heaven. Hallelujah!

First John 14:12 says, "Ye shall do greater things on earth, then Christ."

Jesus said to his disciples, "They shall do greater things on earth than what Christ did if they believed (St John 14:12)." Jesus's ministry was short on earth, as we know, but the impact he had on the earth was incredible beyond any prophet in the Bible. The Holy Bible is the most sold book on earth; every year it outsells fiction, biographies, autobiographies, cookbooks, and Romance novels. The Holy Bible is the greatest book ever; every Sunday morning, ministers preach and repeat the words of Jesus; and by his words, we are healed, delivered, saved, and filled. We are condemned or redeemed by his words. The words of Jesus make miracles happen. Demons tremble at his words, and they are cast out of people at the words of God. Jesus's ministry impacted the gentiles, multitudes, and the disciples; but it had no effect on the Jews because they thought the King of Jews would bring war on the Roman Empire. What they didn't understand was that the war Jesus brought was an inward war, better known as "spiritual warfare."

Jesus took the sting of death out of death so Christians could have hope after death, and that hope is eternal life. Man is no match to war with God in any capacity. It took Jesus saying on the cross, "Forgive them, Father." Had he not asked his father to forgive us, angels from heaven would have wiped out Roman's empire in seconds. Glory to God! No father sits back and allows his innocent son to be killed. God was so angry that the earth opened up, the dead rose, and old patriots walked the earth again. The sky darkened, the winds blew hard, and the earth cracked open. Jesus said, "Father, forgive them for they know not what they do." Because of Jesus's pleading to his father to forgive the world, God turned his face away from the torturing of his Son. If Jesus hadn't pled for God's forgiveness for the scandal created by the Jews and the crucifixion the Romans conducted, there wouldn't be any salvation for mankind. No earthly arsenal, nuclear warheads, or atomic bombs could have stopped God's wrath on mankind if Jesus hadn't intervened.

So God had to turn his face from this crucifixion; that's why the sky darkened, the winds blew, and the earth quaked. God, our Father and man's creator, sat back and allowed the Romans to crucify his only begotten Son solely because his Son said, "Forgive them." If the Roman Empire had only known whom they crucified on the cross, they would have been afraid for their lives and their family's lives, but Jesus covered them with his love and asked for forgiveness for the Romans and the world at large. Jesus's saying, "Father, forgive them for they know not what they do" was the pivoting point for mankind; Jesus became the living sacrifice or lamb, who was literally offered up for the sins of the world; his purpose was to redeem mankind so Jesus would become the pure Lamb, slain as in ultimately sacrificed for all mankind's sins.

After the crucifixion, God's Holy Ghost fell down on the disciples in the upper room. "Ye shall receive power after the Holy Ghost shall come upon you." This is God's power being dispensed to mankind for the purpose of having God's keeping power, miracle power, healing power, staying power, and the power to move mountains in your life. Stop settling for the status quo when you can have the entire mountain. Aim high! Don't be shy. Be strong in the Lord and in the power of his might, because there's greatness within you. Warning: if we do nothing with this greatness within us, we will never experience victory or success or have confidence in God, who will give us rest while others are perplexed. Change is here, and we all must manage our circumstances better. Stop being the victim and become the victor.

Sadly enough, most people continue to live defeated lives no matter how much we preach about the greatness within, talk about it, and sing about it; they will hold their heads downward and feel insignificant because habits are hard to break. Scripture says in John 7:13, "Making the word of God of non effect through your tradition, which ye have delivered; and many such like things do ye."

Hanging on to bad habits and old traditions to the point that God's word has no effect in your life isn't worth losing out on God's plan for your life. Let us run from things that hold us back from reaching our goals and destiny. Take heed to the word of God so you can be a doer and not a hearer only of the word of God. Living in mediocrity is an easy way out for some. Mediocrity is when you do only what's necessary, never striving for excellence, brilliance, or commitment. You just accept and adapt to whatever life brings you. The purpose of salvation is to live free from sin; it is to leave darkness and dark deeds done in the dark so you can come to the light and tap into God-given greatness, which are your talents, skills, gifts, ideas, inventions, and much more. The purpose of salvation isn't to be miserable, stressed out, and defeated; it is for you to stand on the promises of God. God's salvation purpose is for you to be victorious no matter what your background brings to the table. Step into your greatness and own up to it, expose it, and let the world know God gave you great talents, gifts, and abilities; and that you aren't afraid to use or display them. It is your season to come forth and do great things for the Lord. Greater is he who is within you than he who is in the world.

John 14:12 says, "Verily, verily I say unto you he that believe on me, the works that I do shall he do also; and greater works than these shall ye do; because I go unto my father."

It's almost impossible to fathom us on earth doing greater works than Jesus. He is the Son of God. Why does he say these things? Jesus's time was short on earth, but what he installed in us will allow us to do many more things than he has done. So, we can choose to believe what Jesus says or continue to have low self esteem, feeling inadequate, unable to stand up for truth, apprehensive, procrastinating, being frightened—and the list goes on. Or we can choose to be everything Jesus says we can be.

David was a little lad who wasn't scared of anything; when others ran from bears, David stood up to the beast and challenged him. And when the lions roared at David, he stood there as if he hadn't heard anything. David intimidated the beast of the field, yet his family couldn't see his greatness or kingship. Imagine harboring and raising a king and great warrior in your home but never realizing what a great man he would be until your country was faced with the greatest challenge and threat in history. Goliath, the giant, threatened Israel's army; and your child, only twelve years old, accepted the challenge and destroyed this giant with one swing of a slingshot. The parents didn't see David's true potential, but God knew what David possessed.

David's parents continued to put David in charge of sheep. In their eyes, he was only a sheep herdsman. Nothing more, nothing less. They didn't have a clue what David had to encounter by being a sheep herdsman; David had to conquer any threat from vicious beasts in the fields, or else the sheep would be eaten. I am quite sure David mentioned these episodes to his brothers, but they believed in his stories like fairy tales. They didn't give much attention to his so-called victorious battles over the beasts in the field. So when God told the prophet Samuel to go to the house of Jesse, who had several sons, there he would find a king. So as Jesse's sons passed by Samuel, the prophet said, not one of them God chose to be king of Israel. All David's brothers were tall and strong in stature, but David was only twelve years old, still a growing young man.

After Samuel saw all the brothers, he asked whether there were any others, and Jesse replied, "Yes, there remains yet the youngest and behold he keeps the sheep." "Certainly,,David father apparently did not consider David as a fighter and certainly the one keeping the sheep could not be appointed king of Israel.." Samuel didn't ask their father, Jesse, what David's occupation was. He simply asked him to bring David to him. Once David walked in to see the prophet Samuel, immediately God said to Samuel, "Rise up and anoint him king."

Even Jesse, David's father, didn't recognize the gift of God in his son's life; nor could his brothers identify the gift of God in David's life. David had tried to tell his brothers about what was happening out on the field with the sheep. They had all ignored his voice. After David killed a bear and lion in the field as he kept the sheep safe, Goliath was no challenge for him. Goliath was just a dog to him.

My brothers and sisters, your greatness within isn't always noticeable to others and sometimes not always identified by friends, families, church members, spouses, pastors, bosses, counselors, and so forth. It's up to you to come to Christ so he can allow your greatness to shine. Your greatness within—God put it there for you to find. Use it and glorify God with it. Get on your knees and pray to God so he will reveal your true greatness within. Many have discovered their greatness and made many contributions to the world at large, and the world is waiting for you to do the same. Shout, "Glory!" Shout, "Hallelujah!" Greater is he who is within us than he who is in the world. (1 John 4:4)

CHAPTER 8

Stop Stressing and being Perplexed, BeHappy

During 1988, there were plenty of shocking and horrific incidents happening in the world and in America; bad news was repeatedly plastered on the news channels, causing depression, despair, and a cloud of gloom hovering over the world at large. A 727 jet plane crashed near Venezuelan borders, killing 143 passengers. Oliver North and John Poindexter were indicted on conspiracy charges to defraud the United States of America. The Dow Jones industrial average fell 140.58 points, causing a mini crash in the stock market. One of the world renowned televangelist confessed to an affair with a prostitute. In Bangladesh, a cyclone left five million people homeless and thousands dead. Pan Am flight 103 blew up in thin air, and America later found out the tragedy was by the hand of a terrorist group in Scotland; 270 people were killed. Then an earthquake, 6.9 on the Richter scale, killed twenty-five thousand people, injured fifteen thousand, and left four hundred thousand families homeless. The world was experiencing turmoil, the smell of death was in the air, and dead bodies were everywhere.

Look what God did. He sent a man with a song that would change the atmosphere for Americans and the world; the man's name was Bobby McFerrin, and in 1988 he released the song "Don't Worry Be Happy." This song was so appropriate and suitable due to all the things happening in the world. It was a hit song and on Billboard charts for months. People were in the streets singing "Don't Worry Be Happy."

God sent an angel of a song during some of the most terrible times we face; before the song came out, there were frowns on many faces and a look of bleakness. Many felt doom and gloom, but when the song was played on the radio, attitudes changed into a happier state, many danced again, and others repeated titled song, "Don't Worry Be Happy" to coworkers. They sang the song in churches, and on many sitcoms, they repeated those words. This phrase became the most famous phrase of all time. When the song wasn't playing on the radio, people sang it in the street; and when they didn't sing it, they repeated the title over and over.

When you get a chance Google the song for your enjoyment. The title of the songs stuck with all that listened.

This song had no instruments, just the artist making music with his lips, hands, and feet. By doing so, he lifted America's spirit, but it didn't just stop there. People from all over the world sang this song in different languages. All religious groups joined together in one voice to sing this song everywhere they went. People began to see the light, that it was important to be happy no matter what comes our way.

Frankly, when you read the book of Psalms in the Holy Bible (King James Version), David, the king of Israel, always reminded Israel to be happy in the Lord (Proverbs 16:20). To be grateful is to be full of praise and thanks for all the things God has done for you. Later, we will discuss some things you and I should be grateful for, but if you read the book of Psalms for yourself, it will reveal what I mentioned earlier. David, the king of Israel, always reminded his people to be happy and rejoice and do not be stressed and be perplexed.

In the New Testament, in the book of James, one, who happened to be one of Jesus's disciples, wrote a short sentence that had such a gist to it.

James 5:13 says, "Is any merry? Let him sing psalms."

Merry means happy; are you happy today? The reason for my asking this question is because in New York City and many other cities there are so many people wearing frowns during rush hour and in the house of prayer, better known as church. Some Christians serve God with a sad countenance on their faces, almost as if to say they wish they could be doing something else, something that's more exciting than serving God. Sometimes when you look at the facial expressions of people in church, you would think someone had shoved salvation in their hearts like a mother does her babies when they aren't drinking their mother's breast milk. Some of the most depressed and stressed people are found at work on a Monday morning and sometimes on Sunday morning during church services, especially when it comes down to the tithes and offerings, the audience expressions aren't too inviting. You would think you were at a funeral service in some churches. Yet we sing loudly for all to hear that Jesus is the answer, Jesus satisfies, Jesus paid it all, and Jesus is the best thing that ever happened to us.

Excuse me if I may respond; from the looks on your faces when you come into the church, while in church, and while leaving church are so convincing that there must be a better place you prefer to be. If we were totally honest with ourselves, there shouldn't be more frowns than smiles in the house of prayer. The devil is a liar! God loves a cheerful giver(2 Corinthians 9:7) because the word *cheer* means to have fun with it, and that's the kind of attitude that attracts others to do the same. In addition, even God's angels rejoice when one soul comes to Jesus Christ (St. Luke 15:10) while many of us sit in disbelief with no emotions during worship services. Angels in heaven dance and praise God. Can we praise God without wearing frowns? Praise was never meant to be painful. Has God been good to you at all? These same people who refuse to smile in church and refuse to lift up praise to the only one that wakes them up in the morning create a type of frowning ministry, which can be contagious, but oh, how quickly those same frowning faces quickly turn into smiles; and their voices become elevated and boisterous at the nightclub or company's holiday party. Finally, the same frowning people you witness at church will turn into the life of the party; oh boy, you should see them when they win the lottery or play scratch-and-play and win. They scream at the top of their lungs. They run and jump and dance all night long.

Oh, you think the things God gives you aren't valuable enough? Try enjoying new cars, new houses, a new job, and lots of money in your pocket without an ounce of breath in your body. I thought so! Well, each morning God wakes you up, and he deserves some praise, because not everyone got up this morning.

If you don't believe this, check the newspaper obituary. Stop stressing about everything that's not important. Stop stressing and being perplexed smile and be happy. Why?, because when you are stressful, it causes you to wear a sad countenance and that is contagious.

I will admit that there are things happening in our lives and in the world at large that will bring all of us stress and make us perplexed and it shows on our faces each day we live, but we must learn to choose to be happy regardless of the elements that appears in our lives.. The 9/11 terrorist attacks on American soil killed thousands of innocent people. The devastating Hurricane Katrina killed hundreds of people and left thousands of people homeless. The war in Iraq killed thousands of American soldiers. More currently, American faced with Covid-19 a devastating virus that took the lives of millions. After such devastating and unexpected things like these how can you not stress and not be perplexed? Well If you can find a smile or laughter, it will relieve some of the pressure and tension. The biggest element that kills people in America is stress, which breaks down our immune systems, making us susceptible to foreign diseases and sicknesses as well as mental illness which is belatedly increasing in America tremendously. I have been witnessing young adults that have the whole world as their oyster and so gifted and talented and they have a bright future ahead of them only to find out they are suffering from mental illness more so when Covid-19 started and even more so during the duration of Covid-19.

We understand that sudden disasters, hurricanes, terrorist attacks, computer hacking, and identity theft and Covid-19 can all destroy our quality of living. Also, we could be facing extreme gas hikes, higher taxes, lower pay, disobedient children, family troubles, the loss of a loved one, unemployment, homelessness, the loss of medical coverage, and so forth. Stop Stressing and being perplexed because we cannot let these elements dictate our happiness or damage our attitude and facial expressions. Be happy for life itself. Be happy. To know God is your helper should be enough to make you happy. No matter how high the bills reach, be happy. To know God is a healer and has all the wealth of the world in his hands should be enough to make you happy. Be happy to know God can fix your problems. Are any merry? (James 5:13) Let them sing songs, let them lift their voices, let them dance, and let them shout praises to the king. Who is the king of kings? Jesus Christ the son of the living God. Therefore don't stress or be perplexed be happy for God is a helper in the time of trouble (Psalms 27:5) (Psalms 46:1)

Our topic is "Don't Stress or be Perplexed Be Happy."

Proverb 17:22 says, "A merry heart doeth good like a medicine: but a broken spirit it dries the bones."

Ever wonder why comedy shows and comedians have become so popular and rich? Laughter is good for the soul like medicine is for the body. Laughter cures anxiety, gloominess, sadness, sorrow, anger, stress, misery, grief, and sorrow. People are attracted to happy-hearted people, and they tend to want to be around this kind of energy. A smile makes most people look good, and it says to others that you are approachable. On the other hand, frowns make people keep their distance and ponder the thought of whatever could be wrong with you. Frowns make people wonder about you, and they definitely make them judge you harshly.

The Bible says that if you want to make friends, show yourself friendly (Proverbs 18:24). Happy people smile! Practice smiling and being happy about something God has done for you. Is this what worship and praise leaders are experiencing when they try to sing praises to God in the church? Worship and praise leaders sometimes receive no response from the audience when they lift their voices and sing praises to their Savior in the sanctuary. Instead, in most cases, they have to pump the congregation up and make them come alive. Hopefully, the only reason why some congregations have no participation in worship and praise service is because they are tired, but if this isn't the reason for their silence, then maybe salvation alone doesn't excite them anymore, maybe their hearts are waxed cold toward God and his house, or maybe they think it doesn't take all the emotional high of clapping their hands shaking, their heads, dancing in place, singing with a loud voice, and moving to the beat of the song.

In Proverbs 17:22, King Solomon prescribed a remedy or medication that will solve most of our headaches, heartaches, pain, misery, depression, stress, hypertension, and so forth. Develop a merry heart, and it will do well for your body, soul, and spirit; but if you choose to have a broken spirit, it will dry your bones and cause decay and callousness. Stop frowning. Every day above ground brings hope, a new day, a new way, new mercies, more help, new ideas, new people, and the list goes on. A merry heart doesn't mean everything is okay; it simply means you aren't going to entertain elements of misery that try to dictate your happiness or joy. You choose to be happy regardless of circumstances. Let no man or situation take this away from you. Jesus said, "We are the light of the world." How will the world see our light if we carry a frown each day we live? Frowns are cancerous; they spread all over our body movements and expressions. They deaden our thinking patterns, darken our vision, keeps friendly people away from us and corrupt our minds and language. It takes thousands of muscles to wear a frown and only a couple of hundred muscles to smile. Do the math.

How can I smile when my doctor just gave me a bad report? How can I smile when my child was just murdered? How can I smile when I just found out my sixteen-year-old daughter is pregnant? How can I smile when I just caught my spouse with another person? These are some of the worst examples, but they are real, and each episode is disturbing and shocking. These types of cases could cause people to become violent, suicidal, and dangerous, causing strokes and heart attacks. In times like these, we pray, call on the elders for help, and read our scriptures. Sometimes we must get counseling, but most importantly, we limit the time spent mourning and groaning because they handicap our thinking capacity; they blind our reach for solutions and strategies that can help our situation, and they cause us to regret things we have done and things we didn't do; and none of these are going to make us smile.

So give grief a period—nothing more or less. Then breathe again and let the praises of God flow. God is good all the time, and all the time God is good. Despite our issues, flaws, mistakes, or bad times, our God is an awesome God. God himself had to witness his only begotten Son be killed by the same people he had created. Later, Jesus said to forgive them because they didn't know what they had done, (Luke 23:34) God was so heated and aggravated that the winds blew frantically, the thunder roared like a thousand lions, lightning glistened throughout the darkened skies, the earth quaked, the graves of many old Bible patriots opened up, and the dead rose and walked among the living. The angels in heaven were ready to be dispatched by God to destroy the Roman Empire and their armies, but because Jesus said to his Father, "Forgive them for they know not what they do(St. Luke 23:34)," our Father in heaven held back his fury of anger toward mankind, all because Jesus had said to forgive them.

So in whatever you're going through, God understands better than you think. He knows what betrayal, death, pain, suffering, and torture feel like. Now imagine your innocent son hung on a cross to die for a nation that betrayed him, and you had the power to wipe them out singlehandedly, but your son said, "Forgive them." Do you get the gist of the story? Jesus died that we may obtain eternal life, and in return he was crucified, publicly humiliated, tortured, and nailed to a cross, while many laughed and taunted him. Oh, but on the third day there was no more laughter in the air or jokes about the Romans brutally murdering the king of the Jews, Jesus Christ the son of the living God. There were no more tears, no more shackles, no more nails in his hands and his feet, no more thorns on his head that helped him to bleed out, no more suspicions about Jesus being the Son of the living God. Only God could rise from a tomb. Jesus rose from the dead, dear reader; therefore, you can rise in your community, home, in your business. Wherever life finds you, you can get up because the greater one is within you (1 St John 4:4). "Hallelujah!"

God can change the end results of your problems and make it work out for your good. The crucifixion was a tragedy for the disciples and multitudes, but the end results was that Jesus rose on the third day. Now what was meant to destroy the kingdom of God turned out to be the best thing for mankind's redemption. Jesus lives! That's why you should talk to him every day. Don't let a day go by without praising his name. He is truly worthy!

Keep a smile on your face and be genuinely happy. Don't stress and be perplexed; be happy about the small and obvious things. One example is that you are alive and breathing. You can walk and run. You can think and process information. You can read and comprehend. These are all so important. You don't want to imagine not having these blessings from the Lord. You and I have the opportunity to have a strong relationship with God. Why are we so sad and angry? Did God do something wrong to you? I thought so. Happy people live longer, and they can cope with challenges better than unhappy folks. Smile. Jesus loves you. A smile is a picture that says something on the inside is more beautiful, and it wants to blossom or come out.

But a broken spirit dries the bones. There was a prophet named Ezekiel who was told to prophesize to some dry bones in a valley. So God questioned the prophet and asked him, "Can these bones live again?"

His answer was, "Thou knoweth." Then God told the prophet to prophesy to these dry bones.

Ezekiel 37:5–6 says, "Thus saith the Lord God behold I will cause breath to enter into you and ye shall live: and I will lay sinews up you and will bring up flesh upon you and cover you with skin and put breath in you; and ye shall live; and ye shall know that I am the Lord."

Understand that the giver of life is the only one who can restore life to the dead. Dry bones represent death, no activity, emptiness, and nothingness; but when God gets involved, he makes those bones live again and forms the muscles and ligaments. He starts cosmetic surgery. Finally, God breathes in the soul of man, and man becomes a living soul. Wearing frowns and being miserable are similar to these dry bones. God brings these dry bones to life because dry bones profit no one, but they handicap people's lives and are infectious and contagious. No one benefits from its wretchedness; it's just like a frown. A frown displays that something is terribly wrong with someone, and if that person refuses to smile again, his or her frowns will rot his or her bones to the core, leaving the person miserable, depressed, dejected, and dependent on medication that causes sudden death, mental illness and much more. But I heard the Lord say to the prophet Ezekiel to prophesize to these dry bone people all around, so they could come back to life again. There's no glory in dying or being a walking zombie, which represents the walking dead. We should walk in faith, praise and worship, love, peace, longsuffering, and walk in the Spirit of the Lord. We should never fathom walking in death as zombies do. Jesus rose so we can rise and live more abundantly.

When you walk around, feeling sad and sorry for yourself, thinking no one loves you, all these kinds of emotions will dry your bones and keep people far away from you, because they don't want to catch the blues like you. The difference between a happy person and a sad person is that one sees life differently than you, and his or her confidence is in someone bigger than his or her problems, so the person chooses to be happy because the end result will be that the person wins.

Being happy is a choice. We all face circumstances, problems, and dilemmas with a choice of how will we handle them and which attitude will we select. To be happy, we must have faith in God; do what you must, and God will do the rest, believing that faith unlocks our closed doors and that there is nothing too hard for God to solve. God can open any door of blessing for you; as a matter of fact, he has already opened the doors for you. Believe this and receive it. If a person can decide to kill himself or herself and go through with it, like Judas did in the Bible after betraying Jesus for money, then we can make a serious decision to be happy and follow Jesus through our trials, temptations, tribulations, hardships, and complications, which appear in our lives like big mountains that are so hard to climb. It has never been a problem for God to forgive mankind, but it has always been a problem for mankind to forgive themselves and each other. Judas made a serious decision not to forgive himself and not to ask Jesus for forgiveness. He decided to carry his guilt and dirt with a hung-down head and a broken spirit—so much so that he put a noose around his neck and hung himself until he died. Rid yourself of this broken spirit. It truly brings gloom and doom, sorrow, bitterness, pity, grief, unforgiveness, darkness, and a dreary outlook on your situation; these are the symptoms of dry bones. Look at how happy children are; though they don't always understand things around them, they choose to be happy. Bad things shouldn't dictate your happiness. Keep smiling! Be merry, Don't Stress or be perplexed. Sing songs.

I knew a family that birthed a child with many birth defects, including kidney failure, a hole in the infant's stomach, and an artificial sack outside his stomach for him to urinate and have bowel movements. The child's parents blamed themselves and continued to wear frowns at times, but when we visited their son at their house, he smiled and laughed as if nothing was ever wrong. Hallelujah! He ran into corners and giggled; he played so hard with other children around about him, making his parents worry so much that they chased him, caught him, and make him sit down. To their surprise, he was the life of the party. He lifted everyone's spirit, and all who watched him rejoiced that he was a happy child, although at night time they connected him to a machine to help him breathe and assist his kidneys. This child was so close to death; but instead of feeling doom and gloomy, he chose to be happy despite what life offered him. It was almost as though he knew that in whatever life had for him, he was committed to being happy. Glory! What is your choice today? You may not be in a hospital today, but wherever this book finds you, choose to be happy. You're worth it.

Matthew 6:33 says, "But seek ye first the Kingdom of God and his righteousness; and all these things shall be added unto you."

Keep God in your life and continue to pray and read God's word (Bible). Please attend church; it is so important to associate with other believers. As you keep serving the Lord, God promises to take care of all the things you need to be successful and prosperous. God will give you the things you need but not always the things you want. That's why we should be happy and not have a broken spirit or be stressed and perplexed, because God is in control of our destiny, and only you can destroy your destiny with a broken spirit.

What is a broken spirit? A broken spirit is being overwhelmed by sorrow, "to have a contrite heart," to be completely repentant and shamefaced, regretful, and wishing for atonement for your sins. Instead of giving the situation to God, you take matters into your own hands, and your resolve becomes physical or spiritual suicide or both, just like Judas. God never made us to reside and wallow in depression and regretfulness for an extensive period.

You might ask me, "If God didn't design us to live in depression, then why should I feel happy if my spouse was caught in adultery? Why should I be happy after working fifteen years to be laid off? You are telling me to be happy when, in fact, I have done some unforgivable things." Being happy isn't an idea or assumption; it is a choice you make. Some people make a thousand excuses why they shouldn't be happy, and they believe every one. Not only is this attitude unhealthy for your progress and success; it is poisonous and toxic for your mind and soul. A broken spirit will destroy your emotions, health, and spirit; finally, it will take your life and soul. To be happy doesn't mean you will never be angry, upset, mad, regretful, or sorrowful; it simply means you give space (a period of time) for negativity, but you never bathe in it because it's unhealthy. To be happy is a choice. What are you choosing these days?

The old Bible patriot Job was very wealthy equivalent to Bill Gates; he was probably ten times richer, but he loved God with his whole heart and eschewed evil. God allowed the devil to test him. Imagine having everything at your disposal; suddenly, you lose everything dear to you. Would you curse God and die if you lost everything dear to you? Job chose to trust God and said (Job 13:15), "Though he slay me, yet will I trust him." Job chose to suffer the afflictions of his health and not curse God and die. Job's wife told Job to curse God and die. When everything was rich and plentiful, no one asked Job to curse God and die, but now when Job's body was decaying and full of bleeding sores, friends and family told him to curse the same God who had made him rich. They even questioned Job's relationship with God because of his sudden sickness and the disappearance of all his riches. Job was under an attack by Satan, but he chose to trust God. Job lost income, children, land, crops, and friends; even his body was afflicted with disease. Nevertheless, Job went through this attack like a champ. His faith was in the God of the universe, and because God found favor with Job, he gave him double the riches after God conducted this test of faith. God gave him more children, cattle, sheep, fine jewelry—and the list goes on. After many years of affliction and sickness, Job stood healed from all sickness, disease, sores, and scars; and he was a better man who had more riches than ever.

It is said that you can have one hundred rainy and stormy days right behind each other, but only one day of sunshine will make you forget all those bad days. Believe me when I tell you that after all Job endured, the memory of his sufferings was the last thing on his mind. He had so much to be grateful for, and his house was filled with joy, praise, entertainment, and an immeasurable amount of faith in God; whatever life tossed Job's way, his faith elevated him to a higher degree ever known to man. Nothing was too hard for Job's God.

So if you are going through some afflictions, trials, and tribulations, keep your faith strong in the Lord God, and you shall come out better, stronger, healthier, and richer; and the world around you will know it was the Lord God who brought you through it. Hallelujah! If you believe it, say, "Yes! Stop stressing and being perplexed be happy. says, (Psalm 146:5) "Happy is he that hath the God Jacob for his help, whose hope is in the lord his God."

Why be happy? I'll tell you why. It's because God is our helper and shield. That's why we trust him and want to live righteously and be happy. Please understand that God doesn't shield us from our personal responsibilities like rent, tithes, credit card bills, schoolwork, child support, parking tickets, tardiness, or alimony. Jesus told his disciples to render unto Caesar what was Caesar's and to render to God what belonged to God(St Mark 12:17); but even in the neglect of our personal responsibilities, God is merciful to help us and direct our pathway. It is our job to take care of our responsibility, and God will do the rest. God will step in when things become overwhelming. Be happy, people!

Psalm 128:2 says, "For thou shalt eat the labour of thine hands: Happy shalt thou be. And it shall be well with thee."

Depending on welfare and government assistance isn't what God meant for people, but thanks to God for these services, because they have helped millions get on their feet. Although life circumstances can come along and change our quality of life, it has always been declared that men are to work with their hands and by the sweat of their brows. Happy shall he be to eat from his labor and not wait for a handout. Working a full day or forty hours a week allows you to make an honest income. Earning an income is what a real man does, but beggars looking for something without working for it will break any man's spirit and leave a man in a pitiful state. Remember, we spoke of the broken spirit earlier, and we learned that a broken spirit can lead to misery, extreme depression, and possible suicide. Not working is trifling, especially when you can work and have the ability to do so. It's such a wonderful feeling and a sense of achievement to legitimately earn your own money. Money doesn't grow on trees, but it is earned through hard work. Work has its rewards besides money; you receive respect from friends and family, and your work helps the American economy. Your employment allows you to benefit from medical services and investment services while learning a skill and stabilizing a career that benefits your future. When your children see you working, they are going to want to work for a living too. Be happy. Don't stress or be perplexed because life has so much to offer you if at work you're not being treated fairly, pray about the matter and seek God's help first, but always make sure you maintain good work ethics; and for the unemployed people, here is some advice. Please pick yourself up, dress for success, negotiate your way back to employment, or start your own business.

Don't leave God when he blesses you with a new job or a raise. Keep praying and be happy. Smile while working because you are doing so as unto God.

Psalm 144:15 says, "Happy is that people that is in such a case; yea happy is that people whose God is the Lord."

If you belong to God, you should be happy. If you claim to have salvation, you should be happier. If you say you love God, you should be really happy for each day above ground.

John 13:17 says, "If ye know these things, happy are ye if ye do them."

Happy are those who do and live out God's word of truth.

Disobedience to God's word brings about sadness, grief, fear, misery, loneliness, frowning, and much more. Be a doer of the word of God, not a hearer only. Obedience to God's word brings forth happiness. Are you happy today? If not, repent and begin to smile. Life isn't as bad as you may think. Currently, many people are starving, with their stomachs are aching for food and nutrients. Are you starving today? Millions of people are sick with AIDS and other deadly diseases, having no real medical coverage or medical attention. There are so many things for us to be thankful for. We are privileged to enjoy so many amenities and support here in these United States, yet many of us are so unhappy.

Most of this unhappiness comes from an attitude of entitlement, thinking we should have what others have, even if we don't deserve it or can't afford it; we want to fit in with others, and when we can't get what we want, we feel depressed, become miserable, and wear a frown. Keeping up with the Joneses can be exhausting and unfulfilling, and it can dry your bones and cause you to frown and make you do mischievous things to get what you want. People wish they have what you have, live where you live, drive what you drive, and know what you know.

Stop it! Be content in whatever state you are in, and if you want more, do something about it. Be happy! Love yourself. Realize who you are and how important you are to God.

James 5:1 says, "Behold, we count them happy which endure. Ye heard of the patience of Job and have seen the end of the lord; the Lord is very pitiful and of tender mercy."

Have you been through some serious stuff? And if you are still alive to tell the story, you should be happy just for that. People who endured many things should be happy folks. Don't let the world or your circumstances dictate your happiness.

King David said, "I was glad when they said unto me let us go in the house of the Lord (Psalms 122:2)." Glory to God! King David was happy just when he heard the mention of going to the house of God. David sinned numerous times, but he never repeated the same sin because in his heart he loved God and enjoyed the relationship he had with the creator. The Bible says we should enter his courts with praise. What courts? God's house should be filled with praise and thanksgiving. If we would rewind the video footage of the expressions on people's faces when they enter the house of worship; you would see frowns for no reason, attitudes from previous events, angry faces, prune faces, frustrated faces, and that blank look so no one can tell whether they are happy or sad. These faces look as though someone is forcing them to come to church at times. You walk in some churches, and no one greets you or says, "Good morning." Can we even get a "Praise the Lord, brothers and sisters" from the ushers?

It's time to smile and be happy. Wipe those frowns off your faces, especially when you come to the house of the Lord. A frown dries your bones and spirit, but a smile and some laughter are medicine for your body, soul, and spirit, meaning we should practice smiling and laughing more than being in the frowning ministry(Proverbs 17.22). Laughter relieves pressure and creates a better atmosphere. Smiles and some laughter will keep your blood pressure down. High blood pressure stems from worrying, frowning, regretting, holding back on your true potential, not exercising praise and making a regiment of exercise and physical activities, and the list goes on. We are born with happiness; it was installed in us from the beginning of time, but life circumstances dares to try to impede on our gift from God, which is being happy every day we live.

John 12:43 says, "For ye loved the praise of men more than the praise of God."

Praising God is an exercise most Christians try to avoid, maybe because their lives are so busy and they have more important things to do; others may say, "Praising God isn't my thing." Certainly, it's not your thing; it's the thing God inhabits and expects from all of us. On the other hand, we pay great respect and give great praise and honor to movie stars, celebrities, famous people, and reality show personalities; and we have the nerve to raise the roof off, kicking and screaming and giving an ovation to these famous personalities, who could care less about us. But when we step into the church, we murmur and complain as though God isn't our superstar. What a great disparity!

Who woke you up this morning? Who started you on your way? When we enter God's house, we should open our mouths, praise God, and end all this murmuring and complaining in the church. Repent and be converted in the name of Jesus. Have these celebrities done anything for you? Do they even know your name? Do they even care whether you live or die? Did they leave you an inheritance for you and your family? That's a good joke. Yet we give these actors and movie stars more accolades than our ever-loving creator, Jehovah God. We rather praise men instead of our great God. Are we that blind? The giving of accolades to men profits nothing compared to praising the almighty with our vocal chords and dancing with happy feet, who has given you what you have now and that is life. Praising God makes you wear a smile.

Psalm 104:34 says, "My meditation of him shall be sweet: I will be glad in the Lord."

Being happy is definitely a choice only you can make; just thinking about the goodness of God should put a smile on your face. Meditate on the scriptures and his love and kindness. Be glad you have the opportunity to come to Christ while you are alive and well. Many people have lived their lives with frowns, and when they died, the frown remained on their faces as if there was no hope for them. Millions of people have died with so much to offer the world and not enough time to accomplish anything substantial because they allowed their circumstances and sadness to dictate their lives. We who remain have more time on our hands, yet we still wear a frown like a badge of honor. God isn't pleased with this. No matter what happens in your life, there are more things to smile about than to frown about. Let us hear from one of the most famous prophets in the Bible: Moses.

Deuteronomy 33:29 says, "Happy art thou, O Israel: who is like unto thee, O people saved by the Lord, The shield of thy help, and who is the sword of thy Excellency! And thine Enemies shall be found liars unto thee; and thou shalt tread upon their high places."

Moses, the man of God, blessed the children of Israel before his soon death. Some of his last words were "Happy art thou." Moses told Israel, "Happy art thou" because there were no other nations under the sun like them. God himself is your king, and because he's your king, he has helped and shielded his people and helped you through the hard times and fought many battles for you with his sword of excellency, and his words penetrated men's hearts; and because of God, Israel's enemies were no match for them. Together with God, Israel was able to tear down kingdoms, principalities, and foreign government; because of the almighty God, Israel was invincible. Imagine God, your king and ruler, giving you victory and making you more than conquerors through Jesus Christ. You still refuse to walk in victory only to accept a defeated attitude. Moses was trying to convey to Israel that although he had to leave Israel's presence, but Israel's real champion, the almighty God, would never leave them. He will remain their king, and with God on their side, that alone should comfort them and make them happy.

This message was extremely important for Moses to share with Israel, while his time to die was very near. Moses reminded Israel of all the victories God had given them during his time here with them. He alluded to say to Israel how happy they should be and not sad, because although Moses had to leave, God would always be with them.

Would you rather have Moses or God? I tell you today, dear reader, "Be happy" because God is with you, and he is more than the world against you. That's some powerful stuff. Moses was trying to lighten up Israel's grief of him dying, so Moses decided to spread more light and awareness of whom they belong to. They belong to the Kings of kings and Lord of lords, Jehovah God, the beginning and the ending, Alpha and Omega. Hallelujah in the building! He is the God of the universe and the world.

Dr. Martin Luther King Jr. wrote a speech before he died; it dealt with a dream. He called it his "I Have a Dream" speech. Without going into the entire speech, let me say that the main idea of it all was that Dr. Martin Luther King finally saw men and women of all colors and races willingly working together without noticing the obvious differences of skin colors, languages, and cultures. But they would coexist in unity and happiness to gain success and leave a legacy for generations to come. Moses, being an old patriot in the Bible, and Dr. Martin Luther King Jr., being a modern type of Moses, knew their time wasn't long on earth. Instead of complaining about their soon death, they encouraged and promoted unity and happiness. There were a lot of things these men accomplished, but so much more needed to be done. Instead of leaving the people with doubt and fear, these men left people with hope for the future, hope for their children and generations to come. Be happy because happiness is a highly priced treasure; it's very valuable.

Many of us think that if we commit all our hearts and lives to God, this will swallow all the fun and excitement out of our lives and force them into total seriousness, quietness, and solitude. And it will leave us in exile. On the contrary, God sent his Son to fulfill our lives so we can discover true happiness. Can the church say, "Amen"? Sad Christians aren't what God wants to develop.

Jesus said in Matthew 6:33, "Seek ye first the kingdom of God first and all things shall be added unto you." Why would God create us to be sad? This doesn't make any sense. Sin brings sadness, grief, emptiness, frowns, strife, regrets, troubles, misery, and wickedness, but righteousness exalts a nation. Whether you are rich or poor, the choice is yours, whether you will be happy or sad. Let me give you some advice; be happy about God's freebies, bringing you out of darkness into the marvelous light of salvation. It is free. Be alive, be able to breathe, be able to eat and drink freely, be able to walk freely without any help, and enjoy the breeze of a summer day and raindrops that fall by night and day. Enjoy the beautiful, white snow falling from the heavens to brighten our day, the birth of a newborn, having a sound mind, and the list goes on. If you insist on being sad, you will dry up like a prune, and the inspiration you will leave for others is a frowning ministry, and that ministry will dry up their bones, and they will become lifeless like you.

Television advertisers clearly understand that the impact and effects of a smile and being happy attract business and motivate people to buy. In most commercials you see, people are smiling and laughing, giving the world and all who view them a picture of being happy with a product or service, because being happy is contagious. Happy people *are* contagious. Try it sometime. People in the dating scene can tell you how effective a smile is; not everything has to be perfect for you to smile, but knowing the perfect one, Jehovah God, is all you need to spark your happiness. Just the mere fact that you were once lost and now are found should make you smile. You were blind, but now you see; once you were dead, but now you are alive. Praise God from whom all blessing are from ! Praise his holy name!

These are the obvious things that should excite us. Having a Mercedes Benz is nice, and winning millions of dollars from lotto is a good thing, but give me Jesus because "what profits a man to gain the whole world and lose his soul(St. Mark 8:36)." If you die today, will you be ready to meet your maker? Riches are good to have. Society proves this to be true, but there are more important things to consider. Can you take the Benz with you when you die? Can you take millions of dollars to the grave? God's economy doesn't run off oil, cash, credit cards, gasoline, technology, Internet, Facebook, Twitter, Gmail or cell phones. This stuff burns at the presence of God. These are all man's inventions to assist our world and its endeavors, but to think you can build your heaven on earth and take these earthly goods with you when you die is to live in total falsehood; your thinking is totally warped, twisted, and distorted because earthly riches have no heavenly value. Consider your relationship with God and then your family's relationship with the creator because that's more important than having a billion-dollar corporation. Little did you know that the first corporation to exist is family incorporated by God, and depending on how you run it, it will determine the outcome and success of it. Including God in your home creates a peaceful atmosphere, a fun place to be, and freedom from harmful secrets; and it displays unity and love. Not only do families live in truth and happiness; they can create and invent things that benefit others and start up their own companies incorporated by their state.

Riches can't buy real love. Love comes from God. Health and strength come from God. Salvation comes from God, and God's love gives us a pass to enter God's heaven, but our earthly currency is invalid in heaven; only heavenly currency is accepted: faith, love, peace, joy, goodness, gentleness, happiness, giving, and longsuffering. Stop trying to measure up to the status quo of the rich and famous, secret societies, and reality shows, because your heavenly daddy is rich in houses and land and holds all the power in his hand. Hallelujah! The gold, silver, pearls, and precious stones we value so highly on earth are guarded by security guards who have guns; and they are kept in thick, steel vaults with highly sensitive alarms; in heaven the angels walk on gold, silver, pearls, and precious stones as pavement. That's how rich God is. Many billionaires think they are on top of the world because of their billions but little do they know the entire wealth of the earth are just crumbs compared to Heaven.

John 20:29 says, "Jesus saith unto them, Thomas because thou hast seen me, thou hast believe: blessed are they that have not seen and yet believe."

We are included in this blessing. The disciples saw Jesus and had a hard time believing some of the things he said. Jesus said blessed are those like us in this 21 century who didn't see Jesus physically and yet believed his words. That's faith, people. We are some blessed folks because we believe in the footprints Jesus left for us in his Holy Bible, and that's even a better reason for us to be happy. Be happy! Please remember that whenever someone tells you to be happy, that means it's up to you, and only you have the controls in your hands to decide to become whatever someone tells you to be.

After reading messages of impact, I hope many of my readers will learn to be happy and stop wearing frowns. Frowns will give you nothing but pity, but a smile will win friends and give you great opportunities, a good reputation, a promotion, and great success in your life; but beware of those frown hunters. These are those who see you in your worst state of grief and despair, looking for an opportunity to gain from your bleakness. Frown hunters patiently and softly wait, fully determined to coerce you into fulfilling their desires and conquest. Beware! You want to be around people who look on the brighter side of life, people who look at your true potential; they want to see you succeed and be happy. The frown hunter's society needs to see and hear those who are worse off than they; this gives them a great reward and helps to create a pity party.

Who wants to soak themselves in pity? There are no smiles or laughter in pity parties. You and I were never created to drench, marinate, and saturate our lives, thoughts, and time into pity parties, but we were created to be victorious, courageous, bold, strong, loving, friendly, intelligent, spiritual, inventive, wise, encouraging, motivational, inspired, sensational, exceptional, and extraordinary. None of these words demonstrates or spells pity.

For all those who thought God has only one facial expression on his face, you have been deceived. The expressions on God's face are many. Did you know God smiles? Scriptures have said heaven rejoices over one soul that comes to Christ (St Luke 15:7). Who's in heaven? God! And one of God's biggest smiles is the colorful rainbow that gets everyone's attention. God made a covenant with all mankind that he would never again destroy the entire world with water, and the sign of this covenant is a colorful rainbow made as a giant smile from heaven. Of course, this is my interpretation. We sing a song in church, "God Has Smiled on me," and truly God has smiled on all mankind, all races, all colors, and all cultures. Thank you, Jesus! We are all brothers and sisters in Christ, and there are no little you's and big me's. In the book of Acts, the Bible records that God winked at our ignorance (Acts 17: 30). Here we see God showing his mercy with a wink; that's an expression. We seemingly hear more of the angry face and judgment face of God and very little talk about God's other happy facial expressions. It's also reported in the book of Psalms that God laughs at our calamities (Proverbs 1;26-28), especially when we refuse to listen to him and are hardheaded, so we go in our own way, totally refusing God's instruction and guidance, and we end up capsized. God laughs because we refuse to listen to his good instructions.

God even repents of some things he has done (Exodus 32:14). God, the almighty and great one, shows emotions. Who are we not to show any emotions as if we are statues made of stone? Be happy! Live happily! It's okay to laugh sometimes people of God. Laughter is good for the soul, and it's like medicine for the body & soul (Proverbs 17:22). It's okay to smile; smiling represents people who have chosen to be happy despite the drama going on in their lives.

Lastly, Jesus spent 90 percent of his ministry making people happy by healing the sick, raising the dead, saving souls, conducting miracles, delivering those in bondage, turning water into wine, feeding multitudes with five fishes and two loaves of bread, giving sight to the blind, making the deaf to hear, making the lame to walk, and casting out demons. Tell me, which of these would make people frown? Jesus was putting smiles on people's faces throughout Bethlehem, Bethany, Samaria, Galilee, Nazareth, Jerusalem, and Judea because the glory of God and the power of God were in full operation to turn men's and women's hearts toward God.

Look at the woman who suffered from the issue of blood. She was constantly bleeding and didn't know why and doctors couldn't make her well, but she heard about Jesus coming to town, and she pushes her way through a tough crowd to touch Jesus's garment while crawling through the large crowds to get to Jesus. Jesus felt her touch of faith as she pushed through the crowd and touched his garment. He replied, "Someone touched me." As Jesus turned to tell the woman with the issue of blood, "Go thy way and be made whole," her bleeding stopped immediately. The doctors' bills and visits ceased, and the scorning from others immediately reversed. Her redeemer lives and now she was made completely whole, and she was totally cleansed from her disease. Her frown turned into smiles forever, and her heart filled with joy and praises. Fix those frowns on your faces and turn them into smiles. Be happy and stop stressing and being perplexed because God has it all in control. Stop Stressing and being Perplexed . Be happy!

CHAPTER 9

Be about Your Father's Business

Now Jesus parents went to Jerusalem every year at the feast of the Passover and when he was twelve years old, they went to Jerusalem after the custom of the feast. And when they had fulfilled the days, as they returned, the child Jesus tarried behind in Jerusalem; and Joseph and his mother knew not of it. But they, supposing him to have been in the company, went a day's journey; and they sought him among their kinsfolk and acquaintance. And when they found him not, they turned back again to Jerusalem seeking him. And when it came to pass, that after three days they found him in the temple, sitting in the midst of the doctors, both hearing them asking them questions. And all that heard him were astonished at his understanding and answers. And when they saw him, they were amazed: and his mother said unto him, son, why hast thou dealt with us? BEHOLD, thy father and I sought thee sorrowing. And he said unto them, How is it ye sought me? Wist ye not, that I must, "Be About My Father's Business." After which, they moved onward to Nazareth and were subject unto them: but his mother kept all these sayings in her heart. And Jesus increased in wisdom and stature, and in favoring with God and man. (Luke 2:41–52)

H ere we see Mary and Joseph keeping the old customs of the Passover feast. Even to this day, the Passover feast is still honored and celebrated by Jewish customs. Jesus was only twelve at this time, and they all traveled to Jerusalem for this great feast. After the feast, Mary and Joseph were journeying back and noticed Jesus was missing in action. So they traveled back toward Jerusalem to see whether Jesus could be found. After much searching for Jesus, they couldn't find him, so they journey onward to Nazareth; and when they arrived, they found their son, Jesus, in the temple.

He was speaking, asking questions, and giving some astounding answers to lawyers, priests, scholars, and doctors of divinity. These men were considered the brainpower of Jerusalem, but Jesus, being the humble Son of God, listened to these men as they explained their versions of the scriptures and their perceptions of God to him. And when they asked him questions about various things concerning the scriptures, Jesus answered, and the words that came out of Jesus's mouth were so intense and profound that all who stood there, hearing him, were amazed and astonished at the knowledge he demonstrated at only twelve years old; these scholars who heard his voice didn't know Jesus was the embodiment of the word of God. In other words, Jesus was the word of God. Imagine a twelve-year-old speaking on the level of a highly educated doctor or scholar with several prestigious degrees and honorable awards, which had taken years and years to obtain. And here was a kid who had more smarts, wits, history, and wisdom than all of them put together.

Mary and Joseph finally found Jesus in the temple, and she asked him, "Why did you tarry behind making your parents worry about you?" Both Mary and Joseph had thought Jesus was lost or captured.

Jesus replied, "Didn't you know that I must be about my father's business?" If Jesus asked Mary "Didn't you know," that means Mary must have forgotten Jesus's purpose on earth, which the angel of the Lord had told her.

> And behold thou shalt conceive in thy womb, and bring forth a son, and shalt call his name Jesus. He shall be great, and shall be called the son of the Highest: and the Lord God shall give unto him the throne of his father David: And he shall reign over

the house of Jacob for ever; and of his kingdom there shall be no end. Then said Mary unto the Angel, how shall this be, seeing I know not a man? And the angel answered and said unto her, The Holy Ghost shall come upon thee, and the power of the Highest shall overshadow thee: therefore, also that Holy thing which shall be born of thee shall be called the son of God. (Luke 1:31–35)

These are the things the angel of the Lord told Mary before she was even pregnant. Mary had evidently forgotten these sayings of the Lord, but she didn't understand the things Jesus spoke of when he said, "I must be about my father's business." She kept these words deep in her heart.

If anyone should have known what Jesus meant, it should have been Mary and Joseph, because the angel of the Lord had appeared to both Mary and Joseph and told them. Mary had been "chosen and highly favored of the Lord to conceive in her womb a son and his name shall be called Jesus. He shall be great, and shall be called the son of the highest and the Lord God shall give unto him the throne of his father David: and he shall reign over the house for ever; and of this kingdom there shall be no end."

Did Mary forget this entire miracle from God? When did the angel of the Lord appear to Mary, telling her she was chosen to carry the Son of the living God? Not many days after the angel of the Lord appeared to Mary, the baby leaped into Mary's belly, as the angel of the Lord had predicted. What a miracle in operation! This was a holy thing God did in Mary's life.

So now Jesus was twelve, and he demonstrated his godly wisdom to the scholars at the temple, and for the first time, Jesus was making his debut in the temple, and all this was in the will of God for him to do so. Mary and Joseph had intruded into God's business. So Jesus said very sternly to his parents, "I must be about my father's business." Jesus was the perfect example of demonstrating being about God's business. Jesus considered his Father's business as more important than his parents' business for him. Jesus understood that God's business profited more than man's business. Jesus's business was to save the world from sin and wickedness and to give mankind a remedy for sin, which would lead to healing, miracles, salvation, and eternal life. Jesus didn't let any setbacks, problems, rumors, betrayals, beatings, haters, jail time, false accusations, torture, or even a crucifixion stop him from doing the will of God the Father.

What's stopping us from doing the will of God in our lives? Are we just talking the talk and not walking the walk? It appears that we are busy for the Lord in our church duties, but in reality and in our hearts of hearts, we care more about our own agendas and less about God's business. Wouldn't a lifestyle of caring less and less about God's business make us enemies of the cross? Enemies of the cross care nothing about the crucifixion or resurrection of Christ. All they care about is their selfish scheme of things and rewards for themselves; more importantly, enemies of the cross influence and point people away from Christ. Jesus has no effect in their lives; nor do they want their lives affected by Jesus's word or spirit, so they usually point people in the opposite direction from Jesus, having no commitment or guilty conscience. Their hearts have become callous and hardened toward God, giving space only for the enemy of their souls to use them as instruments of mass destruction in other people's lives.

The message today is to be about your Father's business.

The ultimate question we all must answer is, "What business are we really in?"

Believe it or not, you and I are all in business whether you believe it or not. We are all busy about something. What is your business with the Lord God? Is your business with the Lord just to receive help, riches, healings, instant gratification, or popularity? Are you going through a phase and following in the footsteps of your parents to become a pastor, getting close enough to God to attract a spouse? Maybe you are running for public office, and you need some votes, working hard in a church to earn a position. Are you in church just for comfort? Are you using the church only as a platform for you to display your gifts and talents?

What is your business with the Lord God?

Because if we aren't about God's business, then what business are we really in?

Jesus's mission was clear, defined, precise, and specific. It was to redeem mankind from the penalty of sin. The only way people could be redeemed from their sins was for someone to pay a price for all mankind's sins rather than to offer a pure and living sacrifice as a ransom for all sins. No one on earth was qualified to be the perfect sacrifice; it had to be someone pure like a baby lamb, one without any sin in its life. Only Jesus could do such a thing. Give praise to God, because on the cross Jesus paid the price for all the sins of the world.

Jesus was innocent as he lay on that cross. He was tortured and disfigure for all mankind to see. Jesus's business was to sacrifice his life to provide a remedy for sin. He became our living sacrifice on that old, rugged cross. Jesus did all the things his Father wanted him to do: healing the sick and diseased, raising the dead from the grave, giving sight to the blind, giving the deaf their hearing back, delivering many from evil spirits and mental disorders, making the lame to walk, changing water into wine, and finally preaching and teaching the word of God through parables and the demonstration of the Holy Ghost and power. These things were done to glorify God the Father and to get the attention of the multitudes. There was no one like Jesus during these times. Nor will there ever be anyone like our living Savior. How could they not see Jesus was truly the Son of the living God?

Clearly, Jesus left a perfect example of being about his Father's business; he was a great steward over his Father's business. The question still remains: what business are you really in? Judas walked with Jesus and talked to Jesus. He and the disciples cast out demons, healed the sick, and laid hands on the tormented, who were delivered. They left their businesses to follow Jesus and began to learn the work of the Father and to be about God's business; but among them was Judas, and in his heart was a desire to get close enough to Jesus so he could gain financial compensation from the Roman government. Also, he possessed a spirit of greed, and it was so strong that he was willing to betray and deceptively pose as a follower of Christ; but in his heart of hearts, he was the son of perdition or the enemy of the cross and a threat to the work of God. Judas was a plant from hell, though he appeared as though he represented the Roman government. But in actuality, hell sent Judas to stop God's business by betraying Jesus and destroying the work of God. This was a prophecy from the Old Testament.

You see, Jesus was very popular during this time because he healed people who were talking about him; former dead people were talking about Jesus, former demon-possessed people spoke of Jesus, former blind people talked about Jesus, and former deaf people began talking about Jesus. These rumors were reaching the Romans Empire, and someone had to stop Jesus before the multitudes started to believe Jesus was the real King of kings. As has been said so many times over again, our worst enemies are those nearest us.

Judas was in the betrayal business for money. What a horrible thing! Judas said in his heart and to the Romans soldiers, "I can give you Jesus by betraying him but make it worthwhile for me." He wanted profit for betraying the Son of the living God. You've got to be kidding me! Who dares to stand in the way of God's business? Judas was definitely an enemy of the cross. I guess he expected to be living large after he betrayed Jesus. So Judas carried on as though he were Jesus's best friend while planning a mischievous and evil deed he kept highly confidential. No one was to know, but Jesus knew, and he kept it until they dined together.

The worst thing to do to a thief or scandalous person is to let him or her play out his or her dark secret. Then just before it unfolds, you tell the person about his or her intentions and dark plans, which will shine light on his or her dark affairs against you, causing an uncovering and leaving the person with a guilty conscience and a broken spirit. You see, a scandalous person's reward is to do evil without you ever knowing when, why, or who had any part in it, which gives the betrayer great satisfaction and another latch on his or her belt representing an accomplishment. Hallelujah to the uncovering God we serve!

But Jesus exposed Judas right in front of his comrades, his brothers in the Lord. Judas's plan failed because Jesus told him to go and do what he must. These words must have eaten Judas up alive. In other words, they tormented him tremendously, but he thought that if he went through with the betrayal, he'd feel better. Jesus was on to Judas's dark secret. Jesus took the fun out of Judas's dark escapade. No one can devise a weapon or scheme to come against God and win. Glory to God!

Jesus knows your thoughts, plans, and strategies; and he knows your heart. How could you trick the almighty God? No way! Jesus left Judas with a guilty conscience and a tormented spirit, which haunted him day and night. Judas had only to look forward to a couple of hundred dollars, which wouldn't have lasted long. How could he face Jesus after this betrayal? How could he face the disciples again? The Christians during these times wouldn't have embraced Judas for such a disgraceful deed. Judas looked at the reward he had received for this evil deed, and now the money he had betrayed Jesus for became worthless. Judas had betrayed God's Son. Being full of mischief and evil, scandalous behavior, Judas refused to forgive himself and was too proud to ask for forgiveness. Instead, he conspired to take his own life because he couldn't daily live with his guilty conscience for betraying Jesus. This particular scandal had to torment his mind every minute of the day, so his only way to escape from the reality of it all was to take his own life.

Suicide will allow you to escape your current problems and

responsibilities at hand, but after death, those minor earthly issues you escaped from after death will add greater torment and penalty to your soul and a more horrible eternal destination, which you cannot escape. This leaves you to forever be tormented, while the burning in your soul to escape this horrific place will never be fulfilled. Hell is a place where torment is pumped up to 100,000 percent compared to your earthly issues, and the ambiance you enjoy will come from fire and brimstone and the eternal regret of all the bad decisions you made in life forever. Your best friends will be demons, and the agony and memory of all your wrongdoing will never leave your bedside; and all the opportunities and chances given to you to make things right will never cease to exist. Torment, burning, weeping, and the gnashing of your teeth are all you will live for. *That's what darkness rewards you with.*

But Jesus came to give you life. He came to light up your life and make you brand new inside. Why do we choose darkness? Why do we run to dark deeds? That is enough talk about darkness, because Jesus is the light of the world. Jesus wants to light up your world.

Tell me, what business are you really in?

Judas is old news.

We who live in the twenty-first century currently go to church, attend Sunday school, sing in the choir, and visit a prayer service from time to time. Musicians play instruments in the band at church. We preach and teach the scriptures, we fast and pray, we give to the poor, and we visit the sick; but do we search our hearts to find out what business we are really in? In other words, why do we do the things we do?

If our business with Christ is only to go to church to look good and make a fashion statement with our garments and big hats, then our business isn't to do your father's business. Or is it to create a big name for ourselves throughout the church communities? Maybe we are in the Christian business, because it makes your parents feel good about us. Or could it be that we want to get closer to the minister or his wife. Maybe we need some financial assistance from the church. Who knows? Only God knows your heart, but Jesus's business was clear and very much defined. He was about his Father's business. Are you about God's business? When some of us were small and young children, our parents made us be about God's business. Now that we are adults, it's up to us to be about our heavenly Father's business. We all have agendas and aspirations in life, which are good; but the Bible speaks about putting God first so he can help direct our path. What is your business with the Lord?

A gentleman was very instrumental in his church; he worked with choirs and helped with the order of services and so on. He was married for some years, but after a while, some of the church women became heavily acquainted with him and befriended him. One particular female in the church was really fond of him and wanted to take their relationship to the next level of intimacy, called "adultery." Although he participated in adultery, he didn't know this woman had HIV, so of course, when he found out, he had to tell his spouse. Somehow they were able to cope with this disease among themselves with some counseling and medical treatment, but the husband after a while became so vindictive that he started a mission to infect other women because this woman of the night had given him this disease, which he never asked for. All he had wanted was a good time no one would find out about; instead, he got something that could give him a death sentence.

So he started his quest to sleep with multiple women from his church. His plot was uncovered after several women came forward with symptoms of HIV, and all these women finally reported him to local and federal authorities. This man was finally jailed. What business was he in? He was in the adultery and revenge business. Yet he was instrumental in the church, but his business over time became recruiting women for his sinful pleasure.

I repeat: what business are you really in today? You don't need to tell me, the author of this book; but whatever your business with the Lord is, tell it to Jesus and be honest. Ask him to cleanse your wicked heart, evil secrets, and dirty mind. Stop the pursuit of this scandalous behavior in the name of Jesus Christ, the Son of the living God. Expose those dirty deeds to destroy others and terminate those evil plans to destroy someone's life, family, church, and business. How dare you think you can get away with your evil intentions and live happily by making others miserable. Get out of the scandalous business, because it rewards you with eternal misery, destruction, death, and hell.

Whose side are you leaning on? Hopefully, you are leaning on the Lord's side, but if not, choose who you will serve today, and please choose whose business you will carry out. Will it be God's business or the devil's business?

> For the bread of God is he which cometh down from heaven and giveth life unto the world. Then said they unto him, Lord evermore give us this bread. And Jesus said unto them, I am the bread of life: he that cometh to me shall never hunger; and he that believeth on me shall never thirst. (John 6:33–35)

> The Jews then murmured at him, because he said, I am the bread which came down from heaven. And they said is not this Jesus the son of Joseph, whose father and mother we know? How is it then that he saith, I came down from heaven? (John 6:41–42)

> The Jews therefore strove among themselves, saying, how can this man give us his flesh to eat? (John 6:52)

Whoso eateth my flesh, and drinketh my blood, hath eternal life; and I will raise him up at the last days. (John 6:54)

Many therefore of his disciples when they had heard this, said, is an hard saying, who can hear it. (John 6:60)

From that time many of his disciples went back, and walked no more with him. (John 6:66)

When Jesus, the Son of God, preached, taught, and performed miracles, his discipleship expanded and grew large in numbers. But Jesus spoke of eating his flesh and drinking his blood, which represented commitment to righteous living, commitment to serving the Lord, commitment to working for the Lord, and commitment to being about his Father's business. This type of preaching turned the multitudes about-face. The Jews took Jesus's sayings literally and didn't believe him. Why? Because it was forbidden in their religion to drink human blood and eat human flesh, which we call cannibalism. For some reason, I believe the Jews were too smart to think Jesus really meant eating Jesus's natural flesh and drinking his blood. Really? Jesus spoke spiritually using parables to convey a natural point, and he spoke strongly about commitment. They considered these words a hard saying, so they turned away from Jesus's teachings.

Their business with Jesus was clear. As long as Jesus taught and performed miracles, they stayed for the show; but when Jesus started talking about committing their lives to a carpenter's son, who claimed to be God's Son, a great disinterest fell on the multitudes. If you're not about God's business, then whose business are you really about? There are three things God wants to do for us: save our souls, keep us saved, and see us communing with him daily. On the other hand, there are three things Satan wants to do to us: steal, kill, and destroy everything good. Satan's business is also clear and to the point. His plan and ultimate goal are to deceive all mankind to believe a lie rather than to believe God's true word. He is the archenemy of the cross. His daily thoughts are to destroy all the works of God and his righteousness; kill and steal our great dreams and aspirations; and steal our opportunities, destinies, and promises God gave us. Satan wants to destroy our seeds of greatness: children, ideas, family structure, marriage, church, good leadership, business—and the list list goes on and on.

Be about your Father's business, and when you are about your heavenly Father's business, he will attend to your business. Hallelujah!

Satan tempted Jesus in the wilderness several times while Jesus was in the wilderness for forty days and forty nights. Who dares to tempt the Son of the living God? If he tempted Christ to fall and worship him, you can only imagine what kind of temptation he will use to lure you in your own demise. It would be better to choose to serve the prince of darkness who is Satan than to become an undercover hypocrite . That isn't the solution I am suggesting, but if you need my opinion, choose not to be an enemy of the cross (Hebrews 10:31). An enemy of the cross is someone who tries to halt the progress of God's work. It is a dangerous thing to fall into the hands of an angry God, who can destroy both the body and the soul; only God can destroy both. Working against the plan of God is a dangerous thing, and it could cost you your life and your soul. It could also have a great effect on your family's lives. God will expose phonies in the church. Hypocrites will need to make a decision whom they will follow and obey or be damned. God isn't playing with us. God is merciful, but he is also a God of judgment and wrath. You and I don't want to fall into the hands of an angry God, nor face his fury or rage. Who could stand against an angry God?

If you read most corporations' statements of purpose, they

tell you the type of business they are in and also the direction they are headed to and what they intend to achieve. But in all honesty, it is how they run and operate their day-to-day business that determines what business they really are in; that is the core mindset of the company. A statement of purpose is just a thought written down on paper, waiting for people to make it a reality. So it is with our lives.

We are in the church, our intentions are good, and we have good plans to do great things for the Lord, but it is how we live each day that shows where our hearts really lie and the direction we really want to go in. We examine and judge people based on their eye contact, dress code, body gestures and shapes, conversations, and character. God looks beyond all these outward appearances and sees the heart of a man and woman. Ultimately, a person's heart is most delicate and most important; our hearts are vital organs in our faith, and they are just as important as the hearts in our bodies. The heart is the most vital element in our Christian walk with God. God wants our hearts, not our garments (Joel 2:3).

When you travel to foreign countries, the first thing authorities ask for is your passport; and the very next thing they ask is, "What is your business with us?" You must be truthful, because if you're not, they can detain you, arrest you, or even throw you back where you came from. What is your business with the Lord? It's the blessing of God that makes you rich and adds no sorrow (Proverbs 10:22), your total purpose for going to church(. Is this all you want from God? Maybe it's God's power to get wealth (Deuteronomy 8:18); is this all you look for—personal gain? Is it the healing part you seek? But once you get it, do you drift far away from God?

I will mention the ten-leper story again onlyto prove my point. There were ten lepers in a city, and they were cast out from society. They couldn't work, shop in the market, or attend church services. They hid from society because people scorned them and kept their distance, because everyone felt they were contagious.

When these lepers heard Jesus of Nazareth was passing through their town, together with one voice and one mind, they yelled, "Jesus, have mercy on us." Jesus told them to go to the temple and show themselves to the priest, and as they walked in obedience to what Jesus had said, God totally healed them before they arrived at the temple. The priest later confirmed they were totally healed, but only one of the ten lepers went back to thank Jesus. Jesus asked him, "Weren't there nine others. So what happened to the other lepers? They missed out on being made whole."

Only one leper returned and received God's blessing, and Jesus made him whole. Hallelujah! The others received the healing but not the wholeness of God. So it is with us. We get what we want from the Lord, and then we continue serving other gods and giving God less attention while focusing on our real agendas, things that can't do what Jesus does. But the one leper who returned didn't forget what Jesus had done for him, and he wanted more of what Jesus had to offer. Jesus literally and completely changed his way of life, but he wanted more, so he went back to say thanks, because in his heart he wanted Jesus to make him whole. A daily relationship with Christ was what this former leper sought. After one touch from the Lord, this leper came back for more from the Lord. This former leper was going to serve God and be a witness for Christ during the rest of his days. Jesus made him whole.

The leper's healing was a gift from God, but being made whole takes some work. In other words, the healing was just the fringe benefit, but being made whole took going back to the gift giver and asking for more of him. This is exactly what the nine lepers missed out on. Multitudes of people followed Jesus, but only a few were made whole. The woman with the issue of blood, surrounded by multitudes of people, suffered from a continuous bleeding ailment for many years. Finally, one day she found herself stuck in an unrelenting crowd, so she successfully pushed her way through while crawling on her knees to get to Jesus, just to touch the hem of Jesus's garment. Jesus asked, "Who touched me?" And when Jesus looked, it was the woman with the issue of blood. He said, "Woman, be thou made whole."

People of God, there were multitudes of people standing and gazing at Jesus while listening to his words and being full of amazement due to the miracles he performed. But not all of them were made whole. The lack of wholeness keeps us searching for something to fill our voided hearts and souls. Jesus makes us whole with one touch. Do you want to be made whole?

After dating several men for several years, a woman found one man out of the bunch she loved so dearly, but he didn't realize how much she did until one day. While they dined together, she expressed her love and compassion for him, and he asked, "Why do you love me?"

She responded, "You make me whole, and there is no need for any other in my life. I am complete with you."

He replied, "Will you marry me?"

And the answer was yes. This was how the one leper felt about Jesus; Jesus was more than enough for him. Please understand that this one leper had no hidden agendas, no material motive; his business with the Lord was a desire to get more of Jesus and to do his will. This leper was undeniably going to be a witness for Christ.

A man owned a farm, and his dad had trained him to be a farmer. This man's son loved his father so dearly that after his father took ill, he committed to his dad that he would work his business and build it up so his dad wouldn't have to lift a finger to manage it. Little did he know that his father would pass away, and this young lad grieved so intensely for weeks, but he couldn't forget the promise he had made to his dad. So after the grieving ceased, he began to plant seeds throughout his farm, and a year later, his harvest became a hundred times more plentiful than in past years; and this young man continued for many years of harvesting good crops, all because he had committed himself to his father's business.

Are you willing to turn from your wicked ways to follow Christ? Are you sure you want to be about your Father's business? Christianity isn't a fantasy or an illusion ; it is a way of living Christlike. It involves maintaining your walk with God, daily prayer, daily scripture reading, fellowship with other Christians, fasting, and being about your heavenly Father's business. That business comprises witnessing to unbelievers, preaching, visiting the sick, loving your neighbors, and teaching the gospel of Jesus Christ.

Before Jesus went to heaven, He commissioned us to spread the gospel. Are we really spreading the gospel? Are we spreading the good news at work, school, and everywhere our feet tread? The gospel wasn't spoken in some dark and secluded place; rather, it was publicized and demonstrated throughout the towns, cities, states, and countries. Jesus went about preaching the kingdom of God and God's redemption power to all Jews and gentiles. When are you going to share God's business with others? Salvation is free, universal, and worldwide; it is the key to the kingdom of God. No one can enter the kingdom of God without salvation. Are our allegiance and commitment more to the American flag or any flag? Its reputation and strength are good only in America, just like any other flag for that matter. Or is our loyalty more to the flag than to the cross, which happens to be the universal symbol of Christ's death, burial, and resurrection? It has the power to save all mankind. This symbol represents healing for nations and can bring change to the world; finally, it has the power to give us eternal life. Where is your allegiance? Your talents and gifts all come from the Lord Jehovah God, and he wants you to use them for his glory. If you sing, sing to the glory of God and allow your gift to open the doors of opportunity to share the gospel of Jesus Christ. We all have different gifts on earth to glorify God and share it with others.

When you testify of God's goodness, mercy, salvation, righteousness, love, and kindness to the ungodly, you are doing

God's business; and when you do God's business, you are storing up heavenly treasure in God's kingdom. God's kingdom rejects cash, credit cards, bonds, checks, and traveler's checks. No earthly treasure is accepted in God's kingdom, but when one lost soul comes to Christ, heaven rejoices and cherishes this dear soul. What a heavenly treasure for a man and woman to come to Christ! You might feel that you aren't ready to do some of the things mentioned earlier, but if you don't, start small; you will never begin to be about your Father's business. Start with one hour of doing something that pleases the Lord, then eventually after time, that hour will turn into two hours and so on.

Minister to your family first and then spread the gospel to other places. People need to hear the good news. Spread the gospel to the world. Live the life of a Christian and make sure you remain honest and true to your faith in God and his word. Run from deceitfulness, lies, fraudulent practices, and sinful lifestyles. Daily build your faith in the word of God and keep praying. Remember to love your neighbors and enemies, and forgive those who offend you. If God constantly forgives you, you must forgive others too. We aren't above anyone else; that is why we should be humble and continue to keep others in prayer. Being about God's business is spreading the gospel, keeping his commandments, and abiding in his word. We all know what the works of darkness are: lying, stealing, lust, fornication, adultery, hatred, violence, crime, drug abuse, greed, selfishness, murder, strife, trouble-making, hypocrisy, betrayal of the cross, evil, witchcraft, perversion, wickedness, scandalous behavior, trickery, and vengeance. None of these mentioned glorify God; nor are any of these heavenly treasures stored up for you; rather, they bring about hell and damnation to you and your soul.

God gets no glory or praise from evil and wickedness. That's why God said to Israel, "Turn from your wicked ways, and then you can hear from heaven." (2 Chronicles 7:14) *Turning* means not participating in ungodly things mentioned above. God's business is feeding the hungry, housing the homeless, visiting the sick and disabled, helping the poor and needy, loving your neighbors as yourself, treating people with respect and kindness, and sharing the gospel with all those with whom you come in contact. God's business has a lot to do with worshipping God in the temple and adorning yourself with righteousness.

Moses was born a Hebrew and raised as an Egyptian; after much time passed into his adulthood, he later found out he had been born a Hebrew. Once this fact was revealed, he immediately turned from the Egyptian lifestyle, choosing rather to endure the suffering of a Hebrew family heritage instead of enjoying the pleasure of Egypt for a season(Hebrew 11:25). Please understand that worldliness is pleasurable for a moment, but then comes destruction. Moses turned, committed to being a Hebrew, and followed his heritage, which was serving God. After some time, Moses was all about God's business, which was to go tell Pharaoh to let God's people go. You and I cannot serve two masters; you will either love one and hate the other. Moses chose whom he would serve, and now we must choose whom we will serve. Let not your commitment to Christ become a seasonal lifestyle like the weather, but be true to it even unto death. Even when things get dark and dim and scarce, remember that God is our provider and supplier.

God is our help and strength. He is the King above all principalities and governments. He is Lord over the entire world and universal. Don't get it twisted. God remains the same forever and ever. We serve a mighty, true, and loving God. I ask you, "Will you also walk away from God's business?" So many people have walked away from doing God's will. Will you also walk away? Or will you swallow your pride and forgive yourself as God has forgiven you and be more than a follower but a doer of the word of God, demonstrating his work throughout the world, even in your community, knowing that it is by faith we please God?

You can't spread his message without first believing in him.

So today confess your sins and believe on the Lord Jesus Christ. Believe that he has the power to save you and to forgive you of all your sins, and now you are saved. Start doing the things you have been called to do. There is so much to be done because the laborers are few, yet the harvest is great (St. Matthew 9:37). There are more than five billion people on planet earth, but only one Martin Luther King Jr., Billy Graham, T. D. Jakes, Moses, Peter, Paul, Abraham, Oprah Winfrey, Isaac, Jacob, and one you. We need more workers in the vineyard. Are you ready to work to build the kingdom? Are you ready to be about your Father's business? Stop giving excuses like, "I'm not ready yet," "I have too many problems," "I am not righteous enough," "I am shy," and so on. These excuses get larger and larger until you get started doing the will of the Lord. Take one day at a time and then take a few minutes in a day to do something that pertains to God's business, such as witnessing to a friend or family member, starting prayer and Bible study in your home, giving to the poor and less fortunate, feeding the hungry, visiting the sick and praying with them, loving your neighbors and doing all you can to live in harmony with them, and forgiving people, especially family members and your enemies. Promote Jesus! Promote love. Train your children to serve God and have their personal relationship with Jesus. God chose you because he loves you and trusts that you will do the right thing. Handle God's business with no hidden agendas; give God your best, not your garments of excuses. Don't be a faker or an imposter. Be yourself and continue to be about your Father's business. Amen!

Now tell me, what business are you really in?

CHAPTER 10

God Wants Profit

et it be said, written, and remembered that God wants profitable servants in this lifetime and in his kingdom. Matthew 16:25–26 says, "For whosoever will save his life shall lose it: and whosoever will lose his life for my sake shall find it. For what is a man profited, if he shall gain the whole world, and lose his own soul? Or what shall a man give in exchange for his soul?"

To gain the world and all its luxuries and riches may be the profit everyone dreams of and strives for, but it could cost you your soul. It would be better to lose your life and the things you hold dear for Christ's sake than to gain the whole world and lose your soul. The true benefit of life on earth is the promise of eternity, and it is the things we do in our life span that will ultimately determine where we will spend eternity. Although there is much profit here on earth, God promises those who believe and trust in him that the ultimate profit is eternal life, and everything else is temporal. Unprofitable servants will be cast into outer darkness. If you bring forth no profit in your life, you are wasting your life and probably wasting other people's time too. Don't be a time waster. Wasting time may satisfy your quest in life for now, but the sad thing is that wasted time eats away at the quality of your life, stunts your progress, and destroys all your potential and possibilities, leaving your life to waste away in oblivion.

Why should others who value time suffer because there are manythat don't value anything, including time?

Matthew 25:30 says, "And cast ye the profitable servant into outer darkness; there shall be weeping and gnashing of teeth."

It makes no sense to live all your life just to be told you're unprofitable. God's people often question their faith in God and wonder what profit there is in serving the Lord. If you are thinking like this, maybe you are an unprofitable servant. What profit is God looking for? First, he wants your attention. He wants your heart and your willingness to do what he asks of you in the Holy Bible. He wants you to love God with all your heart and your neighbors and your enemies as yourself; and with these two commandments is the glue that holds the entire Ten Commandments together. Without loving God and his people, it's impossible to please God. He wants you to spread the gospel, which is the good news of God's love. God wants you to commune with him each day through prayer and scripture reading.

God wants profit. How do we bring profit to God? It's the same way when you spend quality time with your children, teaching them, reading to them, playing with them, correcting them, and instructing them to behave. Over time they bring profit to their parents by becoming responsible and law-abiding citizens. We were created to have dominion on earth along with keeping a strong relationship with God the Father; many of us got the dominion part down pat, but it is just the one-to-one relationship with Christ that we struggle with ever since the beginning with Adam and Eve. So God reconnects with mankind through Jesus Christ, the Son of the living God, to make it easier for men and women to connect with God through his Son, Jesus Christ; and yet we often struggle to communicate with him. Our heavenly Father cherishes every moment we commune privately with him and put our confidence in him. This is the profit God loves and desires.

Malachi 3:14 says, "Ye have said; it is vain to serve God: and what profit is it that we have kept his ordinance, and that we have walked mournfully before the Lord of host?"

During Malachi's times, the priests in Israel were corrupt and involved themselves in wicked practices, which gave the people of Israel a false sense of security in their relationship with God. These people of God began to see no profit or gain in serving the Lord or keeping his commandments. They felt that while they kept God's commandments and laws, the world around them was being blessed and walked around with no cares, having fun, while God's people were being persecuted for their faith and enduring trials and tribulation. The priests Israel looked up to were worldly and full of sin. So Israel became so sinful that God's word no longer had any impact in their lives. Sound familiar? God used Malachi to warn Israel to return to the Lord.

Malachi 3:7 says, "Return unto me, and I will return unto you, saith the Lord of host. But ye said wherein shall we return."

Israel involved themselves in hypocrisy, infidelity, mixed marriages, divorces, false worship, and total arrogance toward God; and they had no respect for the house of God. So God lifted up Malachi to probe Israel's shortcomings and lifestyles by using questions like these: Will a man rob God? Malachi directed a constant message of judgment to Israel to repent and come back to God.

Israel became sidetracked because their hearts turned away from serving their God; they were looking at the priests in the temple, because the priests were engaging in sinful acts while leading Israel into worship at the temple. Israel, seeing these things, turned their hearts against God. They stopped going to the temple to worship and stopped paying their tithes and offerings. They felt that serving the Lord wasn't profitable for them. Israel watched the unrighteous elders and priests prosper in their communities, while true servants of the Lord suffered persecution and hardship.

All this didn't sit well with Israel. God sent Malachi to Israel so they would repent first and return to God with their hearts, then with their tithes and offerings. Just because others fail to live by God's commandments and laws, that doesn't justify or qualify you and me to walk away from God. There is truly an underlying purpose as to why people turn from God; not everyone honestly loves the Lord God, yet they come to church, sing the hymns, pray in the congregation, and attend church activities; but their purpose is far from God. Israel felt there was the same old stuff going on in the temple, and nothing was being done about it; so why would it be profitable for Israel to do the things God required of them while overlooking the evil deeds of the elders and priests who would lead them in worship? Didn't Israel know they weren't judged by other people's transgressions, since relationships are judged by individual accountability? But when you get sidetracked by watching others indulge in sinful acts and remain in leadership, don't fall into a backsliding state because of other people's sinful indulgences. You pray for them and tell them the truth, but allowing them to change your relationship with God is almost hypocritical, because your commitment to God has nothing to do with your leader's pursuit for sinful pleasures and worldly activities,, but it has everything to do with your heart drawing near to the heart of God. But if you give space to temptations in your heart and become influenced by your peers participating in sinful activities, you will do the same as evil men.

In the last couple of decades, prominent bishops, evangelists, and pastors have been publicized and exposed for leading secret lifestyles of indulging in adultery, homosexuality, drugs, criminal acts, and hiring prostitutes with church funds while still conducting services, preaching, and teaching the gospel. Many of our pulpit ministers' sinful lifestyles have been plastered on our television sets, in the newspapers, and on the Internet. Yes, many of our prominent leaders in the pulpit have fallen from grace. Churches abroad were suffering from a great falling away from men of the cloth in the pulpit. This falling away from grace and righteousness has impacted church attendance, whereby fewer people come to church, church membership has decreased, loyal parishioners become visitors, and tithes and offerings shrink to just lots of George Washingtons (dollar bills). People have become discouraged after seeing the same leaders who preach holiness or hell fall into the same sins they preach against.

There is no justification for these episodes, but the Bible speaks of mighty men falling(Isaiah 3:25). That is why our faith should be in Jesus Christ, not in men and women, because they will fall and fail you. But God doesn't fail or fall. He is the same today, yesterday, and forevermore(Malachi 3:6) "I am the Lord; I change not"). (James 1:17) He is the father of lights with whom there is no change or variation. Someone may have drawn you to church, but that shouldn't be the only reason why you attend church. Check your heart to see whether you're in the faith. Be converted again because people willfully fall and make mistakes. People sin. That's why we desperately need the Lord God in our hearts. Why not put your trust only in God, who is the author and finisher of our faith (Hebrews 12:2) and the forgiver of our sins?

Jesus came down from heaven, not for the well but for the sick. Sin is a sickness, so if you are full of sin, Jesus wants to save your life today. We put our trust in the Lord God, so if and when others fall in sin, we can stand because our faith is in God the Father, not man. Knowing this, we should restore our brothers and sisters back to grace and not persecute them with our gossip, scorn, and ridicule; instead, we should encourage them and pray for them because it could have been us. Today's church as we know is just a building where God meets us if we invite him in, and it's a place where we worship God's holy name. But the true church isn't a building; it's your heart of hearts where he lives; and because Jesus dwells within you, wherever you go, he's there by your side ("Lo I am with you always, even unto the end of the world, Amen St Matthew 28:20) which means God will never leave you nor forsake you"). This is what Jesus said to his disciple upon leaving to go to his Father in heaven.

Jesus dwells within you. That's the real church. So when you meet other Christians in church, the room should be filled with the presence of God, where God's healing powers, miracles, saving power, and Holy Ghost power are in full operation. Glory hallelujah! What is a temple without people, and most importantly, what is a temple without God? Where is your heart? Multitudes of people go to church all over the world; some join their local church, others commit to leadership positions, and others just attend because it's something to do or maybe because it's a tradition to be in church on Sunday. Over the years in my Christian walk, I have noticed that the church services that have the fewest amount of people are prayer services. Why is this? It's because prayer is not about you or some well-known speaker;or famous choir instead it's about you and God alone. Jesus said, "My house shall be called the House of Prayer (St. Matthew 21:13)," but we have made it a concert hall, playhouse, Bingo and gambling house, dating game, and showtime at the Apollo, academy award show with actors and competitive artist. Jesus said, "My temple shall be called the House of Prayer." Otherwords, God house of prayer is where we worship God everything else should be secondary or not at all.

Do you want to try an experiment? For one month, call all your people and church memebers to prayer. Stop all programs and special events, no music; use only your hands and feet to keep the beat and your prayers. You will witness so many empty chairs; your congregation of one thousand will turn into double digits. Prayer is talking to God the Father, and when you have done it, he speaks back to you; he reveals and exposes your wrongdoing, and he will deliver you and set you free from whatever ails you. If you want to be a profitable servant, you must pray. Let your request be known in prayer. God wants to hear your prayers and to have daily communion with you through prayer and supplication. If there is no prayer, there is no profit for the church. (Jeremiah 2:11)

There was a lady who prayed for twelve years for God to deliver her son from drugs and prison; after those twelve years were over, authorities released him. She rejoiced with exceeding gladness and brought him to church; he gave his life to the Lord. God is good.

My mom prayed for me, and she was so diligent and constant. The end results of her faith were that God kept me from drug addiction, jail time, having babies out of wedlock, gangs, and rioting. There is profit in prayer. Profit is something everyone desires, whether they admit it or not. Big businesses want to see profits, and they need big profits. Profits help businesses stay in business. Profits help employers employ people; they help companies expand and grow into giant corporations, such as

Facebook, McDonald's, General Motors, Verizon, Microsoft, AOL, Google, and many more. This happens all because of profits.

What is profit?

Profit is gaining something from your labor. It is increase from diligently working at something; it is earnings after a forty-hour week plus health benefits; it is interest on the dollar, productivity, commissions, and royalties. The world and its economy thrive off profits; without profits everything we enjoy now would cease.

Ecclesiastes 5:9 says, "The profit of the earth is for all the king himself is served by the field."

In our personal lives, we want to profit. Marriage involves both a man and a woman, and both desperately want something out of their relationship. When neither feels there's any profit in the relationship, they will seek a divorce. People want profit in their marriage. Why? Because if you put work into something for years and you commit yourself to another, you judge your progress by the profits you get. What did you get out of the contract of marriage? Most people don't remember their promise to stay married "through sickness and health, for better or worse, for richer or poorer, till death do us part."

It is the same with finding a church home. We look for various things we can gain when we make a sound decision to become a member of any church. We look at how it will benefit our lives and our family's lives. That's called profit, people!

We choose our careers and jobs based on the companies, salaries, and benefits package (profit). The question on our minds is, how will this job benefit me? Employers want to make profit from their employees. They look for workers who are productive, on time, hardworking, dedicated, and willing to follow directions well. This is a person who gets along with others. That's why you should work as unto the Lord, who sees all things.

Do not work unto man, who has favoritism and maybe is unstable with his personal affairs. Always strive for excellence in your working environment. When other coworkers see you perform beyond the call of duty, they will either follow your lead or get jealous and try to give you a bad name. You should do more than what is required at work. When you see something that needs to be done, do it. Be helpful, kind, and productive, because when someone works like this, he or she becomes irreplaceable; the person becomes an asset to the company. An asset is something or someone who offers much value and substance. That sounds like profit to me.

God wants profitable servants. The word *profit* is often used and sought after in the business arena, but it is every person's goal to get some profit in life. Well, God wants profitable servants.

Proverbs 14:23 says, "In all Labor there is profit."

Profitable servants eventually soar, and unprofitable servants fade into the sunset. If you work a little, you reap a little; but if you work hard, you reap plentifully. The Lord God wants profit from his people, and he's tired of unprofitable servants being lazy and using excuses as a way of life.

Are you profitable toward God? Matthew 25:14–30 says,

> The kingdom of heaven is as a man traveling into a far country that called his own servants and delivered unto them his goods. And unto one he gave five talents, to another two, and to another one; to every man according to his several abilities; and straightway took a journey. Then he that had received five talents went and traded with the same and made them other five talents. And likewise he that had received two, he also gained other two. But he that had received one went and digged in the earth, and reckoneth with them. And so he that had received the five brought other five talents, saying Lord thou deliver unto me five talents, behold I have gained five talent more. His lord said unto him, well done thou good

and faithful servant. He also that had received two talents came and said, Lord thou delivered unto me two talents: behold I have gained two more talents. His lord said unto him, well done thou good and faithful servant. Then he which had received one talent came and said, Lord I knew thee that thou art an hard man, reaping where thou hast not sown, and gathering where thou hast not strawed: and I was afraid and went and hid thy one talent in the ground; there thou hast that is thine. His Lord answered and said unto him (listen very carefully) thou wicked and slothful servant thou knewest that I reap where I sow not, and gather where I have not strawed. Thou oughtest therefore to have put my money to the exchangers and the at my coming should have received mine own with usury. Take therefore the talent from him, and give it unto him which hath ten talents. For unto every one that hath shall be given, and he shall have abundance: but from him that hath not shall be taken away even that which he hath. And cast ye the unprofitable servant into outer darkness: there shall be weeping and gnashing of teeth.

As you can see and read, the above verses prove that our Lord God wants profit from our lives, and the gifts and talents God freely gave to us are to be used as unto glorifying God, not man. Please examine the first two servants who received their talents. One had five talents, and the other had two talents. Each of these servants doubled what they had received from the Lord. How did they do this? They put their talents and abilities to work through trade and drew enough interest that over time they were able to double what they had. Trade represents economy, marketplace, and high-yield investment. Many of us sit back on our talents, abilities, and gifts, becoming selfish, stingy, and prideful—never undertaking the opportunity to make our talents work for us. When our Lord comes back to claim his talents from you, will you be prepared? It is our job to be good stewards over the talents and gifts God has given us. As you read farther, you see God distributed according to each of the servants' abilities. Here's where many of us drop the ball.

God distributes his gifts and talents proportionately accordingly to our abilities; instead of handling what God gave us, we choose to desire and envy those who have more talents than we do while hiding our own talents. Listen up, people. God loves diversity. You and I are definitely not the only Christians on planet earth; nor can one person do it all, but being unified, we can all be profitable to God. With this in mind, take your one talent and work it like the Lord God gave it to you, and then he will add to your one talent and uncover many of your hidden gifts.

Let us look at the verse dealing with the unprofitable servant, who had only one talent and decided to hide it instead of investing it. God called him wicked and slothful. *Wicked* means sinful, immoral, corrupt, and intentionally capable of harming others as well as yourself. The word *slothful* means lazy, idle, indolent, inactive, and lethargic. Jesus used both words, *wicked* and *slothful*, to describe an unprofitable servant. This means the unprofitable servant allowed sin and corruption to enter his heart, thereby causing him to be purposely lethargic in the things he knew were right to do. The unprofitable servant knew what was necessary but refused to do so because of his evil ways and sluggish attitude. God called him wicked and slothful.

The servant who had one talent took extended time to dig a six-foot grave to hide his one talent. Digging a grave can literally take two to four hours depending on the texture of the ground; this time could have been invested in the viable economy. Instead of investing quality time to bring forth profits, he now found himself digging deep in the ground to hide his talent. Imagine hiding your gift from opportunities that could make your career soar like a rocket ship. Now the God who takes inventory of your profits, working capacity, and progress finds that you are burying your gifts and talents in a grave while envying others, who are working their talents and gifts to the maximum. So instead of reporting your profits, you gain from hard works and try to authenticate excuses of why you're not profitable. Excuses equal zero. He knew God would "reap where he sowed not and gather where I have no straw," but then the unprofitable servant said this. He was fearful, so his fear had caused him to bury his one talent and then give it back to God. So God became angry, took the one talent, and gave it to the most profitable servant, who had the most talents. Why did God do this? The one with the most talents had proved to be the most profitable and responsible; he had proved he could handle more. Can you handle more, or are you afraid?

God loves to invest in profitable servants because they bring forth profits to him.

In the New Testament, Saul was a scholar and highly educated man, but he had this thing for killing people who believed in Jesus, called Christians. Saul brought forth much profit to those who wanted to keep Judaism alive and well. Also, the Roman Empire wanted Christians to be killed and tortured because they believed in another king.

Saul was committed to getting the job done to slaughter Christians for a living, which brought forth profit to the powers that be in Rome. It was considered treason to speak of an upcoming king while a king yet sat on the throne, and worshipping another king while a king was on the throne was total betrayal. Killing Christians was in the best interest of Rome. Saul killed hundreds, even thousands, of innocent Christians because they believed in another king, Jesus, the King of kings, not in the king of Rome. So instead of killing Saul instantaneously, God decided to turn Saul's world upside down by bringing him to his knees so he would be converted. Saul was on a horse on his way to Damascus, sending threats of slaughtering the disciples of the lord; and as he journeyed onward, the light of God shone on him, and he fell to the ground and heard the voice of the Lord say, "Saul, why persecutes thou me?"(Acts 9:4) God took this murderer and converted him to be a Christian. God changed his name from Saul to Paul, cleaned him up, and sent him on his way to do God's work. The name change was necessary because the history behind Saul's name was as a murderer, but after his encounter with the Lord Jesus Christ, the history behind his name was as apostle, disciple, and prophet.

Do you need a name change? Why on earth would God do such a thing for a vicious and brutal man? It was done for God's glory! Both the Romans and priests profited from Saul's way of life. Now God profited from Paul's new lifestyle. Saul eventually became an apostle for many churches, teaching and preaching the gospel of the Lord Jesus Christ; and he wrote most of the New Testament. Of course, the church didn't accept Paul as easily as you would imagine, since Paul had once been an enemy of the cross. Why would God need him? Profits! And may I add that this has everything to do with God's business. God wants profits! Paul was a highly educated man, who possessed a quality that the job must be done at whatever cost. Who wouldn't want someone like this in his or her business?

Life is a gift from God. What have you done with your life since you entered this world? God from heaven gave you your life. It wasn't merely a conception; it was the plan of God the Father. You were chosen out of millions of sperm to become who you are today. Take inventory of your life and see what your accomplishments are. Take notice of the things you're doing and people you are helping. Life is a gift from God—you better believe it; and one day we all will answer to God for the deeds done in our bodies and lives. God wants profit.

The scriptures mention, "For bodily exercise profit little: but

Godliness is profitable unto all things, having promise of the life that now is, and of that which is to come" (1 Timothy 4:8). Regardless of whether you choose to serve God, either way you will make a choice, and someone will profit from your choice one way or another. Why not reroute your life to being a follower of Jesus Christ because he *means you no harm*? Nor does he want you to die and lose your soul. On the other hand, Satan wants to attract, lure, deceive, and swindle you to follow his agenda, which is to steal, kill, and destroy your life and soul. But that's not all; he wants to disintegrate your dreams and goals, and load you up with fear and doubt to detour your opportunities, destroy your marriage, scatter your church, and divide your family. But Jesus wants to give you life, freedom, salvation, healing, unity, deliverance, and miracles. Jesus doesn't sound like someone you should run from; instead, he's someone you should run to.

Bodily exercise is profitable, but compared to your heart and soul, there's no comparison. Bodily exercise profits little, but 1 percent of a million is ten thousand, so a little profit is always better than no profit at all. Had the man with one talent produced a little profit, God would have pleasurably rewarded him. Instead, he chose not to do anything, and because of his nothingness, God cast him into outer darkness. God rewards profitable servants and calls them a good and faithful servant; he rebuked the unprofitable servant and called him wicked and slothful. Then he cast him into outer darkness. You are alive for a reason, and clearly it isn't to do anything or nothing, but it is to serve God while working out your mission in life.

Once there was a young man who found a job with a very good company, which had great benefits, retirement plans, and investment plans. It wasn't readily available for new employees, but after two years, they could apply for these benefits. After two years, employees were to report to human resources and enroll in many of these benefit packages. This young man kept putting off each year applying for the benefit package each year.. They even sent him letters concerning enrolling in his benefit packages. He was used to making $700 a week; if he enrolled in these benefit packages, his payroll check would be reduced by $200. He couldn't come to grips with this transaction, so he waited and put off the decision for years. Finally, he approached retirement age and witnessed his coworkers buying houses, purchasing boats, starting new businesses, and retiring early with lots of money. He asked one of his coworkers where all this money had come from. His fellow coworker said thirty years ago, he had gone to human resources and enrolled in a benefits package, and his employer took the maximum amount out of his check, investing the money in his retirement 401K. And because of those past investments, he accumulated $100,000.

The man asking the question put his head down and walked away. A couple of years later, he was fired and didn't have any savings or investment plan, only a paycheck, which ceased because the company giving him the opportunity to become well off was downsizing. They laid off several hundred of their employees.

The paycheck was the talent or seed money, nothing more, but the extended benefits were the tools or marketplace to invest their talent in to double or triple his investment, which would have added extra value to his future. But because he did nothing, he was forced to find another job and start all over again. After many years of not finding a job, his end result was to get government assistance to live.

If we take inventory of our lives, we may find that we aren't as profitable as we think we should be for Christ. Don't concern yourself with your past; just deal with the present. Today you can make things right, so repent and be converted. Start living a profitable life for God. God is merciful and loving, and he promises he will never leave you, so trust him each day. Turn from your wicked ways and live righteously. Remember, our Lord Jesus Christ is the only perfect one; we are imperfect, but Christ makes us perfect in him. Hallelujah!

How can you be profitable to God?

1. You must be born again (salvation is free). Confess your sins to Jesus, repent of them, and turn from your evil ways. You must confess the Lord Jesus Christ as your Lord and Savior, and you are now born again. This is the first step toward accepting salvation. After you have done this, you must move step by step to mature in your salvation so your commitment to Christ will withstand anything that tries to halt your progress. Here are some steps to mature as a born-again Christian.
2. Read your Bible.
3. Pray every day.
4. Attend a church that has good teaching, preaching, and outreach.
5. Find your purpose in life and get busy for the kingdom of God.
6. Obey God and love others as you love yourself and keep his commandments.

How you can be profitable in your church?

1. Be faithful and prompt in attendance.
2. Pay your tithes and offerings because they help the ministry.
3. Find your position in ministry and work it with all your heart.
4. Participate in worship and praise, service, and witness to nonbelievers with your group.
5. Ask God, "What would you have me do in this ministry?

How can I be profitable to my family?

1. Love one another and tell each other of your love.
2. Forgive each other and keep the communication open.
3. Pick a day out each week and time when you conduct prayer, sing, and have a Bible study. Plan a fun night and create or build something together. Create a family time without TV, Internet, cell phones, and so forth.
4. Read the scriptures and let everyone speak and express himself or herself. Share one another's struggles and accomplishments.

How can you be profitable in your community?

1. Get to know your community leaders and what they represent.
2. Attend community meetings to find out what's going on in your community and where you live. Give ideas and solutions to be a better community. Lend your time and energy to help your community.
3. Pray for your community and its leaders.
4. Be profitable to your employer.
5. Be punctual.
6. Work hard, finish projects given, and go beyond mediocrity. Do exceptional work, let your work speak for itself, and put your signature on it.
7. Render your service to help others, who are overloaded with work.
8. Have a conversation with your bosses, pray for them and the success of their company, and celebrate their birthdays and accomplishments.
9. Visit the human resources department and get information on investment opportunities, benefit packages, higher

positions, new opportunities for education reimbursement, and so forth.

How can you be profitable in your marriage?

1. Focus on things your spouse likes and cares about.
2. Pray together five to ten minutes a day. Read your Bible.
3. Attend church together.
4. Take vacations together and learn to have fun.
5. Learn to be kind and forgive each other.
6. Set goals for your lives and celebrate your accomplishments.
7. Discuss your struggles, good and bad. Don't hide. Expose little things that can become cancerous.
8. Don't let anyone, even family, come between you and your marriage. Keep secrets out of your marriage. Express your weaknesses and strengths with your spouse. Marriage isn't a fifty/fifty experience. On the contrary, marriage is 100 percent from both spouses.

The mere fact that you both entered into marriage simply means both of you saw profit in each other so much that no one else could fill each other's mold; that's why your relationship went from dating to marriage, which is a true commitment. As much as possible, do your best to make the good outweigh the bad, because the good stuff is the profit you're looking for. It helps when other elements of surprise appear or try to invade your happiness. Prayer is the glue that will seal your marriage; no matter what comes your way, your marriage will last.

One of Job's friends asked Job a question. Job 22:2 says, "Can a man be profitable unto God, as he that is wise may be profitable unto himself?"

We can be profitable to God by committing our lives to Jesus, being obedient to his word, following him, and putting our gifts and talents to work for God's purpose. Job was such a profitable servant to God that God bragged to Satan about Job. Can God brag on you?

Job 1:6–8 says, "Now there was a day when the sons of God came to present themselves before the Lord, and Satan came among them. And the Lord said unto Satan whence thou comest? Then Satan answered the Lord and said from going to and fro in the earth, and from walking up and down in it. And the Lord said unto Satan, hast thou considered my servant Job, that there is none like him in the earth, perfect and an upright man, one that feareth God and escheweth evil."

I wonder whether God could brag on our lives and lifestyles. The Lord bragged to Satan about Job's righteous living and that he feared God and ran from evil before it occurred. What a great strategy it is to run from evil the moment you see it appear! Satan asked God to take away the hedge he had put around Job's health, work, substance, and children; and he would curse God to his face, Satan claimed. Holiness brings about God's protection over your health, income, family, and life. You and I are under God's protection, and Satan can't touch us unless God gives him permission to do so. Hallelujah! God gives permission only when he can depend on that person or if that person deserves God's judgment.

Job is a prime example of a profitable servant. He lived his life by serving God and teaching his children about God. He prayed and didn't brag about his riches, which God had bestowed on him, because Job was richer than rich. In those days, they determined their riches by the cattle they kept, family size, and the spread of land they possessed. Job was rich and happy, and he was a profitable servant to God. God brags about his profitable servants. Living righteously brings profit to God and to us too; unrighteousness makes us a liability to God, the church, and our family.

Unrighteousness brings destruction, damnation, curses, darkness, and death to the body and soul, but righteousness exalts a nation, and with unrighteousness, it destroys a nation or people. Being a profitable servant doesn't mean you will never suffer temptation, tribulations, hard times, surprise attacks, or health issues; it merely means you will serve the Lord no matter what occurs. You choose to trust in the Lord because there is a greater reward awaiting you. Job lost his children, all his cattle and herds, friends, and family members. Yet he trusted in the Lord, never doubting but always trusting in God and not in the arms of flesh. The arms of flesh are people, government, and the world system. Job said to his wife and friends, who stood by watching him deteriorate slowly, "Though he slay me yet will I trust him."

His friends and family still persisted to ask Job, "Why don't you curse God and die? Why don't you just give up and denounce God?"

Job exclaimed, "Though he slay me yet will I trust him." How powerful are these words, even unto this day and time! These words spell out a total dedication to serve God with every fiber left within you no matter what life hands you. This was Job's position and stance with God, even though his wife tried to convince him to curse God and die. Job repeated, "Though he slay me yet will I trust him."

Imagine being wealthy for many years and lose everything overnight. What a horrible travesty to have experienced, and this occurrence could very well happen to anyone. The elements of being poor are very much different than the reward of being rich because the poor are very acquainted with lack and deficiency, sickness, and misery. Job was rich, healthy, and well known; he also had a large family and lots of cattle, land, and properties. Then one day Job lost everything, even his health, in one day. Wow! Job's health worsened, and the money was gone. He had only his faith in God. God lifted the hedge of God's protection from Job's life and allowed Satan to mess with Job's children, his business, and his health; but God instructed Satan not to touch his soul. So within moments of time, Job began to lose everything dear to him, but the main idea of the story was that Job was already a profitable servant of the Lord; and God put Job through a test. Job came out with double of everything he had lost. Hallelujah!

Job 41:10 says, "And the Lord turned the captivity of Job, when he prayed for his friends: also the Lord gave Job twice as much as he had before. Then came there unto him all his brethren, and all his sisters, and all they that had been of his acquaintance before, and did eat bread with him in his house; and they bemoaned him, and comforted him over all the evil that the Lord had brought upon him; every man also gave him a piece of money, and a new beginning."

You always come out with more when you are a profitable servant. God rekindled old friendships, reunited family members, and gave Job double for his troubles. Job kept prayer in his life and testified of God's goodness over and over to all those who would listen. Job never lost faith in God. His faith in God increased despite losing everything except his mind and soul. Job refused to curse God and die; instead, he blessed God's name all throughout his sufferings and poverty state. So God rewarded Job with stable health and wealth, which was double the size he had before, and he brought his family back together. What more could you ask for?

Jeremiah 2:11 says, "Hath a nation changed their god's which are yet no god? But my people have changed their glory for that which doth not profit."

And the word of the Lord came to the prophet Jeremiah, asking a question of Israel: "Have you changed gods from the one and only God?" Is it true that some of us have changed gods from the one and only God? It was clear and known to Jeremiah that Israel changed gods like they changed underwear. When they suffered, they repetitiously cried aloud to the Lord God, but when they prospered, they forgot God and followed other gods. They ignored God's glory for what didn't profit them anything. What do you get out of worshipping a dead god? A god that can't answer you back, a god you can destroy, a god that is weaker than you, a god that doesn't move or show any expressions on its face, a god that cannot come to your rescue? Why waste your time and energy serving and worshipping a counterfeit god; wouldn't you prefer a real God, who speaks back and performs miracles? Or do you rather continue to see whether your dead god will one day awake from the dead? Serve and obey the only true Jehovah God. Israel would see the hand of God move during their turmoil. God's hands opened the Red Sea, God's hands put a consuming fire in front of the Egyptian army to protect Israel from the Egyptians' revengeful fury, and God's hands flatten the wall of Jericho, which was never done before.

God's hands destroyed Israel's enemies by night and by day. Many nations admitted and advertised to their people, Israel, that God was and is the Lord God. Nations and world leaders in Moses's days feared Jehovah God. Miracles after miracles God executed on behalf of Israel, and yet none of these things were enough to keep Israel committed to God; Israel suffered from attention deficit disorder, no matter what God did for Israel. They found reasons to turn to dead gods.

There's no profit in serving dead gods, only destruction. What is the name of your dead god? Drugs, sex, pornography, adultery, liquor, stealing, killing, statues, money, jewelry, scandalous mischief, lying and cheating, greed and selfishness, gambling, perversion, gangbanging, houses and land, fame and fortune, prostitution, pimping children and women, witchcraft, pride— these are all false gods and cannot give you life or perform miracles. They need your involvement to exist, but you can exist without any of these. So, who is more powerful than all these things we entrapped ourselves in? God the Father doesn't need us to exist because he created all of us in his image, so if we fail to heed his call, God will continue to exist and have his being. Dead gods need people to serve them to exist, and those who serve them are destroyed.

It is those inner cravings of the heart that want everything except God because man was born in sin after Adam and Eve sinned. We change our profitable relationship with God to commit adultery with dead gods, which bring us destruction, misery, pain, and spiritual cancer of the heart. What is spiritual cancer of the heart? It is when your heart for the true God slowly dies out and deteriorates because of your forcefulness to run to unprofitable gods. Your acceptance and warped understanding to think a relationship with God doesn't profit anything causes you to feel you are missing out on something better, so you seek worldly pleasures over God until you find yourself in the land of hopelessness and sinfulness. Only then do you regret the wages of what sin pays you. Just living a righteous life profits your current life and future, but living a sinful life without God pays a wage of death. The scriptures have told us that the wages of sin are death, but the gift of God is eternal life. No matter how good your sinful pleasures make you feel mentally and physically, the wages or profit you will eventually receive is death. After you have completed your quest to quench your fleshly desires and sinful appetite, Jesus Christ, the Son of the living God, stands waiting for you to come back to him in prayer and supplication before it's too late. Come back home!

Every time Israel lusted after the gods of other nations, the presence of God left them, and their enemies overtook them, enslaved them, raped their wives and children, beat them, tortured them, and killed their elders and priests. Why would you want to enjoy sin for a season and end up like Israel in bondage? We weren't created to live in a box or jail cell, nor were we created to live in quicksand, which is a metaphor for involving and participating in things or with people who continuously put us down in a pit of bondage and in sinful activities every time we try to do better or be better. Stay on the Lord's side. Don't even be attracted to the darkness this world has to offer, because your only reward will be self-destruction to the tenth power. God has great things in store for you and your family if you just wait on the Lord and trust in the Lord God. Don't turn to the left. Keep your eyes on Jesus, for there is profit in serving the Lord. Hallelujah!

> And Esau said unto Jacob, feed me, I pray thee, with that same red pottage; for I am faint: Therefore was his name called Edom. And Jacob said, sell me this day thy birthright
>
> And Esau said, behold, I am at the point to die, and what profit shall this birthright do to me? And Jacob said, swear to me this day, and he sware unto him: and he sold his birthright unto Jacob. Then Jacob unto Esau bread and pottage of lentils; and he did eat and drink, and rose up, and went his way thus Esau despised his birthright. (Genesis 25:30–34)

God's blessings and promises of wealth and prosperity were given to Abraham and his seed, and they were passed down to Israel through Isaac and his children's children. It also was a tradition that the firstborn would receive the birthright, which was the inheritance of all God promised Israel. Being the oldest brother, Esau was to be selected to be given the birthright by Isaac because Isaac loved him dearly, and Esau was the eldest child. Esau was always in the field, working the field with the cattle and herd of horses. On the other hand, Jacob, the youngest brother, stayed close to his mother and was sort of a spoiled child. It is my assumption there were discussions about the value of having the birthright, because Jacob understood the value of having a birthright more than Esau, his brother, did. Esau rose early every morning to work the field from sunup till sundown.

One day Jacob went up to check on his brother, and he brought with him some red pottage to eat. But after Esau worked so hard, he began to get faint and weak, and he asked for some pottage from Jacob. Jacob said, "You can have it. Just sell me your birthright now."

Esau answered and said, "Behold I am at the point to die." Jacob didn't stutter or blink; instead, he insisted on using this opportunity to make Esau make a fast decision which would dearly cost him, so Esau proceeded to say, "And what profit shall this birthright do to me?"

Here's where we all fall short. We allow others to convince us that unrighteous living is more profitable than righteous living. Instead of valuing what we have in Christ Jesus, we voraciously cast ourselves to worldly pleasures; and when the fun is over, we cry out to God the Father for help. If you don't value what you have, someone else will, and he or she will take it from you. Value your relationship with God. Value your family and church family. Value your marriage because there are people who want what you have. Value your employment and work it so it can work for you. If you don't value what God gives you, you will end up being a lukewarm Christian, fragile and easily turned to and fro. Salvation is free. Read your Bible and find its true value so you won't throw it away as easily as Esau did.

Esau worked hard and long hours, and at the end of the day, he could see the profits of his labor, but he couldn't see the relevance of his birthright. Sometimes when you give a child something so valuable, he or she doesn't know how to handle it. Better yet, the child cannot understand its true value. The birthright was an inheritance of wealth, which wasn't something you cashed in immediately; rather, over time you reaped rewards and became wealthy. Here is where some Christians, poor people, greedy people, and evil people lose. They focus on the time factor. It takes much time for valuable things to yield their worth.

Esau sold the birthright for a bowl of soup. For the love of God, the soup was instant gratification, but the birthright was a generational and eternal blessing for Esau and his children's children. Why would you sell all that for a measly bowl of soup?

Desperate measures for desperate people. This is what backsliders, carnal Christians, do. They sell all their inheritance with God for some measly drugs, crime, adultery, fame and riches, sexual escapade, alcohol, gangbanging, clubbing, pornographic material, stealing, and lying just to become an enemy of the cross. Please understand that no matter how much you live a lie or refuse to commit to God, you and no one else can take the power away from the cross of the Lord Jesus Christ. Also, despite everything you don't want from God, many others will accept all our Lord Jesus Christ has to offer them. Jacob wanted the blessing of God so much that he planned a strategy to take Esau's inheritance from him, and Esau freely gave his brother such a valuable document, only to willfully toss it away like a baseball without any knowledge and regard of its rich value. Would you sign your deed over to someone just because you missed one mortgage payment? No. You fight to keep your house because you will benefit from it in the long haul—and your children too. This is what we do with our Lord Jesus Christ.

Many Christians have asked, "Is there profit in serving the Lord?" Maybe that's why we don't witness to the unsaved or go to see the sick and disabled; it's because we don't value what we have, and maybe we think what we have isn't valuable enough to share. Esau forgot one thing; the same field he worked on belonged to God, and God gave him the strength he used to till the land. Esau was set up to be blessed immeasurably and highly favored among the heathen and his people, but he didn't want the blessing badly enough. Sometimes this is the attitude some people take; they don't want to be as Christlike as they say they do. They will participate in various positions in church, but when it comes down to commitment, they walk away just like the multitudes did to Jesus. As long as Jesus conducted miracles, healings, and deliverance, the multitudes stayed; but as soon as Jesus spoke of commitment, the multitude vanished into thin air. Jesus turned to his disciples and asked, "Will you also go away?"

The disciples hesitated, but Peter immediately lifted his voice and said, "Lord, to whom shall we go?" Peter caught the value of having Jesus in his life. It is more valuable to have Jesus than the whole world. It would be better to surrender to your dead gods than to be an enemy of the cross. But as for me, the writer of this book, I will follow the Lord Jesus Christ.

Proverbs 10:2 says, "Treasures of wickedness profit nothing."

Please understand there is profit in wickedness, but the profit it contains leads to destruction, which would be your reward. Sin and wickedness may look good at face value, but they are all lies; and at the end of the day, they have no substance of value. They lead only to destruction. There are those who have built an entire business by profiting from wickedness, just to name a few: prostitution, street pharmaceutical sales, hit men, high-level thieves, terrorists, computer hackers, false prophets, witches, and warlocks. They carry out their daily tasks to bring deception and fraud to people's lives. If they don't turn from their wicked ways, God will suddenly cut them off without warning. Only righteousness exalts a nation, but wickedness brings the wrath of God and damnation to a nation or people.

Matthew 26:14–15 says, "Then one of the twelve, called Judas Iscariot, went unto the chief priests, And said unto them, what will ye give me, and I will deliver him unto you? And they covenanted with him for thirty pieces of silver. And from that time he sought opportunity to betray him."

Judas wanted profit for a scandalous betrayal.

Judas didn't want a committed relationship with Christ, the Son of the living God. He would much rather create a scandalous relationship, which made everyone think he was a disciple, but over time he betrayed Jesus so he and the priests of that day could profit from Jesus's capture. This would make him infamous and reap a cash reward. But Jesus knew of Judas's craftiness and deceptive ways. Jesus told Judas, "Do what you must quickly." And at the Last Supper, Jesus mentioned there was a devil among them. (St. John 6:70). Jesus uncovered Judas's plan to betray him.

The most irksome thing you can do to disturb a scandalous person or thief at heart is to uncover his or her scandal before the person can complete his or her deceptive plan. You see, the reward for the scandalous person isn't to get caught before the scandal reaches its full fruition. So Jesus informed Judas that he knew what he was up to, and he proved it by telling Judas to move quickly. But Jesus announced to the disciples that there was a devil among them. This statement must have tormented Judas to the tenth power, especially when Jesus did nothing to stop his plot of betrayal; instead, he allowed him to play out this ungodly, selfish, greedy, phony, and wicked action against God's Son, Jesus Christ. No wonder he committed suicide; his reputation, which would follow him, wouldn't be an honorable one. And then there was the mere fact that Jesus was the Son of the Living God, and Judas helped kill the Son of God for measly coins. He risked his entire reputation to become the most scandalous and evil person to have ever lived. Judas's only selfish way of escape was to kill himself, not knowing that after death he would receive damnation with the devil with his angels of darkness laughing at how foolish and naïve Judas had been to betray the King of kings and Lord of lords, only to receive hell and damnation for an eternal reward.

Sapphira and Ananias kept their portions or profits from the Lord God. Acts 5:1–5 says,

> But a certain man named Ananias, with Sapphira his wife sold a possession
>
> And kept back a part of the price, his wife also being privy to it, and brought a certain part, and laid it at the Apostles feet but it was not what they agreed to give to the church and ministry. But Peter said, Ananias, why hath Satan filled thine

heart to lie to the Holy Ghost and to keep back part of the price of the land? Whiles it remained, was it not thine own? And after it was sold, was it not thine own power? Why hast thou conceived this thing in thine heart? Thou hast not lied unto men but unto God.

And Ananias, hearing these words, fell down, and gave up the ghost: and great fear came on all them that heard these things.

Lying to the Holy Ghost, which is God's spirit, is a dangerous thing to do. This is what both Sapphira and Ananias did. All the Christians made promises to God and their parishioners to give a particular portion of their profits to the church for the building of God's kingdom so everyone would benefit equally, but Sapphira and Ananias secretly decided among themselves to withhold some of their profits, which no one would really know but God. So when Ananias arrived to give his portion to the church, Paul told him, "Why did you lie but you did not lie to me you lied to the Holy Ghost?" And suddenly Ananias fell dead, and after some time, his wife came with her portion, and the same thing happened to her. What a tragedy! It isn't good to lie to the Holy Ghost, because it can cause sudden death, even slow death. Be careful of your promises to God.

It is the spirit that quickeneth; the flesh profiteth nothing: the words that I speak unto you, they are spirit and they are life. But there are some of you that believe not. For Jesus knew from the beginning who they were that believed not, and who should betray him.

And he said, therefore said I unto you, that no man can come unto me, except it were given unto him of my father. From that time many of his disciples went back, and walked no more with him. Then said Jesus unto the twelve will ye also go away? Then Simon Peter answered him, Lord to whom shall we go? Thou hast the words of eternal life. And we believe and are sure that thou art that Christ, the son of the living God. Jesus answered them, Have not I chosen you twelve and one of you is a devil. (John 6:63–70)

The Flesh Profits Nothing (John 6:63–70)

"The flesh" here means walking and trusting in your resources more than God's power. It is leaning and depending on the arms of humans, not God. This is a perfect example of walking in the flesh. Judas positioned himself around Jesus, posing to be a disciple, but instead, he was a plant or terrorist for all those, including the priests, who refused to believe Jesus was the Son of God. Judas played out a righteous role, but in his heart, he was committed to doing an ungodly deed to gain an earthly reward. You cannot mix unrighteousness with righteousness; it will blow up in your face and cause much harm to you, just like mixing both bleach and ammonia. When combined, they bring about destructive results. A man cannot serve God and the devil at the same time. He will follow one or the other.

Judas is the best example of a hypocrite. Hypocrites, you can be converted today. It would be better to live your life to the fullest than to perpetrate a fraud in the house of prayer. Be truthful to yourself and God. Repent, ye workers of iniquity(St. Matthew 7:23), and be ye saved by the washing of the blood of Jesus Christ. Confess your sins, and God is faithful to forgive them all. Hallelujah! I remember the times I went to church after participating in sinful acts all week, and then on Saturday evening, I prepared my repentant prayers so I could feel better about myself during the Sunday morning service. I was committed to going to church but not committed to God.

I didn't start off that way, but after much time, I ended up that way. There is a big difference between the two. You see, I was living in the flesh, but I knew how to put on my spiritual hat on Sunday. I knew the church language: "Praise the Lord, brothers and sisters, giving honor to God and the whole house of faith," "I'm blessed and highly favored," "I'm blessed and am better than blessed," "I am only human. Keep me in your prayers," and the list goes on. But these sayings are just words, and they cannot spell commitment. Commitment comes from within; it is with the heart that men believe Jesus is the Son of the living God. God is a spirit, and those who worship him must worship him in spirit and truth.

It's easy not to be committed to anything, to just live vicariously while experimenting with new things and participating in sinful activities as you please; but to make a decision and be truly committed to something takes work. Be committed to walking in holiness. Be committed to upstanding the law. Be committed to loving your enemies and those who try to use you. Be committed to helping others find Christ. Be committed to true praise and real worship in God's sanctuary; stand immovable, never yielding to temptations of the flesh. Do what's right.

Doing wrong is easy. Just submit to whatever comes, but doing something right takes some work and persistence. That's why our prisons are filled, and their waiting lists are increasing each day, because men would rather have darkness than the light of Jesus. Walk in the Spirit of the Lord God so you won't fulfill the works of the flesh. There's good profit in serving the Lord. In life you must get the right kind of profit that will bless you and your family. God's profit adds no sorrow to your life, but workings of darkness will destroy you and your family. There's good profit and there's corruptive profit but you must make your choice which one you will be your credo,

Tithes and Offerings Bring Profit

God wants you as well as his church to prosper simply by giving cheerfully and committing your 10 percent of sacrificial earnings to the house of the Lord. Some may ask, Why does God want our hard-earned money? This world currency isn't allowed in heaven; in fact, it burns at the sight of God. God doesn't need this earth's zillion dollars, which have been made from the elements of God's creation. God has ordained people to make sacrifices to God from the beginning of time. Don't your false gods make you render certain sacrifices to please them? The only thing is that they cannot answer your prayers like Jehovah God can.

Our tithes and offerings belong to God, and giving them back to God's house of prayer is our way of appreciating all the things God gives us to enjoy in life while being obedient to his command. Giving a portion of our substance back to God shouldn't be done grudgingly or in a detestable way, because it is better to give than to receive(Acts 20:35). Whether we give to God, he is still faithful to us. He will still wake us up in the morning whether we give, and we will still live as God intended us to. God is never stingy with his gifts. God's gifts are free. If you feel some pressure about giving to your local churches or to the ministry you are involved in, pray about it, and when you feel it's suitable to give tithes and offerings, at that point do so as unto God and definitely not unto man.

Please understand and note that tithes and offerings to the house of prayer aren't paying for the oxygen you breathe, the functionality of your brain, your eyesight, your hearing capacity, your vocal cords, your body movements, and your heartbeat. All these are gifts from God. You breathe and exhale because almighty God gave them to you as a gift. So how much could you give God to show your appreciation toward this precious life he installed in you? No dollar amount can pay for the life you possess. The most valuable things in life are those you cannot buy with cash, silver, or gold. God made us all into living souls, and their value is definitely immeasurable. That's why we cheerfully give offerings and tithes because we cannot repay the debt we owe. How could you pay a debt to a heavenly God with earthly money? Think about that. The money we give to our church—God doesn't need or benefit from it. It is to finance his work of God on earth and to bless those who are less fortunate than we. Giving is a heavenly thing, and God rewards those who give with the right intentions and with a cheerful heart. Please refrain from giving to God's house if giving isn't in your heart, because even though you give grudgingly, the minister may accept your gift, but God won't honor it. I repeat, God doesn't need your money. You need your money, but if you want to grow your money, you've got to do something with it. Even the riches of men give to the poor without regrets. Who are you to think you can grow your money without giving back to some capacity?

God sees our hidden motives in giving. If our hearts aren't in the transaction, the transaction becomes void with God; I repeat, God doesn't need our money. I must repeat that "God doesn't need your money." The purpose of giving is for you and your family to be blessed while helping others less fortunate. We hold too tight to this green paper like it's our best friend or a close family member, and it's only paper, but our economy protects money more than it protects people who use it. Money is driven in an armored truck while guarded by licensed security officers carrying heavy artillery, then escorted to a two-foot-thick steel vault with a combination lock only one or two people can open. Not only is the vault guarded by security guards, but it is also guarded by surveillance cameras and touch-sensitive lasers. It is as though our society and economy value money more than human life. In some instances, men and women have proved they value money more than people. Many people would rather have money than God.

This world can keep its green-colored paper and credit cards. Just give God a willing soul that wants to do things God way, and people will give unto his or her endeavors and vision with no remorse, pain, or soreness. God is truly the real deal. Some rich people spend most of their time giving back to ministries, schools, food banks, education, science, health care, churches, businesses, and so forth. Because they create tax shelters or tax breaks for themselves to dodge paying higher taxes, in addition to this, they feel as though they are contributing to society. The American system is designed so we give or pay more taxes. One of God's principles is giving, and when you give, it comes back to you in many different ways.

It's like planting one apple seed in the ground; it grows into an apple tree, harvesting hundreds of apples with thousands of extra apple seeds to plant and to harvest more apple trees in the future. When we obey God's law of giving, we are planting for a great harvest in our lives and in our family's lives in ministry so the gospel will spread throughout the world.—

> Will a man rob God? Yet ye have robbed me, but ye say, wherein have we robbed thee? We robbed God in tithes and offerings. Ye are cursed with a curse: for ye have robbed me, even this whole nation. *Bring ye all the tithes into the storehouse*, that there may be meat in mine house, and prove me now herewith, saith the Lord of host, if I will not *open you the windows of heaven*, and *pour you out a blessing*, that there *shall not be room enough to receive it.*
>
> And I will *rebuke the devourer for your sakes*, and he shall not destroy the fruit of your ground;

neither shall your vine cast her fruit before the time in the field, saith the Lord of Host.

And *all nations shall call you blessed*; for ye shall be a delightsome land said the Lord of hosts. (Malachi 3:8–12, emphasis added)

There are six points mentioned in this chapter of Malachi that will benefit you much.

1. "Bring ye all the tithes into the storehouse." Storehouses represent the house of God, and it is there where we should bring 10 percent of our income, commissions, percentage, royalties, dividends, salaries, inheritance, alimony, all income to the house of God. God wants to multiply your income, and when you do this as unto the Lord cheerfully and freely, ask what you will, and he will supply all you need. Your tithes and offerings are instructed by God, but their purpose is for you to prosper. I repeat, you aren't paying for a debt you owe God. Neither you nor I could afford to pay the debt we owe, even if all people in the entire world put their incomes together. Jesus paid our debts so we can achieve eternal life. Hallelujah!

   Offerings are the surplus, and it is up to your discretion as to the amount of offering you desire to give your church organization. Remember, if you give sparingly, you will reap sparingly (2 Corinthians 9:6); and if you give bountifully, you shall reap bountifully. And if you decide not to give at all, it's your choice. God won't make you do anything that's not in your heart to do. It would be better to keep every dime in your pocket than to give grudgingly. Remember, God doesn't need your money, but you do, and if you want more of it, give it, and it shall be given to you more abundantly.

2. "Prove me now herewith." God is challenging us to try his way or formula to be blessed people. Put God's instruction to work; bring your 10 percent tithe and offering to the house of God and watch it work for you. The only way to understand this method is to try it, believe it, and do it. Without notice, our government can take up 50 percent of our earning, and every year thousands of dollars come out of our payroll check, and we don't know what our government does with all our tax dollars. But if you decide not to pay your taxes, you are setting yourself up to possibly lose everything you own.

Please understand that Jesus said to render to Caesar what is Caesar's and render to God what is God's. It is in God's will that we pay for our responsibilities and debts. That is why giving to God's house will make money come to us instead of our having nervous breakdowns and heart attacks trying so hard to get money. God says, "Prove me this day." As we give to the house of God, we are following God's instructions, and there isn't one prophet in the Bible who followed God's instructions and ended up unsuccessful. Instead, they were blessed immeasurably.

3. "Open the windows of heaven." It's God's good pleasure to open the windows of heaven and pour out a blessing on mankind. The windows of heaven represent opportunities, especially windows of opportunities that appear closed for you, but as you pray and give, God begins to open the windows of heaven and doors of opportunity for you. Then good things happen, miracles take place, and supernatural things happen. Do you need something good to happen in your life? How about a miracle? The Israelites were in the desert for years, and as time went by, they complained to Moses about being hungry, so God opened the windows of heaven and poured out manna from heaven. This manna was bread from heaven that filled their bellies (Exodus

16:15). Imagine bread falling from the blue skies. Oh, what a wonderful sight to see!

God wants to open the windows of heaven for us and pour out a blessing for you and your family. We sing a song in church, "Can't nobody Do Me like Jesus," and it's so true. No one can do me like Jesus. Hallelujah! God takes care of his people and those who refuse to believe him. As mentioned before, the opening of the windows of heaven represents opportunities for you to use your success. So that job you applied for three months ago calls you and offers you a large salary to come aboard. That's the window of heaven opening for you. Finally, your banker approves your loan for your business, and the list of opportunities begins to start adding up. Waiting for opportunities doesn't mean you sit dormant and wait. No. It means that while waiting for opportunities, you keep working. God wants to pour his blessings on you so you can bless others too. God's blessing is rich and adds no sorrow (Proverbs 10:22). God's blessings come stress free. Some people just want God to sprinkle his blessings on them. I would rather that God would pour his blessing on me than just a sprinkle of his blessing. A sprinkle from God is more than enough to sustain us, but a pouring of God's blessings can cause a flood, and a flood affects communities, cities, states, and countries. I won't mind being flooded with God's blessings. Hallelujah!

4. "No room to receive it." Didn't I tell you that pouring causes flooding? God said he would pour his blessings on us—so much so that we wouldn't have room to receive it. This means his blessing would come in such abundance that we have more than enough to share with others. Why else would God give us so much that we wouldn't have room for? The purpose is to help others. There is really no secret why there are filthy, rich people in our world. God arranged for certain people to be rich so they could

give millions of dollars to help feed the poor, clothe the naked, help educate our children, help provide affordable housing, and so on. Lots of the filthy rich remain nameless because they don't want a trail leading back to them. There's no room to receive it; isn't just dealing with money. It is your health, your family's well-being, your business striving, your living quarters expanding. You become owners of property and your church and much more. After Bill Gates created the most used processing system in the world, Microsoft Windows. he and his wife spend all their time giving back to education, businesses, health care, and science, because once God pours out blessings on your life, they keep coming. People who are hoarders usually die miserably and empty hearted, so give as God gives you, and he will continue to shower down blessings on you. God wants you to be profitable. God wants your church to be profitable. God wants your family to be profitable. God wants your marriage to be profitable. God wants your business to be profitable. As God desires and seeks profit from his servant, you should seek and desire profits from the things you do. Amen.

5. "He will rebuke the devourer." This is considered God's insurance policy over your blessings. As you know, once you attain wealth, it is advised that you get several insurance policies because people always want to sue people with wealth. Some people have made it a career to sue companies and individuals. So God says if we pay our tithes and offerings, he will rebuke the devourer. Who is the devourer? The devourer comprises those companies and people who try to steal your blessings due to you. God says he will build a hedge around us so nothing can block, stop, or take the blessings he bestows on us. Why? So we can take care of our responsibilities and help others. As

we help others, the blessing will come back to us again and again. Can the church say, "Amen"? Hallelujah?

God loves investing in people, and you are a prime target or candidate for God to shower down his blessing. If we could only see every element and instrument meant to harm us, slow us down, or even destroy us, we would trust in God's system of doing things even more. In my fifty four years of life, I know God has kept me alive and well for a purpose because I am confident that bullets have passed by me without noticing. Cars and trucks have missed me by only inches, and I have been untouched from plane crashes, I escaped from fires in my home, and the list goes on. God protects us each day. This same God promises to rebuke all who dare to intercept our progress and blessings from God. God says he will rebuke them. He will use their devices of evil as tools for their demise so we can soar like eagles. Are you tired of falling for anything and everything? It's time to soar high above the vibrations and currents of life and be what God made us to be. Conquerors and conquerors are profitable people.

6. "All nations shall call you blessed." This is the part I like; when all is said and done, people will speak good things about you and about how God has blessed you and made you to prosper. As you continue to follow Christ, they will speak of God's goodness toward you, and some may even follow in your footsteps because God's way is working for you. All nations, meaning people from all nations in your communities, will call you blessed. Some people in my past neighborhood had a bad reputation. Some were known as fighters, drug dealers, killers, and thieves, so when they came to the barbershop, the whispers of how they lived filled the atmosphere. God said, "If you do it his way, those same people will call you blessed." A good reputation is better than all the money in the world. You

can't get a loan without a good reputation; it's hard to get a job without a good reputation. Even businesses like doing business with people who have a good reputation. You can't adopt a child without a good reputation; it's hard to get and keep a credit card without a good reputation. It's hard for doctors to keep patients without a good reputation. Imagine what happens when your name is blessed. Hallelujah! It will open more doors of blessings for you and draw the right people to you, and all nations will call you blessed. Praise God from whom all blessings flow. That's true profit.

In conclusion, being a profitable servant isn't hard when your heart is in the right place, but you will have a tough and torturing time if you're just having some good intentions. Good intentions aren't enough to be profitable. You need to be committed to the Lord God so when the spiritual emotions are gone and trouble rises, temptations surround you, and tribulations come your way, it will be your commitment to the Lord God, who will last. Yes, that's what makes a profitable servant. Keep your heart and mind on the Lord, live a committed lifestyle for the Lord, and love your neighbor. By doing so, you will profit greatly.

You have the potential to be and live as a profitable servant for the Lord. Stop adding up your mistakes, shortcomings, weaknesses, and pitfalls. Just repent and commit your life to God today. Put your faith in the Lord Jesus Christ, and it will be your faith in him that will keep you committed. You can do this! Live a profitable life. And your family and friends will all benefit from it. But most importantly, you will gain eternal life. Thank you, Jesus!

CHAPTER 11

What's My Name?

Y ou should know my name already because your thoughts of me are constantly running through your mind. My name has stood throughout history. Some people have even given their lives for me, and others have taken lives for me within the Old Testament and in the twentieth century.

I am the one who makes you happy when I'm around. When you're sick, I can make you well with the best doctors at your bedside. When you're depressed, I'll make you free from all your stress and troubles; and when you're in debt, I will bless you outstandingly.

What Is My Name?

Don't leave home without me, because without me your life will be most difficult and miserable. People are jealous of you because you have more of me than others. Do I satisfy your needs? The answer is, yes, I do.

I love it when you talk about me to others, giving them a testimony of how good I am to you; don't ever think you can fight my battles because you can't. Didn't you know I can fight your battles and my own battles too?

What Is My Name?

"Worship me, and I'll be your God." If you will love me more than everything and everyone else, I will give you more than you can imagine.

What Is My Name?

Think of me at home late at night, at noonday, in the morning, and when you go to work and school. Let your thoughts be on how great I am.

What Is My Name?

Whether the world knows it or not, they need me to survive. What would the world do or be without me?

What Is My Name?

I'll make your enemies your footstool; I'll help you deal with your family problems.

If you need anything, just call me, and I will answer you.

What Is My Name?

Bring me with you everywhere you go. Carry me around safely, because people want what you have. For years men have written books about me, and those books have sold hundreds of millions of copies each year. School teachers and students talk about me. Finally, I am a big topic in churches around the world. When ministers call my name in church, some people become disturbed and don't participate, but I know they love me deep down inside.

What Is My Name?

When you're down and out, feeling sad, who can help? Who do you call?

When you're looking for friends and can't find one, who do you call?

When you are sick and can't afford to get well, who do you call?

When you're homeless, who do you call?

When you're poor, who do you call?

When your business needs help, who do you call?

What's my name? I can't hear you! Say my name louder. Say it again.

Let your voice ring my name. Praise my name. Lift your hands and clap your hands and rejoice.

Glorify my name, praise my name, and let the earth honor my name!

What Is My Name?

But that's not my name. Thanks for giving me the highest compliment, but Jesus isn't my name.

My Name Is Money, Honey!

That's right, people; you know, if you had more of me, things would be better for you.

I make people rich, and I make people poor.

Money is my name, and people are my game.

Banks spend millions of dollars just to guard me, and their security guards will kill anybody caught trying to steal a dollar. People hide me in armored trucks. They cast iron safes with a secret combination, and the safes are fireproof. Is your house or apartment fireproof? *I thought so!*

It would take an atomic bomb for these safe to be opened. Yes, darlings, I am special and highly favored. I know that's right. Say my name. Money, honey.

No one really likes to give me away because he or she has to work so hard to get money. What's my name? Honey, it's Money.

The lack of money causes heart attacks, sugar diabetes, cancer, stress, mental disorders, and a thousand other different diseases and even death because people are depressed without me. Child, you are a mess without me. You heard me. You are a mess without me. You better not leave home without me. Don't you do that! Don't you dare! Without me, you will become homeless, go broke, starve, get sick, be depressed, and become suicidal. Please sing this song with me. "Money, money, money." That's my name.

Say my name.

People act insanely over me.

Drug dealers kill people for a little money. Many of our political officials lie because they want more money. TV commercials will say and do just about anything to get you to spend your money, and guess what? You fall for it. It works all the time; and to my surprise, prisons have become a multibillion-dollar industry for certain ethnic group such as blacks and hispanic's, but you know who you are out there; these ethnic groups don't benefit from prison, but somebody does, and it's certainly not you. Some investors spend millions of dollars investing in locking up black and Hispanic men and women, and the profits are remarkable. Some of these prison investors may be sitting next to you right now. Look around!

You get up in the morning so frustrated with your life and everybody else in it, and because of the lack of money, you yield your time to crime and get caught up in the prison system. More money is being made off your incarceration than you can ever imagine, darling. It's a shame that more money is devoted to prison than to public schools. Did you know this? It's the Bible truth. What's my name? Money! Money! Money! Money! Money! Sounds like music to my ears with a type of symphonic sound.

People betray family members for me. Remember Judas? He loved me so much that he betrayed Jesus for thirty pieces of silver and then took his life. Maybe if the pieces of silver had been gold, he would have stayed alive. Judas sold out the Kings of kings for a measly thirty pieces of silver. Look at the power of me, Money! Don't laugh because some of you will sell out your family and church family for money.

People will lie and keep secrets even unto death for me. Say that again?

People will falsify legal documents for money. Oh yes, they will. Have you ever done this? You all know ya'll done this once in your lifetime. Be honest. Look at you; don't get scared.

Some bishops, preachers, pastors, deacons, missionaries, televangelists, and ushers currently play lotto. And why do they gamble? Because they want more of me. Money! Honey!

Not everybody on welfare and public assistance has told the truth on his or her application. You know why. It's because they want more of me, Money, honey. People will marry someone just for money and divorce them just to get me, Money. All of you probably thought infidelity and breaking up someone else's happy home were all about love. Child, please. People do this nonsense for money too. We look down on the prostitutes selling their bodies on the street, but many church women and others have put prostitution out of business because there's money to be made, and desperate people take desperate measures when they need more money. I feel like a movie star because everyone wants me, more Money. Many churches and ministries all over the country get caught up in scandals, and when the tabloids uncover the scandal, we find out large amounts of money were the reason for the scandal. People will do stuff in the dark for me; oh, yes, they will. Millions of dollars change people quickly, maybe because what money really does brilliantly is expose and reveal what's really in people's hearts and intentions. I, Money, sit back and witness every day with my eyes wide open, seeing criminals, committing dark deeds, injustice, perversion, sinful acts, trivial, trifling episodes, and wicked people involve themselves in wickedness just for green paper called money; and we all thought Judas was bad. Child, let me tell you something. Judas would turn over in his grave if he saw the stuff I witness people do for money.

Say my name! Don't be shy. Say it.

Money is my name, and people are simply my game. Can I get an "Oh, yes" in the building? Don't get mad at me. I am just telling you the truth.

Countries go to war for me, and terrorists sometimes risk everything for me. Everybody wants to be a millionaire in today's society. Men and women are becoming millionaires every thirty minutes per day. You can't stop it because people value money more than God. Did I offend you? I don't apologize, because it's the truth. Tell it, brother. Cash; money speaks for itself.

Computer hackers penetrate through all kinds of security codes just because of me, Money. You don't believe me? Just ask some of the banks, investment groups, super retail stores, online dating companies, and so forth. They will all tell you what I'm saying is the truth. These hackers want money, and they will track down your history, financial status, personal information, and bank account. Like a lion hunting for food, once they find it, they indulge in this kind of ransom from you; and if you don't pay up, you lose millions of dollars, business, and income.

This world makes me feel so special because I am treated with the utmost respect and handled with extreme care. I am treated better than all of you in this room and in this world. I am highly protected from all danger that comes my way. People risk their lives for me every day.

I am so special and royal that you can't seem to live without me, people. Just look at you. All of you are hooked on me like a "drug addict looking for their next high!" You do not believe me? Try living without me. Some people will do anything for money. Money makes people betray best friends, spouses, mama, papa, pastors, employers—and the list keeps growing.

Do you know how it feels when everyone desires you more than God? People give their entire allegiance to me, money made of paper, more than to God and his human race. I get more attention than runway models. People willingly devote their entire careers to finding more of me money. People are willing to betray loved ones for me. They leave their spouses for me. They kill others for me and steal for me; they create porn sites to get more of me. My name is Money, honey. People lie for me; they have sex just to get more of me, Money. They conduct sex trafficking for me. They conduct abortion clinics for me and burn down their houses or businesses for me so they can get the insurance money. Churches kick members out of church when they fail to pay tithes. It's all about Money, honey. Don't you get it? People do all this just for me, Money. Wait a minute. This sounds like a song.

> Just for me,
> Everybody wants me,
> Just me.
> Everybody wants me:
> Money!

People desire me more than God, and I have the power to duplicate myself over and over because I pay somebody to make copies of me. Plus I cannot walk, so people must carry me around, but anyway, having all this royal treatment, you would think nothing bothered me. You would think I had it all together. You would think I'm too blessed to be stressed and better than blessed. You probably wish you were in my shoes, no doubt, right? With all this recognition of how wonderful I am (Money), there's one thing that troubles me a whole lot; in fact, it torments me from time to time. It's something I don't quite get. It even blows my mind; it makes me feel strange sometimes and jealous most times. While I'm in great demand and still the world's greatest superstar, I remain the loneliest in the entire world.

Everyone is after me insanely and intensely, and I get that, but what I don't get is this. I would trade all my royal treatment and wealth just to be alive like you all. My forever recurring dream is to live as a human being, a person like you: breathing, moving, and thinking like you. This would be the best thing in the world that could ever happen to me. You see, all of what I am is some paper mixed with some cotton and other things stripped from the bark of a tree, and there's no life in me, only the life you give me. But most times I am miserable; I am stuck in a vault for days, weeks, months, and years. It's so lonely in there. There's no one to talk to, no one to love me and keep me company. You try living in a vault and see how it feels. I am constantly being traded for something, driving around with criminals, thieves, murderers, and evil people; and I just don't understand all the measures people take to get more of me (Money). And they sometimes risk everything for just the touch and smell of hundreds of dollars bills, and then they apparently lose everything dear to them in the process.

People treat me better than their own family members and their God. I wish I could get you all to realize how important you are and how important your relationship with your creator is. You see, God made trees before mankind, but he gave mankind the power to get wealth. Preach, Money! God blessed man and told him to be fruitful and multiply and to replenish and subdue the earth. Finally, he instructed man to have dominion over the sea, air, and earth. Ask me, How do I know this to be true? I know this to be true because many of my clients, who desperately seek after my presence, are preachers, men and women of the cloth, who use deception to lure people to give them money and valuable things. Then, instead of the money going to the house of worship, they pocket it for themselves. What a shame! They tell people to believe God for the increase while they steal other people's last dime. What a great disparity to con people into doing something that benefits only one person. These false prophets give God's people the illusion that it's all for God's kingdom, while literally their only purpose is to steal from God's house.

Oh, how I wish I had those promises God gave to mankind. You see, I was there in the Garden of Eden when man received those promises, and I was there when man was kicked out of the Garden of Eden too. Who would think the status of money would be what it is today in the twenty-first century? Money is sought after more than anything I know on earth. How many dreams have you had about being rich? How many dreams have you had about marrying someone rich? How many times have you played lotto, hoping to strike it rich? How many times have you robbed banks, grocery stores, clothing stores, drug stores, discount stores, churches, and family members—and from your job, where you are employed—just to get money? How many times have you stolen people's identity to get money? How many times have you falsified documents to get cash? How many times have you lied on your tax documents and employment applications to get more money? How many times have you committed sexual favors just for, guest what, money? How many times have you faked your injury so you could collect the insurance money? How many times have you sued people who weren't really at fault just for Mr. Number One, Money? Yeah, you really love me. *All of you* have proved your true love for me. I appreciate it. But this still doesn't erase this feeling of emptiness I explained to you earlier.

You see, all of you want more money so bad, and I understand why, but I wish your God would breathe on me and in me just for one day so I could experience what it's like to be alive—breathing, walking, talking, having eyes to see, and operating with all five human senses and faculties. *Help me, somebody! Help me, Jesus!* Nobody thinks I need help, maybe because you desire more of me than a relationship with your creator. Oh, how warped you all are! You have been truly deceived. Money in itself is full of emptiness and empty dreams, which delight you with a mirage of temporary pleasurable things; and when it's all over, you will find yourself still unfulfilled just like me.

I am only paper that wants to breathe the breath of life like you. Lord, help me please! I am only paper, people, but I would willingly trade all my wealth to breathe like a human being.

Just as much as you want my dollar worth, I would like to breathe and have my own being like you.

I too would like the chance to be a human being like you. You guys don't value it anyway. If I could trade places with you, you could keep your money and give me life. Keep your money but give me Jesus.

If I were a human being, I would be happier than a trillion dollars times a trillion dollars, because at that point money wouldn't matter to me like it does to you. Coming from my background, people are the prize, but they don't get it. They don't even have a clue as to how more important they are than I am. It's almost like everyone is in this dark cloud, never coming to the light of how valuable they are. People can exist without money, but money can't exist without people. You want me so desperately, but you don't realize how dirty I am. I've been handled with some of the worst dirty hands in the world, from criminals to derelicts on the street. I am sometimes found in dirty, filthy dumpsters, in dirty rivers, in toilet bowls, in sweaty socks, in stinky shoes, in grimy underwear, and in the inner bra for most women. Often people find traces and evidence of blood on money due to a deal that went bad. I am so dirty that the tollbooth clerk refuses to handle me without latex gloves. Yet none of these things ever stop desperate people who want me more than God.

Imagine having no eyesight, voice, brain, friends, or family just hidden in a vault. Imagine that you can't walk, having no soul, no spirit, no expressions while hanging around criminals every day and having people who want you so badly; but in reality they want only what I can do for them. And then here I go again, back in the vault. I'm miserable, wretched, lonely, and full of emptiness. I feel abandoned, purposeless, and worthless when I'm stuck in that vault; and anybody who chooses to worship me will eventually end up like me too. Worthless!

Give me life. I want to live. Give me life! I want to live so God can use me. I want to live. And they tell me I can't even pay for it or bargain with God for life, because I could easily gather up a trillion dollars within minutes to pay for what you have. But there's no dollar value on the life God gives you.

Life is a gift from God. That's what they say. That's what's written in the scriptures. (St Romans 6:23)The wages of sin is death but the gift of God is life and eternal life if we seek first the kingdom. God has given mankind this special gift, which sounds like a song written by Marie Della Thomas, "A Special Gift." Google "Her song." Regardless, I could never be a candidate for life in general or eternal life. Never! Figure that out. Being the wealthy of the wealthiest, I still can't even buy life. I can only fantasize about it because what I see is people wasting their lives on worthless things every day *just to obtain money, fame, fortune, houses, and land.*

So why do you love me more than people? Why do you love me more than God? Are you insane? You all have more going for you than what money has to offer ya'll. Take it from me, paperback money. I'm not all you think I am cranked up to be.

Clearly you have much more than I do. It's evident. You have more than I. Yet you pursue me like a god, and you ignore the real Jehovah God. What's wrong with you people? Money will never actually talk back to you, nor will it befriend you. Money has no allegiance to anyone, because it's dead and has no life in itself, and anyone who worships money will live an empty life.

You know what? I don't understand.

You have so much more than I do, and yet you are still so unhappy, dissatisfied, disgruntled, and discontented. I see your faces during the church offering times. Your faces look like sour prunes, all because you don't want to let go of me. I say, loose me, woman. I say, loose me, man. Let me go! It's better to give than to borrow. It's better to give than to be stingy and tightfisted. Generosity and openhandedness leave room for your hands to receive prosperity, opportunity, and blessings. Am I talking right, church folks? I'm about to preach in this place. Hear me!

You are living beings. Don't you get it? God breathed his breath into your nostrils, life, and he made you in his likeness. Do you understand who you are? So that means if God is great, you have his greatness inside you. So instead of looking to God for help, you seek me., Money! Why, people? You are more than I am. Money is dead without you. You give money life. Money doesn't give you life. Don't you all get it?

People are more important and more valuable than money. Your life is more important than money. Your friends and family are more important than money, and finally the Lord God, your creator, is far more important than your relationship with me, Money. What's wrong with you all? Some people are abducting children, prostituting, fighting, killing, lying, betraying family, and stealing from your neighbors just to receive money. Wow! Why do you work so hard to scam and cheat your way to success and then expect to live happily ever after? Your schemes and con games will catch up with you sooner than later, and they will bite you where the sun doesn't shine and reward you with tons of regrets and gloom and doom forever.

How I wish I could be you. How I wish I could be you. You all are the prize, but you don't even realize it or understand the greatness God has installed in you.

What's my name? Money! Yes, Money is my name, but I am only paper; there's no life in me but the life you give me. Money in itself isn't evil. The love of money is the root of all evil (1Timothy 6:10), but the gift of God is eternal life(Roman 6:23). The gift God gives you is life, people, not money. Money isn't a gift. It's just paper you and all humanity give life to. Money doesn't qualify for eternal life; nor does money qualify for life in general. Worship God, not money. Do not worship dead gods. No matter how many things you think I can buy for you, money is still dead, people. People give money life.

Worship God, the life giver. Who is the life giver? Who is the mind regulator,? Who is the Alpha and Omega? Who is King of king and Lord of lords? What's his name? What's his name? It is Jesus. Worship that name.

What's my name now? Mr. Paperback himself, but most people in America call me, "Mr. Cash." Yes, I'm nothing but paper. The name you should adore and worship is Jesus Christ, the Son of the living God. Worship that name! Don't idolize me, Money. What am I, and who am I, so majestic and magnificent to be reverenced, when in fact people made me? But God made you all. For there is no other name under the sun whereby man can be saved and obtain eternal life but by the name of the Lord Jesus Christ (Acts 4:12) "Neither is there salvation in any other: for there is none other name under heaven given among men, whereby we must be saved".,. Worship that name! What's his name? It's Jesus. Worship and adore that name.

Printed in the United States
by Baker & Taylor Publisher Services